masculinity &
Morality

masculinity &
Morality

LARRY MAY

Cornell

University

Press

Ithaca

and

London

Library of Congress Cataloging-in-Publication Data
May, Larry.
    Masculinity and morality / Larry May.
        p.   cm.
    Includes bibliographical references (p.   ) and index.
    ISBN 0-8014-3418-1 (cloth : alk. paper).—
    ISBN 0-8014-8442-1 (pbk. : alk. paper)
        1. Masculinity—Moral and ethical aspects.
2. Sex role—Moral and ethical aspects.
3. Men—Sexual behavior—Moral and ethical aspects.
I. Title.
HQ1090.M385   1997
305.31—dc21   97-37785

Cornell University Press strives to utilize
environmentally responsible suppliers and materials
to the fullest extent possible in the publishing of its books.
Such materials include vegetable-based, low-VOC inks
and acid-free papers that are also either recycled,
totally chlorine-free, or partly composed of
nonwood fibers.
Cloth printing   10 9 8 7 6 5 4 3 2 1
Paperback printing   10 9 8 7 6 5 4 3 2 1

For Marilyn and Elizabeth

Contents

Acknowledgments

This book truly represents a collaborative effort. At each stage I have benefited greatly from discussions with colleagues, students, and friends. Indeed, two of the chapters were literally written with others. My greatest debt of gratitude is owed to Robert Strikwerda. Our joint papers on masculinity were the inspiration for this book. Bob has graciously allowed me to use one of these papers as the core of Chapter 5, and James Bohman has also kindly allowed me to use a paper I wrote with him as the core of Chapter 3. Of equal importance, Jim and Bob have spent hundreds of hours discussing the issues of this book with me. I readily admit that I am a "social" philosopher in the sense that my best work is merely an extension of conversations I have had. This book represents the fruits of this form of "social" philosophy.

I also owe a large debt to Carl Wellman, Richard Hiskes, Iris Young, and Kenneth Clatterbaugh, who read the entire manuscript and supplied me with much needed critical feedback at a late stage. Edward Soule spent a summer as my research assistant, also carefully reading an early draft. Marilyn Friedman, Hugh LaFollette, and Margaret Walker read most of the manuscript, at various stages of development, and also provided a valuable sounding board for me. This small group of people could be thanked in every section of the book, for their suggestions, large and small, have shaped my ideas into something coherent. In addition, a somewhat larger group of people gave me help with various chapters. Those I can remember are Victoria Davion, Diana Meyers, Karen Warren, Duane Cady, Virginia Ingram, Jason Clevenger, Sally Scholz, Alison Bailey, Ron Broach, Johann Klaassen, Susan Bordo, Sandra Harding, Gretchen Arnold, James Sterba, Naomi Scheman, Eva Kittay, William Rehg, Thomas Digby, Harry Brod, Richard Nunan, Elvia Herrera, Joel Anderson, Andy Clark, and Roger Gibson. My thanks can be only partial recompense for their hard work.

I have presented versions of these chapters at several meetings of the American Philosophical Association, the North American Society for Social Philosophy, the American section of the International Association for Law and Social Philosophy (AMINTAPHIL), the Society for Women in Philosophy, and the Radical Philosophy Association. Chapters 3 and 5 originally appeared in the journal *Hypatia*. Chapter 2 will appear in a festschrift for Virginia Held, edited by Joram Haber and Mark Halfon, to be published by Rowman and Littlefield; and Chapter 8 will also be published in a collection of essays edited by Thomas Digby.

I am also grateful for excellent editorial assistance from the staff of Cornell University Press, especially my editor, Alison Shonkwiler. Stephanie Bauer compiled an excellent index.

L.M.

masculinity &
Morality

Introduction

What does morality have to do with masculinity? Here are three of many ways that conceptions of masculinity and morality interconnect. First, our conceptions of masculinity affect our ideas of who can best attain moral understanding. Men's lack of certain experiences, such as pregnancy, is sometimes thought to make it hard for them to understand the morality of abortion; and the unlikeliness that a man would be the object of sexual assault is sometimes thought to make it harder for men to understand the morality of rape. Second, our conceptions of masculinity also affect our notions of what counts as a moral excuse. Some people maintain that rapists are sometimes provoked to act, and hence their acts are judged to be morally excusable, attributable to a nearly uncontrollable sexual urge stimulated by their victim's appearance. Others argue that men should consider themselves to be more rather than less responsible for such sexual harms given the history of sexual relations between men and women. Third, our conceptions of masculinity affect the role responsibilities we assign. Men are sometimes thought to have a smaller role than women, perhaps because they are less caring than women, in decisions concerning how to care for, and even whether to have, children. As a result men are expected to have less responsibility for the care of their children and to be less blamable than women for abandoning these children. In both moral theory and practice, conceptions of masculinity play an increasingly important role in contemporary debates.

My approach to the topic of masculinity is explicitly moral but unlike most of the current literature, my approach focuses more on group-oriented issues rather than matters of individual psychology. In my previous work I have developed a model of understanding moral responsibility as a matter of what individuals in groups owe their communities.[1] I have been especially interested in notions of collective and shared responsibility which extend our attention beyond the confines of what individual men (or women) have done, to include what they could have done, especially in concert with others. I have been guided by the insight that most of the world's great social problems can only be solved by collective rather than individual isolated efforts. One important part of the solution to many of these problems, including rape, sexual harassment, and pornography, is for people to see how seemingly innocuous individual actions or inactions combine to produce large-scale harmful consequences, and for these people to be motivated to change their behavior.

My interest in the relation between masculinity and morality is philosophical but also personal. My early writings on masculinity were collaborative projects which brought together philosophical reflections on gender and society with my and my colleagues' experiences of being men, unhappy at the assigned roles we were asked to play. I wrote about subjects that were part of my own experience, such as male intimacy or its lack,[2] fatherhood and its frustrations,[3] attitudes unfortunately conducive to the perpetuation of rape,[4] and images of male sexuality gleaned from my Catholic boyhood.[5] I also surveyed social science literature to make sure that my own experiences were at least somewhat representative of experiences of many other men in contemporary Western societies.

The point of my writings about masculinity is both to develop a criticial consideration of a certain philosophical concept, for instance, intimacy or commitment or solidarity, in a new light and also to attempt to begin reperceiving and reconceiving ourselves as men. Because these two goals were sometimes at odds with each other, or at least competed with each other, the following chapters have an unusual style. Confessional anecdotes are followed by sometimes dense philosophical analysis, and then by a final section of exhortations and practical suggestions about how to change our lives. Traditional male roles are subjected to critical scrutiny, especially in light of the adverse consequences the fulfilling of these roles has had for the status of women, and this scrutiny is followed by positive proposals for reconceptualizing these roles.

The first time I presented some of my work on masculinity was at a women's studies colloquium. There, members of the audience challenged me to explain why I thought I needed to take such a convoluted path to get to the practical recommendations. Would anyone really be more likely to heed the advice at the end because of the hard-to-follow stuff in the middle? Why not cut to the chase, moving straight from anecdotes to exhortations, like the popular writers on masculinity? I now regard these questions as a serious challenge to all of us who write philosophically about masculinity from a progressive standpoint. What are we doing when we mix careful conceptual analyses with commonsense conclusions?

The answer I would now make to such a challenge is in a sense a justification for the style of writing in the essays that follow. Over the last decade, men's writing on masculinity has gotten much more sophisticated in terms of social science methodology and results, but it has hardly progressed at all in theoretical sophistication.[6] Of course, theoretical sophistication is not a value in itself. But the blithe platitudes that are often offered up, especially by psychoanalytically oriented members of the men's movement,[7] cannot possibly be considered plausible unless they are vigorously defended and challenged and defended again. Even when truth is spoken forthrightly, it will not often inspire others to recognize it as such unless it is presented in a critical and even dialectical way that invites the reader or hearer to come to see the truth on his or her own, thinking it through with proddings by advocates and critics alike. I have tried to add some philosophical rigor to the largely popular debates about which I have commented. Forcing ourselves to think hard about what can seem commonsensically obvious or abhorrent will enrich our mental lives and perhaps broaden our shared moral understanding.[8]

In the first chapter I consider the topics of male anger and sexual desire, so often seen as bases for excusing men from moral responsibility for harms they cause. I describe what I call the "badgered male excuse" and the "testosterone excuse" and show that neither is properly a basis for excusing men for their violent actions. I consider and partially reject a standard construal of anger and sexual desire as largely a reasonable response to stimuli in one's environment, but I argue nonetheless that anger and sexual desire can be an important source of knowledge about ourselves. It gives men a glimpse into the mechanisms we need but often lack which would enable us to take responsibility for our emotional lives.

In the second chapter I explore the phenomenon of paternity. "Paternity" is often used ambiguously to refer either to mere procreation or to the full range of experiences constituting fatherhood. A series of court cases in the United States has examined whether and when procreation is sufficient to establish rights over adoption, abortion, or custody. I look at these cases, searching for a moral rationale that would justify denying to some men the same rights afforded to women over decisions concerning the care of their offspring. I argue that only when a man has demonstrated that he is a true father in the nurturant sense, and not merely a procreator, should he be afforded similar rights to those of the mother. Simple paternity should not be conceptually confused with full-blown fatherhood. When they are confused men are given more rights than they deserve and are held less accountable, less able to enter into mature and responsible relationships. I end with a discussion of a positive reconceptualization of paternity.

In the third chapter James Bohman and I look at what it means for a man to take responsibility for his sexuality. We focus on the phenomenon of confessing one's sexual sins. This practice has historically provided boys and men with a mixed message. Engaging in coercive sex is publicly proclaimed to be sinful; yet in the privacy of the confessional coercive sex is treated as merely one of a number of transgressions that can be washed away, without requiring changes of attitude or future behavior. We compare Catholic confessional practices to those of psychoanalytically oriented male writers on masculinity, who also employ a kind of confession about past sexual transgressions. We maintain that neither sort of confession is helpful as long as there remains a mixed message about the nature of coercive sexuality. At the end we propose a progressive confessional mode for discussing male sexuality which we think will lead to a greater collective awareness of the problems of sexual aggression.

In the fourth chapter I discuss the explosive topic of pornography, arguing that its harm is best understood as a group-based harm to women. I consider and reject such well-known group-oriented views of the harm of pornography as Catharine MacKinnon's view of it as a form of group defamation and Cass Sunstein's perception of it as a form of castelike discrimination. I urge that we think of pornography as a cumulative harm to the status of women as a group, analogous to the cumulative harm to the residents of the city of Gary, Indiana, by exposure to industrial air pollution. I argue that pornography can be understood as a form of moral pollution. I end with a discussion of the positive effects of certain forms of egalitarian pornography, and use these effects as a reason for thinking that pornography should not be banned but merely regulated, as is also true of industrial pollution.

In the fifth chapter Robert Strikwerda and I consider men's collective responsibility for rape. We assess the arguments that men are evolutionarily predisposed to rape and that women as well as men are responsible for the rape culture, rejecting both of these arguments. We focus on the fact that most rapists are not easily distinguishable from the rest of the normal male population. In some sense, each of us men could have been a rapist. When this fact is considered along with the fact that men as a group benefit from the prevalence of rape, an argument emerges for thinking that men are collectively responsible for rape. At the end we consider various actions men can take to distance themselves from the rest of the male population that contributes to the prevalence of rape.

In the sixth chapter I consider various ways that men have responded to the increasing prevalence of sexual harassment in education and employment contexts. Even though sexual harassment, like rape, seems obviously wrong, men are not as willing to condemn it as they are willing to condemn rape. I focus initially on the way that sexual harassment has changed from being a relatively obtuse form of intimidation to a much more subtle form of exclusion of females by males. One of the largely undiscussed issues in sexual harassment is its contribution to male bonding and solidarity. I explain and criticize this basis of male solidarity and then end the chapter with a lengthy discussion of positive ways to achieve male solidarity without making women feel uncomfortable or excluded.

In the seventh chapter I focus on male bonding and socialization, especially in military academies. Shannon Faulkner's successful attempt to gain entrance to a private military college, the Citadel, illustrates some of the problems in this form of male socialization, especially the "adversative" training that is favored in military and athletic contexts. I propose an alternative form of socialization that I call "conversative" socialization, which stresses dialogue and role reversal as bases for conflict resolution, rather than the combative strategies of adversative socialization. I give reasons for thinking that such socialization may be best carried out in an all-male setting, thus providing a justifiable basis for all-male academies, albeit very different from such formerly all-male bastions as the Citadel and the Virginia Military Institute.

In the eighth and final chapter I describe the progressive male standpoint that is implicit in the previous chapters. I describe four aspects of this standpoint: personal experience, critical reflection on the traditional roles that form the basis of that experience, moral motivation to change, and the construction of plausible practical alternatives to these traditional roles. Following in the footsteps of feminist standpoint theorists, I argue that men are often best placed to describe male experience but that women are better placed to critique it. Since most men don't give as much credence to women's writings about masculinity as they do men's, men retain a special role in the analysis of masculinity. Men are in a better position to bring about changes in the behavior of their fellow men.

Throughout this book I describe traditional male roles and conceptual frameworks and open them to critique. I hope to persuade men to reassess and change their behavior that has had detrimental effects on the lives of women and of fellow men. I also hope men will think about alternative roles that would give men better control over who they want to be and yet leave room for distinctly male roles, not merely androgynous roles for men and women alike. The underlying moral issue is responsibility: where it should be ascribed, what will motivate men to take it, and how it might ultimately change the way men think about their larger roles in society.

Throughout the book, I take an explicitly progressive approach which shares a lot with feminist approaches.[9] This approach creates a politically difficult position for me and other men who try to write about masculinity in a progressive mode. The problem results from having to write for three very different audiences at once. As members of an academic community of scholars, we write to continue on-going debates on various themes in moral and social philosophy. As aspiring members of a community of feminists and progressives, we males write to achieve legitimacy, to distance ourselves from what Susan Bordo calls "the undifferentiated patriarchal male."[10] As members of a larger community of men, we write to convince one another that there are models of "being a Man" which are quite different from those typically conveyed by the mainstream media. Because of the schizophrenia of writing for such diverse audiences, progressive male philosophers are destined to be regarded with suspicion: as not quite philosophers by the community of scholars, as not quite feminists by fellow female feminists, and as not quite real men by the larger society of men. Perhaps this tension is good — from such tensions provocative thoughts might be conceived. If nothing else, the tension will keep us honest.

Typically, philosophical writing is a demanding enterprise because of the sheer difficulty of giving an account of an abstract concept, such as temporality, in a way which renders the concept clear while preserving the complexity and subtlety of the concept. In social and moral philosophy, the concepts being examined, such as abortion or euthanasia, also often have highly emotional dimensions that present difficulties of two sorts: one needs to look beyond the emotional character of the concepts to be able to describe them in the light of reason; but also such analytical descriptions cannot ignore the emotional dimension which is often a constitutive dimension of the concept. In addition, in writing about masculinity I have set myself a further difficulty of attempting to blend conceptual analysis with personal experience. In talking about my own experiences of being male, I have had to confront my own failures to behave in ways which I now think are indicative of a responsible individual. Confronting these experiences has made it much harder to write about masculinity, but I hope it has also enriched the ensuing philosophical discussions and provided flesh to the often dry bones of conceptual analysis and argumentation.

In a recent class, mainly composed of freshmen, none of my students could understand why a man would think that he should not share equally with his female partner the full range of child-raising duties. Few if any of the men in the class, or the women for that matter, were willing to call themselves feminists or radicals. Many had been raised by only one parent, or were raised in some form of nontraditional family. Even those who had been raised in a traditional family spoke about the value of having parents share tasks. For me the most interesting thing was that when we came to the question of what masculinity means, most of the male students could give no answer, except the negative response that being masculine does not mean that one condones rape or that one must always be in charge.

In what follows I provide theoretical arguments that will set the stage for providing a positive answer to the question of what masculinity might mean. I am not sure though that I can do much better than to point out what masculinity is not. I remain encouraged by the realization that many young men, and women, today are also asking these questions in an attempt to understand what our moral responsibilities are, especially to the next generation. In the end this book is written for my students, especially my male students, who have consistently shown me over the years that many of the old stereotypes of masculinity are falling, brought down by reflection and discussion rather than confrontation. Of course, it remains to be seen whether the social institutions that have undergirded a traditional conception of masculinity will also be changed when exposed to the light of critical reflection. Changing those institutions will take our collective efforts, but such efforts begin with individual steps, such as the one I take here.

I

Anger, Desire, and Moral Responsibility

Overwhelming anger and uncontrollable sexual desire are two of the most common excuses men use in arguing that they should be forgiven for rape, harassment, battery, and a host of other offenses against women. The angry young man and the teenage boy whose hormones are out of control have become cultural stereotypes, and as with all stereotypes, there is some truth to be found here. Anger and rage are so commonly expressed by young adult males that we all come to expect it.[1] Also, men and boys frequently refer to their uncontrollable sexual desire as an excuse for various forms of sexual aggression. In this chapter I argue that it is important for men to take responsibility for ourselves and that a major part of that task will be to take responsibility for our anger and sexual desire which is too often used as an excuse, as a way of avoiding guilt or shame.

The abusive male who says that he only saw red or who was overcome by sexual lust has become too common.

I The Badgered Man Excuse

Recently, I was confronted with a stressful situation when I was told that we needed to replace an expensive section of sewer pipe in the front yard of our house. My response was to get angry at the contractor who had just informed me of the situation. Rather than becoming saddened, or resigned, in the face of stress or danger I, like most men I know, will become angry. I have spent a lot of my life becoming angry, yelling at someone, brooding and seething for a while and then, considerably later, attempting to cool off. It has seemed to me somehow justified to react angrily, either because I could not easily control my temper or because the person who was the object of my anger somehow deserved it.

Male athletes and soldiers, those paradigmatic "men," learn to use what is sometimes called "controlled anger," to channel angry responses toward a particular positive goal. But in many cases such anger is not easily contained and spills over into other aspects of their lives. Recently an outfielder, Albert Belle, was sanctioned by the commissioner of baseball's American League because he threw a baseball at a photographer who made him mad by trying to take his picture against Belle's wishes.[2] Belle, often cited as one of the best contemporary baseball players, by his own admission plays best when he plays angry. The same can be said of certain football players. Perhaps the most talented college player to enter professional football ranks in 1996, Lawrence Phillips, is known to be a "mean player" on the field, and that is just the way he likes it. Unfortunately, he is also mean off the field. He was convicted of beating up his girlfriend and dragging her down several flights of stairs by her hair.[3] Male soldiers are also trained to become angry and then to use their anger to become better fighters. As in the case of athletes, domestic violence is prevalent on military bases.[4]

When Albert Belle throws a baseball at a photographer with the intent to harm him because he is angry at the photographer for taking his picture, it seems clear that his anger and his action are not morally appropriate. And when a man responds angrily to a slight provocation from one of his children, the same can be said. In both cases the men are allowing themselves to be governed by emotions that, in some sense, they could and should control in order to avoid causing harm to others. But while their anger and the ensuing behavior may be morally condemnable it may also be something from which they can learn. In each case, the men can determine what they are allowing themselves to do and to what extent this behavior causes harm that could be prevented.

The morally difficult cases are those in which a man uses his seemingly uncontrollable anger as an excuse for violent outbursts. In its most plausible form, the uncontrolled anger excuse is based on a series of incidents, often unrelated, that push the man past the breaking point. I have felt, for instance, that if one more student comes into my office with a suppposedly legitimate excuse for not turning in an assignment on time, I will simply explode. My anger, eventually expressed to a student who had never before done anything to set the stage for my angry response to him, seems to the student to be unjustified. But to me at that moment in my life it seems completely justified as a response to the ridiculous lengths to which some undergraduates will go to avoid a deadline.

We have developed in our society the male equivalent of the battered woman syndrome excuse, what I will call the badgered man excuse. Just as use of the battered woman syndrome excuse asked juries to look at the history of abuse as a basis for seeing why the woman finally struck back at her spouse, so there is a covert excuse that asks us to forgive men who have reached the breaking point after countless insults and setbacks have pushed them to the limit of male tolerance. As in the battered woman syndrome, it is not the circumstances of the current events that are crucial. Rather, it is the pattern of events, many dating back quite a while, that are crucial for seeing the angry outburst as somehow excusable.[5]

The battered woman syndrome provides women with an excuse for harming or killing their spouses, even though the event that triggered a woman's violent reaction may not be, by itself, sufficient to justify the reaction. Until the development of this excuse, a battered woman had to establish self-defense, had to show that her husband's current behavior indicated that he was on the verge of killing or seriously harming her, before her violent responses could be justified. Recognizing the battered woman syndrome made it possible to bring into evidence the past pattern of abuse, so that the harm is seen as cumulative, and the woman's violent reaction measured against repeated harm, rather than merely an isolated threat.[6]

Some legal theorists have argued that we would have been better off to stay with the self-defense accounts, for when one introduces the battered woman syndrome one effectively implies that the defendant was temporarily insane. Yet, it seems clear that a battered woman may have good reason to attack her husband, given the pattern of past violence.[7] If she had a good reason, then it is not an excuse at all that should be sought, but a defense or justification. This line of reasoning is important. Employing the battered woman syndrome excuse should not be seen as an admission that a battered woman's response was irrational. Rather, on my view, it should be seen as a way of making sense of a woman's response to a pattern of abuse.

One might argue that men's angry and enraged reactions to certain fairly mild stimuli could be understood on the model of the battered woman syndrome. Many men experience increased frustration in certain contexts, and their reactions are not best viewed as merely triggered by a current incident, such as the student who presents an excuse for not turning in an assignment on time. Rather, the response needs to be considered in the context of the pattern of events leading up to the one that proximately triggers the angry or enraged response. It seems similarly unfair to restrict our attention to the present incident in the women's and the men's cases, when it seems clear that the response is to a larger pattern of events.[8] One obvious example of men who have used such an excuse are those authors who complain about male bashing by the women's movement and the popular press. Robert Bly and others in the psychoanalytically oriented men's movement see men as pushed to the breaking point.[9]

There are several reasons for rejecting the analogy between the battered woman syndrome and badgered man excuses. In the case of women who are in abusive domestic situations, the forms of past abuse are often horrific, including beatings, rapes, threats to their lives, threats to their children, etc. It is hard for most people to imagine being stuck in a relationship that is so cruel. While many men feel terrific stress in their lives, few, if any, are in the kind of relationship that battered women typically experience. Men need to realize the strong disanalogies between their situations and those of battered women.[10] Just as the person who is insulted needs to see the difference between his case and that of another person who is physically assaulted.[11]

Men who are in oppressively stressful situations or relationships may be able to claim some sort of excuse for their angry or enraged responses, but it will not be equivalent to that claimed by battered women. The battered woman syndrome excuse relieves the woman of all, or almost all, responsibility for her violent response. The badgered man excuse will at best relieve the man of only some of the responsibility for his reactions. In addition, if the stress that has built up was not based on violent threats to the well-being of the man, then he cannot use this experience to relieve himself of responsibility for a violent reaction to that experience, since his situation is not analogous to that of the battered woman. The badgered man's response must in some sense fit that to which he is responding.

One could argue that verbally abusive, not merely physically abusive, situations are threatening to the survival of the person, and hence could play a role in excusing a violent reaction. Think of the person who is subjected to mounting verbal insults aimed at the person's racial or ethnic heritage, family or reputation. Such insults can seem like a slap in the face. A violent response seems reasonable in such cases and could be justified or excused on a different basis from the one I am considering. On some accounts, anger is morally acceptable just in case an angry response is in some sense reasonable. Men need to show that their angry outbursts are indeed of this sort. I turn next to another kind of excuse that men often use to relieve themselves of responsibility before returning to a more developed treatment of reasonableness and moral responsibility for our anger.

▐▐ The Testosterone Excuse

Moral responsibility for one's emotional reactions and behavior is premised on the ability to exercise control over one's actions. In cases of anger, some men seem *nearly* out of control. In cases of sexual desire, it is thought to be *literally* true that some men cannot act otherwise than in line with their raging hormones. And even when this thesis is watered down, it is often thought that men, much more than women, have great difficulty controlling their sexual urges because of their hormones, and that as a result men should not be morally blamed for at least some of their acts of sexual aggression. Critical examination, however, casts doubt on the plausibility of this excuse.

As normally understood, moral responsibility makes sense only in those cases where a person could have done otherwise than what he or she did.[12] If I shove you or hypnotize you and thereby get you to do what I want you to do, rather than what you want to do, it is I rather than you who is thought to be morally responsible for any ensuing harms. People are thought to be morally responsible for events over which they have some control. When there is no external compulsion, responsibility is generally thought to be possible.[13] The difficult cases concern possible internal compulsions. If someone is severely impaired mentally, that person is often not in control of his or her own actions. Similarly, when someone is afraid, it is sometimes said that the person is not fully responsible because his or her reactions are under the control of various internal compulsions.

Can hormones diminish a person's control over his or her actions and, hence, constitute an excuse from moral responsibility? In one sense it seems obvious that such an excuse could be justified. If the person has such a hormonal imbalance that deliberative thought is literally blocked, then agency and control over one's actions are also blocked, and moral responsibility is at least diminished. Various illnesses can produce such a hormonal imbalance. But are the hormonal imbalances that accompany ordinary male adolescence sufficiently like those in these illnesses for us to think that adolescent boys and young men are blocked from deliberative thought? Surely not. If there is any similarity here at all it would be when hormones, especially testosterone, are linked with specific environmental triggers such as occur in sexual desire. But it is not plausible to think that adolescence itself involves the kind of hormonal imbalance that would block out all deliberation, since nearly all teenage males are able to engage in some deliberately chosen behavior.

Studies of nonhuman animals reveal that those males with higher concentrations of testosterone display more dominance and aggression than males with lower concentrations of testosterone. But the results are inconclusive when human males are studied, except when it is sexual aggression that is at issue. For human males, higher levels of testosterone correlate with greater sexual aggressiveness.[14] Such empirical findings seem to suggest that hormones do influence human male sexual behavior; but these studies do not show that hormones block deliberation or overrule choice. Indeed, the relatively diverse pattern of male sexual aggressiveness in the overall population seems to indicate that the effects of testosterone can be controlled, at least by controlling the environmental cues, such as watching violent pornography, that trigger testosterone to produce male sexual aggressiveness.[15] My point is a simple one: unless deliberative choice is blocked and unless men have no choice but to act in line with their hormones, the strong case for a testosterone excuse has been defeated.

A weaker case for a testosterone excuse would be based on the added difficulty that men have in controlling their sexual aggressiveness due to the presence of testoterone. Such a weak case would establish a basis for partial relief from moral responsibility by some men in some situations, not a blanket excuse. But there are serious objections to even the weak case.[16] The most serious conceptual objection is that such a case seems to depend on the implausible notion that just because something is hard to do, our responsibility for not doing it is diminished. Such a view seems implausible since moral responsibility dictates what people should do in their lives, where the assumption is that people will have to strive hard to do what are their responsibilities.

Consider the selfish person who generally finds it hard to do things for others unless he or she perceives some clear-cut advantage. Now consider another person who is not so selfish and much more inclined to help others without regard to the personal costs or benefits of doing so. If moral responsibilities could be eliminated merely because a person found it hard to fulfill them, then the selfish person would have fewer moral responsibilities than the nonselfish person. Yet, this seems to be the wrong result. The demands of morality should be as clearly addressed to the selfish person as to the person ready to do what morality required.

The weak version of the testosterone excuse means that men who have a greater proclivity to engage in sexual aggression will be less subject to the demands of morality than those who are less likely to engage in aggression. Yet, again this seems to be quite counterintuitive. Those who can do what they morally should do, but who find it hard to do so, would be forgiven for not doing so; whereas those who find it easy to do what they should do would be more subject to the demands of morality. Yet, it is just the person who is less likely to act in a morally responsible manner who needs to feel the constraints of morality more than does the person who is quite likely to be morally responsible anyway.

Morality should not be diminished when the going gets tough. Indeed, it is just at that point that morality should come clearly into view. Those people who are already inclined to act in a morally responsible manner do not have as much need for the social institutions that constitute morality's public expression. In a sense, the public sanctions that attach to morality are there for those who would not normally act in a morally responsible manner. Of course, they also play a role for everyone else, since few people are always inclined to do what they should do. But the main function of such public sanctions would be defeated if people thought that morality applied less to those who had a hard time following it.

Thus the weak version of the testosterone excuse runs contrary to the main impetus for having a morality at all. Unless men are literally blocked from deliberative choice and action by their sexual desires, it would not make sense to excuse them from responsibility. Morality should not be defeated or diminished because its demands are hard to meet. Of course, if moral demands are set unreasonably high, then the institutions of morality might be adversely affected. So the defenders of the weak version of the testosterone excuse, as well as the badgered man excuse, would need to show that it was somehow unreasonable for men to be morally criticized for their behavior since it is reasonable for men to respond to their environment as their emotions of sexual desire, or anger, moved them. I turn next to this topic.

III Reasonableness and Morality

A number of philosophers have tried to provide an account of morality as a form of reasonableness or rationality. On some of these accounts, what it is morally appropriate to do is what it makes sense to do.[17] According to such views, when an agent reacts emotionally his or her behavior is morally appropriate insofar as it is a rational or reasonable response to a perceived violation of a norm the agent accepts. Behavior is inappropriate or immoral when it fails to make sense given the norms that are accepted by the agent, or given some other norms that are relevant. In this section I will explore such a conceptualization of morality to see whether this type of analysis will help us understand the potential excuses of men based on their emotions.

Some emotional reactions are best seen as reasonable responses to a violation of norms by oneself or others. People often feel guilt because they perceive themselves as having failed to live up to a norm; and people often feel anger toward those who have violated norms. But in other cases our emotional responses may be morally appropriate or inappropriate quite independently of whether the person who expresses the emotion has accepted the norm or not.[18] It may be morally inappropriate to feel anger or sexual desire, and to act on these emotions, even though such reactions make sense to that person. If this is true then there will be cases where an emotion such as anger or sexual desire may be morally inappropriate even though it is perceived by that person to be a reasonable response to a given situation.

Most important for our purposes, a person may be angry in a way that appears reasonable and morally appropriate to the agent but not to the larger society. Perhaps the object of one's anger is one's own child who is not at fault but has nonetheless caused a harm. The father finds it reasonable to react angrily, but his neighbors do not. By reflecting on his neighbors' reactions, the child's father may come to see his anger as unreasonable. On the other hand, it may be that the anger does not reside completely outside the realm of moral approval, although it is outside the realm of normal social approval. It may be important for the person who feels anger to have this experience as a way of marking deeply felt connections with others. Here, anger is in some sense appropriate because it connects us to those to whom we are morally bound, even where these moral bonds are themselves not reasonably justifiable. Morality may have to do with certain arrangements that are weighty, yet not sanctioned by norms that the agent or society accepts. Anger may be a kind of marker of these weighty arrangements that cannot be extinguished by societal norms that are seemingly opposed to them.

In defending the moral assessment of emotions such as anger and sexual desire in terms of what it makes sense for an agent to do, we might follow Allan Gibbard and distinguish two meanings of "making sense," the basis of what is reasonable or rational. We might distinguish between "saying that it makes sense *for* a person to be angry [or desirous] from saying that it makes sense *that* a person is angry [or desirous]."[19] It may make sense *for* the person to express anger or sexual desire in that it is at least understandable why he so acted. It may be understandable that he acted a certain way in that given who this person is it is important, or even strongly conditioned, that he act this way. But for it to make sense *that* a person is angry or desirous, in that it is justifiable that he so acted, we must make reference to some set of accepted norms, either of the agent or of the society. There may be norms of education that make an assessment of moral inappropriateness legitimate, however understandable the behavior.

Even though I find this distinction quite helpful and will continue to employ it in a restricted way, it seems to me that some cases will not easily fit the reasonableness model of morality. Think of someone who is in love. In some respect, it makes sense *for* the person to be in this emotional state, but it does not make sense *that* the person has the emotion, in that this emotion may not be normatively sanctioned in a particular context, say, where those who are in love are brother and sister or they are of different races or of the same sex. Yet, we might think that being in love can be morally unproblematic even when it defies accepted norms. Love is an emotion that seems to have moral legitimacy independent of whether it is supported by accepted norms or not. If no one is hurt, being in love may be morally justifiable even though it is socially unacceptable in certain contexts. Here we often appeal to norms that are outside (or perhaps "above") those that are set by a given society. It may be that no one actually lives by these norms; yet they may figure in a possible justification of a person's reaction.

Think also of the quite different example of not being able to stop eating nuts at a party. Gibbard has helpfully pointed out that it may make sense *for* a person not to be able to stop eating nuts, in that he is being motivated by his base or animalistic motivations more than his rational ones. Yet, it does not make sense *that* he so act, and this is only captured when we look at the norms that most of us accept concerning proper party behavior. Should we infer from this that it is only the nonanimalistic motivations that can convey any sense of moral appropriateness? Maybe being in love is like not being able to stop eating nuts, something which is morally acceptable even though it does not make sense *that* the person act this way given the society's norms.

Consider the people who were involved in the infamous Milgram experiment. The psychologist conducting the experiment told subjects to administer what seemed to be large doses of potentially lethal electric shock to other subjects. Two-thirds of the subjects complied and administered the shocks even though these same people later admitted that it was wrong to harm another person.[20] Did these people display weakness of will in giving in to the demands of the psychologist? Or were they in the grip of a norm prescribing obedience to authority that they didn't really accept? Of course it would be frightening to think that they accepted the norm: do what you are told by the experts. I think it is not out of the question that they did accept it in some sense or other. But when they went home afterward many also felt guilty or at least angry for being put in the position of the heavy. And they felt this way perhaps because they did act reasonably, in at least one sense, insofar as they followed the advice of the experts. Like the man who gets angry at his child for things over which the child does not really have full control, the people who participated in the Milgram experiment might have felt responsible for being too loyal to authority and, yet, like the compulsive nut eater, not easily able to change their behavior.

Our feelings and reasons are subject to discussion, both internal and external, but they are not deemed to be moral just because they conform to a set of standards the agent finds acceptable and to which he or she consistently adheres. Rather, we subject them to various intuitions that often defy normal senses of acceptability. This is certainly true when we appeal to our intuitions about what an ideal person would do or what a person would do in an ideal situation. In judging the actions of a male parent, we might ignore what this man thinks about his roles or even how he has consistently acted as a parent before.[21] If morality is to be conflated with reasonableness, it will not be the agent's idea of what makes sense or even some more generalized sense of what makes sense for the society that demarcates the reasonable. Rather, we must refer to some overarching standard of what it means to be a responsible person.[22]

In many cases it seems appropriate to think of morality on the model of what it makes sense to do, but in other cases such a conflation will not serve our intuitions. When morality is disconnected from what seems reasonable, we can sometimes begin to see why certain emotional reactions by men may make sense but nonetheless be morally inappropriate, and also why other reactions that seem inappropriate are not. It may make sense for a man to respond to certain environmental cues and be sexually stimulated to act aggressively toward a woman, and yet we may think that this behavior is morally inappropriate even though we understand why he reacted this way. That it was hard to resist reacting this way or that the reaction made sense in terms of the norms accepted by the man in question or even by the society at large may not settle the question of whether it was the morally responsible thing to do. The man who responds angrily to his spouse for what appears to him and his neighbors to be a grave insult should not be automatically relieved of responsibility for his reaction.

IV Assessing Excuses

So far I have suggested that we can treat the emotional responses of anger and sexual desire in roughly similar ways from a moral point of view. Now I want to delve a bit more deeply into these matters and begin to explore some of the differences between these emotional reactions or responses in order to see how this affects a person's moral reponsibility for these emotions. One of the most obvious differences between anger and sexual desire comes out in the way that we talk about each. While anger and sexual desire each have an object, they have very different relationships to their objects. Grammatically, a person is angry *at* another person, but a person is sexually desirous *of* another person. This grammatical difference reflects a difference in the way these emotions typically get expressed.

Put bluntly, sexual desire normally drives a person toward another person, whereas anger normally drives people apart.[23] Whereas both emotions may cause aggressive or violent behavior toward others, the impetus for such behavior is quite different. The angry person is stimulated by a sense of injury or outrage at what a person has done. The sexually desirous person is stimulated by anticipation of pleasure that physical contact with another person could produce, often reacting aggressively to secure that pleasure.

One way to think about this is that anger is a negative emotional reaction while sexual desire is a positive one; the object of anger repels, while the object of sexual desire attracts.

Sexual desire attracts in an odd way, suggesting that the above difference may be not quite accurate since in many cases the object of sexual desire is not looked upon in a generally favorable light. This is why men may rape or beat the woman who is the object of their sexual desire.[24] Sexual desire is an emotion that needs an object for pleasure to ensue, but the object itself does not have to be held in high esteem or viewed positively in any other way than in terms of sexual attractiveness. And even "attractiveness" makes the response sound too positive, for what attracts a man sexually may merely be some exposed flesh on a woman, whether it be a breast or an ankle. And the ankle or breast need not be "attractive" in the sense that it is judged to be a good one of its kind, but merely one that does stimulate a certain kind of hormonal reaction, and hence literally attracts, draws one toward, without really being "attractive."

Anger and sexual desire are reactive emotions.[25] But they are reactive in different ways. Anger is normally a reaction to a perceived harm, injury, or threat. Sexual desire does not involve anything like this kind of assessment, for sexual stimulation can occur in spite of conscious assessments, even without them altogether. In the case of anger, the assessment could be quite rudimentary as when a man thinks that it has taken someone too long to respond to a question, but there seems to be some kind of conscious assessment here nonetheless. In sexual desire, a man could judge that a woman or another man is dressed in an appealing or provocative manner, or the man could merely be triggered to respond a certain way quite independent of conscious judgment. Of course there still could be some kind of unconscious judgment occurring.

When we assign moral responsibility for actions based on anger or sexual desire, the extent to which deliberation is involved is important because deliberation is often a sign that an action is under a person's control. But even where there is no deliberation or conscious judgment, emotional reactions can still be sufficiently under one's control that one is held morally responsible for actions resulting from them. Habitual behavior is not deliberative or even often conscious. Yet, we certainly can influence what habits we develop and which we do not. And in many cases, it is possible to break, or interrupt, a habit or set of habits and start on the road to a new way of conducting one's life.

Habitual anger or sexual desire are two of the most intriguing bases of male behavior. In my own experience, I can easily get into a rut of responding with anger to certain kinds of actions of others. If I stop myself early enough I can change the pattern and force myself to respond in some other way to the real or imagined injuries that someone is doing to me. Consider the actions of a university administrator who consistently delays in returning my phone calls or in answering my memos. I find it easy to see such unresponsiveness in personal terms, as clear indications that the administrator does not take me seriously as a colleague. My ensuing anger at this administrator, then, is a response to this perceived slight to my professional standing in the community, or perhaps even to me as person. But when I take a step back from the situation, there are ways of construing this unresponsiveness that do not elicit the automatic angry reaction. If I focus on the incompetence of the administrator, or on the fact that the administrator's unresponsiveness really doesn't injure me much at all, then I can form a different take on the situation that brings my anger into check. If I fail to do this, the more times I think about the unresponsiveness as a slight to me personally, the harder it is not to feel angry with him.

Consider another case discussed at length in Chapter 4, a man's sexual reactions to a pornographic photograph.[26] In a sense the object of his sexual desire is the woman portrayed in the pornographic photograph. Long-standing habits may make it easy for a man to become sexually stimulated by viewing even part of the photograph. In my own case, such habits extend back into my teenage years, and sometimes the habits of sexual response to photographs seem impossible to break. What makes these habits especially hard to break is the way they are connected to patterns of masturbation. Yet, the habits can at least be modified, even the habits of long-standing duration. One can retrain oneself to view certain images in such a negative light that the painful thoughts associated with the images begin to counter the pleasurable thoughts. Rape or sexual abuse for instance can be associated with the stories told by the victims of such terror, with the result that it is hard to regard images of rape or sexual abuse without also thinking about the terror of the victims.

As long as it is possible to change or interrupt habitual behavior based on anger or sexual desire, then this behavior is a proper subject for morality, especially for assigning moral responsibility for harms produced by that behavior.[27] Male aggression based on anger or sexual desire is indeed a source of much harm in the world, especially toward women. I make the larger case for such a claim in the majority of the other chapters of this book, especially in the chapters on pornography, rape, and sexual harassment.[28] Once it is acknowledged that aggression based on anger and sexual desire is a source of harm, then men should do all they can to change these emotional responses in themselves.

v Taking Responsibility for Emotions

The image of men as quick to display anger and strongly driven by sexual desire will take time and hard work to overcome. One way to start this process is to point out that this image portrays men as not in control of their lives and, hence, not responsible for what they do. It is worthwhile trying to change such an image, especially since it is greatly at odds with the traditional image of men as being in control of their emotions. And while there are other problems with the way that men view themselves emotionally, such as the distaste for many quite positive forms of emotion, I believe most men would generally think it advantageous if the conception of masculinity could be reframed so that control over emotions was again given center stage.

In a strikingly polemical essay in *Time* magazine in 1994, a counterargument to my posiiton was articulated. Lance Morrow mockingly stated a variation on one of the questions of this chapter: "Why — aside from the fact that they are jerks — do men get angry?" He replied to his own question as follows:

> Does it have anything to do with the fact that they die seven years earlier than women do, with rates of heart disease, ulcers, suicide, alcoholism, and other stress diseases considerably higher than those of women? Are they angry because something in their conditioned or instinctive social roles as men revs them up in order to expose them to the worst dangers. . . . 93% of people killed on the job are men. The more dangerous the job, the greater the percentage of men who are doing it. Federal, state, and local governments spend hundreds of millions of dollars protecting women workers from sexual harassment, while millions of men are still left substantially unprotected from premature death by industrial hazard. Actually the real reason men get angry is not the danger of premature death. It is mostly because they are unappreciated.[29]

I would agree with Morrow that men have a greater tendency than women to get angry because they feel frustrated and unappreciated. Men want to feel good about themselves, about their contributions to society, and yet they are not getting the social recognition they expect; but one reason they are not is the tendency to use excuses like those I have been investigating. It is surely not fair to blame the women who seemingly fail to appreciate men's contributions.[30]

As I have indicated, when men excuse their aggression because of anger or sexual desire, they turn away from their traditional image of being in control of their emotions. In order to regain their self-esteem and social recognition, they need to take responsibility for their faults just as they have sought to gain recognition of their strengths. By taking responsibility for our lives, especially our emotions, I mean admitting that there are things that could have and should have been done differently, and then resolving to change. The notion of men taking responsibility for their emotions, especially when their emotions lead to aggressive harmful behavior, has the two elements I have indicated to be important: it stresses the idea of control of themselves, and it pushes men away from using the implausible badgered man and testosterone excuses.

The key to men taking responsibility for their emotions is that they feel the need to do so from within. Taking responsibility is quite different from being assigned responsibility.[31] A person can be assigned responsibility and yet not feel it, not acknowledge that the assignment is justified.[32] Assigning responsibility is also often an accusatory process that alienates the person claimed to be responsible. Taking responsibility is a matter of self-appraisal, and so it is not very often the case that a person takes responsibility for an action or its consequences and yet does not also *feel* responsible. It is for this reason that taking responsibility is more closely correlated with feeling motivated to change than are the more accusatory forms of responsibility assignment which stress guilt or social condemnation.

In taking responsibility for our lives, especially for our emotional lives, we men are at a bit of a disadvantage in terms of our socialization.[33] Men generally have less insight into their emotional lives than do women and therefore find it harder to recognize and understand their emotional reactions. In order to change their reactions men must first gain knowledge of themselves, and no doubt many men will require help. Friends, spouses, partners, and family members will all have to be enlisted in this endeavor. Most important, men will have to begin listening to what others say about them, without immediately getting angry. Or they will have to figure out how to process constructive criticism after they have calmed down.

Men have traditionally been thought to have inner strength to figure out the answers to practical problems and then to motivate themselves to solve the problems. For many men, the more difficult and risky the problem, the greater they strive to solve it. If we men can devote ourselves to the task of solving the problem of how to change certain habitual emotional reactions with the same intensity as is applied to other practical problems, we men will find a way to change our patterns of emotional response. Perhaps what is needed is to convince ourselves that the process of changing our emotional lives is a risky or dangerous one, as an impetus to take it seriously. Actually, it is a risky business, for men risk losing a lot of the ground that they have come to depend upon as firm soil that they can stand on. But the risk will be worth it, since men stand to regain self-esteem and social acceptance, and also to begin the task of ending the pattern of aggression and abuse that has contributed to harms to women.[34]

When men take a critical look at the way they use anger and sexual desire as excuses, they will be launched on the path of reclaiming a sense of responsibility and respect for their emotional lives. That responsibility and respect are linked is not apparent to everyone. Perhaps the clearest indication that they are so linked, at least in the lives of men, is that when men think of themselves in a positive light they often also think of themselves as in control of most of the aspects of that life. Studies of male self-esteem link positive conceptions of one's masculinity with positive self-acceptance. Education and occupation are not highly correlated with self-acceptance. Locus of control is highly correlated with self-acceptance, but not as highly as is masculinity.[35] These findings have led some psychologists to worry about the effects of breaking down male sex roles in our society.

It is sometimes thought that if traditional male roles are undermined, men may lose their remaining sense of self-worth. I am pointing out another avenue. We can try to reconfigure the meaning of masculinity, so that men can feel good about being masculine without the negative repercussions of traditional patterns of aggressive masculine behavior. It is for this reason that in the chapters that follow I often discuss new models of distinctly masculine roles, rather than merely urge that men give up masculine roles altogether.[36] For example, I describe new patterns of socialization that build on men's traditional strengths as leaders and problem solvers in a way that leaves behind the often violent aggressiveness that has become so characteristic of military and sports contexts.[37] In so doing I try to build on the positive strengths of some of the traditional masculine roles, while leaving behind what is negative and harmful to women.

2

Paternity and Commitment

When we adopted our daughter, the judge told us that the adoption was final and that henceforth our rights, and also our obligations, to raise her could not be overridden by her birth parents.[1] Our lawyer had insisted that we identify and obtain consent from her birth father as well as her birth mother. At that time it was common for young women who wished to have their infants adopted simply to deny that they knew who the father was. Legal advertisements were then run asking for the birth father to come forward and challenge the adoption. If no father came forward, then many lawyers forged ahead with the adoption. But our lawyer was a very cautious person, and she insisted that the birth father be identified. Subsequently we met both birth parents, and the adoption proceeded smoothly.

The well-publicized cases of "Baby Jessica" and "Baby Richard" illustrated the legal problems that can result when a biological father arrives on the scene after an otherwise proper adoption has occurred.[2] It has seemed utterly unfair to adoptive parents that a healthy family, settled with the blessing of the law for several years, could be so easily disrupted by a man asserting a claim of procreative authority contrary to the best interests of the child. In the case of Baby Jessica, the Iowa and Michigan Supreme Courts held that an otherwise proper adoption could be overturned because a previously unidentified biological father claimed his right to raise his biological offspring.[3]

In the United States in the middle 1990s, the rights of biological fathers were given increasing importance in contested adoption cases. I want to look at some legal cases in this domain to identify the underlying philosophical justifications of these decisions. I will challenge the importance of mere procreation and present a conception of paternity that is at odds with the conception of gender equality[4] seemingly embraced by the "Baby Jessica" and "Baby Richard" cases and endorsed by the United States Supreme Court. I begin by looking at the case law that preceded this change as a way of understanding how legal and social views of biological parents, especially fathers, have changed.

❙ Paternal Rights

In the 1970s and 1980s court opinions critically scrutinized the various rationales for giving priority to biological mothers over biological fathers in contested adoption cases. In a string of United States Supreme Court cases, dating from 1972 to 1989, the claims of biological fathers were given increasing importance although the claims of children and mothers were still given greater importance. In the 1990s several state supreme court opinions seemingly embraced father's rights more wholeheartedly and were allowed to stand by the U.S. Supreme Court. I want to argue against the change we appear to be seeing, for it seems to me that the earlier cases in the 1970s and 1980s were sometimes based on quite questionable rationales.

In the case of *Stanley v. Illinois*, the U.S. Supreme Court first acknowledged the rights of unwed fathers. The case provides a fascinating glimpse of how these matters were understood before 1972 and why there was a need for some changes in the law. Peter Stanley "fathered" three offspring with Joan Stanley. Over the years, he lived with Joan and his children off and on. When Joan Stanley died, the state of Illinois tried to place the children in foster care, mainly because Peter and Joan had never married, and the state did not recognize any parental rights of unwed fathers. Justice Byron White wrote the majority opinion of the U.S. Supreme Court in overturning the decision of the lower court. He identified an interest that a man has "in the children he has sired *and* raised." [5] This linking seems to imply a dual standard: biological paternity *and* nurturance. But Chief Justice Warren Burger, in his dissenting opinion, pointed out that Peter Stanley had not been a nurturing father. In fact, he seemed quite willing to let his children go into foster care until it became clear to him that he would lose "welfare payments if others were named guardians of the children." Nevertheless, the majority of the justices apparently concluded that Peter Stanley should have custody regardless of whether he was a nurturing or "good" father.[6]

What is bizarre about the law before *Stanley* is that, regardless of what relationship an unwed biological father had with his children, he was given no rights concerning them. So, it was quite reasonable for the Supreme Court to side with Peter Stanley, whose biological and social connection with the children should not be ignored simply because he was not married to their mother. As a number of commentators have noted, unwed fathers were not given much, if any, legal interest in their offspring before 1972.[7] Of course, married fathers had continued to have privileged legal control over their offspring during this period.

In 1979 the U.S. Supreme Court reached a decision in *Caban v. Mohammed*. In this case, once again an unmarried couple had children and cohabited as if they were married. After they split up, the woman married another man, and her husband petitioned to adopt the children. The biological father tried to block the adoption, but New York State did not give unwed fathers the same rights as mothers; most important, unwed fathers had no right to block an adoption of their offspring. The U.S. Supreme Court declared this state law unconstitutional because the difference in rights accorded to unmarried men and women did not "bear a substantial relation to the State's interest in providing adoptive homes for its illegitimate children." [8] But in a lucid dissent, Justice Potter Stewart best summarized the principle that was most applicable to this case and others: "Parental rights do not spring full-blown from the biological connection between parent and child. They require relationships more enduring." [9]

In *Lehr v. Robertson* (1983), the majority opinion, written by Justice John Paul Stevens, quoted Justice Stewart's dissent in *Caban* and then provided the most developed rationale for this string of cases: [10]

The significance of the biological connection is that it offers the natural father an opportunity that no other male possesses to develop a relationship with his offspring. If he grasps that opportunity and accepts some measure of responsibility for the child's future, he may enjoy the blessings of the parent-child relationship and make uniquely valuable contributions to the child's development.[11]

The key here is that a biological father's rights, for instance to veto an adoption, are premised on his having seized the opportunity to accept "some measure of responsibility for the child's future." According to the court, nature makes women mothers, but it "gives men the chance to become fathers."[12] It is in light of this principle that the Baby Jessica and Baby Richard cases should be viewed.[13]

In these 1990s cases the biological fathers were not given the opportunity to become responsible fathers, since in both cases the biological mothers deceived the fathers about their pregnancies. In the Baby Jessica case, Cara Clausen, an unmarried woman, gave birth to a baby girl. Two days after the birth, Cara "gave her irrevocable consent to the child's adoption . . . as did the man she named (falsely, as it turned out) as the child's father on the birth certificate."[14] Iowa law gave biological fathers the right to veto an adoption which was not tied to raising, nurturing, or even demonstrating a commitment to act responsibly toward the child. Cara Clausen changed her mind shortly after the adoption and notified the true biological father, Daniel Schmidt, who filed a petition within weeks of the adoption to have it overturned.

One of the disturbing aspects of this case was that the adoptive parents, the DeBoers, did all they could to drag out the legal battle. What seemed like such a tragedy, namely for a three-year-old child to be dragged out of its adoptive parents' arms and placed into the arms of someone largely unknown to her, could have been avoided if the DeBoers had tried to expedite the legal proceedings rather than to stall them. It is also disturbing that Cara Clausen deceived the DeBoers and Daniel Schmidt, and that she used Schmidt to affect a situation which she herself had no legitimate basis to influence, having "irrevocably" given up her own rights to Baby Jessica. Clearly this case, like the Baby Richard case, cannot easily be seen as illustrating only the biological father's paternity rights. Rather, it may be that these fathers were not granted the opportunity to display responsibility for or commitment to their offspring, and for this reason, rather than because of their mere genetic link to their offspring, their claims were heard.

The case of Baby Richard involves even more deception. Daniela Janikova and Otakar Kirshner had a sexual relationship and Janikova became pregnant. They moved in together and cohabited for seven months. While Kirchner was traveling in Czechoslovakia, one of his relatives told Janikova that Kirchner had married a Czech woman abroad. Janikova moved out of their apartment and concealed her whereabouts. After giving birth Janikova immediately put Baby Richard up for adoption, listing the biological father as unknown. She also instructed one of her relatives to tell Kirchner that the baby had died. Illinois law stipulated that a biological father must show "a reasonable degree of interest in the child within the first thirty days of the child's life" in order to have a claim to block its adoption.[15] Fifty-seven days after the birth, Janikova relented and told Kirchner that their child had been adopted. Kirchner immediately petitioned to overturn the adoption, and as in the case of Baby Jessica, a long legal battle ensued. He married Janikova, and they ultimately gained custody of the child on April 30, 1995. A year and a half later, he abandoned wife and child.

One of the most striking facts of the Baby Jessica case is that the courts refused to give much weight to Daniel Schmidt's failure to support two children he had "fathered" before. In so deciding, the courts seemed to turn away from the dual test for paternal rights and to move closer to a single test: biological paternity. This shift is in my view quite regrettable. It is true that Schmidt might have a change of heart and now become a good father to Baby Jessica. But this mere possibility should not be sufficient to grant Schmidt the right to overturn an adoption. Nurturance, rather than genetics, should be the key factor in such cases.

❚❚ Procreation as a Moral Fact

In this section I wish to challenge an argument in favor of seeing male procreation as a strong moral basis for rights in adoption and abortion decisions. Daniel Callahan has provided one of the most cogent arguments to this effect. He begins with a moral axiom that I also embraced in the previous chapter, namely: "Human beings bear a moral responsibility for those voluntary acts that have an impact on the lives of others; they are morally accountable for such acts."[16] From this moral axiom Callahan argues that "unless a male is utterly naive about the facts of procreation, to engage in voluntary sexual intercourse is to be responsible for what happens as a result."[17] Callahan goes on to say: "The most important moral statement might be this: Once a father, always a father. Because the relationship is biological rather than contractual, the natural bond cannot be abrogated or put aside."[18] And, so this argument goes, the natural bond gives rise to a moral bond (based on the above moral axiom). According to Callahan, "each and every father has a full set of moral obligations toward the children he procreates ... unless he is mentally or financially incompetent to discharge those duties."[19]

According to Callahan, we cannot accept his argument about a father's obligations and responsibilities without committing ourselves to similar views about a father's rights: "Fathers in short have a moral right to know they are fathers and to have a voice in decisions about the outcome of pregnancy. To deny males such a right is also to reject the very concept of paternal responsibility for one's procreative actions. ... If society wants obligations taken seriously, rights must be recognized."[20] We cannot tell fathers they should share in child-rearing duties and also tell them that they have little or no say in decisions about abortion or adoption. Just as fathers cannot be relieved of their moral obligations as inseminators (not even through the anonymous act of artificial insemination), so they also cannot be stripped of their moral rights. Callahan blames feminists for giving mixed signals, chastising men for not assuming their moral obligations as fathers while pushing men out of abortion and adoption decisions.

This rhetorically powerful argument is not without its merits. I applaud Callahan's attempt to counter what he calls the "infantilization" of men. Much too little is expected of men as fathers in contemporary American society. And corresponding to diminished expectations is a tendency among many men to be the ones taken care of, rather than the ones who do the caretaking. In a previous article, I have argued that fatherhood should be understood as deeply connected to the provision of nurturance, education, and role modeling. Men should not see themselves as merely "intimates" or "playmates" of their children but should assume full responsibility for the caretaking of these children.[21] So, initially my own views of fatherhood are quite compatible with Callahan's.

Callahan, however, has perhaps too glibly assumed that if a person has done something to warrant being ascribed an obligation or responsibility, that person also has a basis for a rights claim.[22] It is true that in many cases rights and responsibilities go hand in hand. It is not true that merely having incurred an obligation also creates a right for the same person. If I harm you, I have by my harmful act incurred an obligation to make amends to you for the harm I caused, but no corresponding right is generated. In many cases, the same act does create both an obligation and a right, but Callahan seems to suggest that it is because one has incurred an obligation that one gets the right. Rather, in those cases where rights and responsibilities do correlate this relation exists by virtue of the act that creates both; the obligation does not somehow form an independent basis for a right.

I also wish to distinguish the responsibilities and rights of "fathers" from those of "procreators." I agree that *true* fathers should have both obligations and rights in the upbringing of their children. But I disagree with equating fatherhood with paternity, where paternity is seen as mere biological procreation. While it is true that sometimes we talk of "fathering" a child when what we mean is procreating, this is a very misleading form of expression. Notice that there is no corresponding connotation to "mothering" a child. That expression, in common parlance, refers exclusively to acts of nurturance and caretaking.[23] It is a sign of how low our expectations are of men as fathers that the term "fathering" can refer merely to the acts of insemination and impregnation.

Those who hold to a view of paternity as mere impregnation are also often committed to the maintenance of strong relationships and community. But such a view is actually at odds with support for community and strong relationships. True fatherhood should attach only to those men who have taken their relationships with mother or with child seriously. By "true fatherhood" I mean the condition of being in a caring relationship with one's children through which one nurtures, supports, and educates them. Fatherhood, as we will see later in the chapter, is an accomplishment, not a simple matter of biological fact. Indeed, adoptive fathers can be just as much fathers as biological fathers. There is no necessary connection between being a father and biological paternity.

A man who starts down a nurturing path with his children has greater rights concerning their upbringing than does a man who merely engages in an act of insemination. In fact, as a rule of thumb I propose the following: the more involvement a man has with his children, the more are his rights concerning their upbringing. But I reject Callahan's view that obligations can be understood in a similar way. In some cases, especially in cases of sexual assault, men may incur obligations even though they have not, and never will, have a nurturing relationship with their offspring. I will later provide an argument against the view, seemingly embraced by very recent court decisions, that paternal rights are biologically rather than socially grounded. Before doing this I turn to a consideration of the strong presumption in favor of the biological mother's rights.

III Maternal Rights

Why should biological mothers have been given such a strong basis, and biological fathers such a comparatively weak basis, for making decisions concerning the welfare of the child?[24] There are several possibilities. First, one could argue that maternal rights are based on mere genetic contribution to the child. But of course, this argument would give no greater weight to the mother's status than to the father's. Second, one could argue that maternal rights are based on the fact that the mother has carried the child for nine months during pregnancy. This view would distinguish her situation from the biological father's, but an additional argument is needed to explain why the fact of pregnancy should be given such overwhelming weight. Third, one could argue that mothers have a much stronger psychological bond with the child than do fathers, but this is not true across the board and is probably a poor generalization. Increasingly, it is being recognized that men can form as strong a bond of attachment to their children as can women. Fourth, one could argue pragmatically that it is easy to identify mothers but very difficult to identify fathers. With advances in DNA "fingerprinting," however, it is becoming easier and easier to identify fathers, and there is less and less justification for giving priority to maternal rights over paternal rights on prudential grounds.

The strongest argument is the second one, namely, that the biological mother carries the child for nine months, "an activity for which there is no precise male analogue."[25] I think there is something to this argument, but it needs to be filled out. There are, after all, many unique traits in each sex for which there is no precise analogue in the other sex. There is no precise analogue for the sperm that men contribute to the reproductive process. There are rough analogues and equivalences, though, even in the case of carrying a child for nine months. A biological father can display nurturance and support through his care for the biological mother during the pregnancy. A father can make plans for receiving the baby into a home, and take parenting classes so as to be better able to care for the child in the first few weeks, realizing that the mother will normally be in a weakened state just after giving birth. All these nongenetic factors, taken together, might constitute a rough equivalence to some women's nine-month pregnancy.[26] For the man, as well as for the woman, it is the caring labor rather than the mere genetic link that creates interests and rights.[27]

It is my view that biological mothers should not automatically be assumed to have strong interests and rights in their children merely because of their genetic link with the child. Indeed, even carrying the child for nine months may not be sufficient either, especially when we consider cases of drug and alcohol abuse during pregnancy which clearly risk harm to the fetus. It is the caring relationship established between fetus and mother in utero, not a mere genetic link or simple biological labor, that should, on my view, create the strong maternal interest and right.[28] One of the most powerful arguments for diminishing the genetic and simple biological criteria is that they have very little to do with the character of parenting that an individual man or woman is likely to engage in. If one thinks that the best interests of the child should have weight, then simple biological criteria would have to be amended.

American social policy countenances very heavy screening for adoptive parents but virtually none for biological parents.[29] Despite some efforts in the direction of screening where drug abuse is suspected, there is no strong likelihood that biological parents will be screened for their parenting skills even in the distant future. But when biological parents seek to overturn an already finalized adoption and remove a child from the home of its adoptive parents, it is not unreasonable to begin to redress this disparity by demanding that the biological parent demonstrate that he or she is likely to be a good parent. It is not too much to expect that judges will take into account whether a biological parent who is challenging an adoption will be a good parent to that child, given that it is already established that an adoptive parent has met this test.[30]

The legal battle in Tennessee over control of frozen embryos well illustrates some of the problems involved in recognizing a strong maternal right based on mere genetic connection. When all that has occurred is that sperm and egg have been joined in a test tube, with no intrauterine gestation, then neither the woman nor the man has a greater claim on the embryo based on genetic connection since the contribution by each "parent" is roughly the same. When there has been some intrauterine development of the fetus, then the woman can claim some priority over the biological father based on the caring relationship she may have developed with the fetus. But my view is that neither biological mothers nor biological fathers have a strong interest or right in decisions about their child merely on the basis of their genetic link with the child. In this chapter, I am advocating that this conclusion influence only cases of contested adoption cases. I make no claims about other parental struggles, although my analysis could be extended to show that divorce-based custody battles should not be biased in favor of mother or father on genetic grounds alone.

IV Commitment to Fatherhood

For too long men have identified themselves as men, as "real men," in terms of their role as procreator rather than caretaker of their children.[31] This identification is expressed in the primary meaning of the term "to father," that is, "to beget."[32] As I pointed out, English has no corresponding term to "mothering" for identifying the role of nurturing and education performed by a male parent. Perhaps the best example of the complete removal of paternity from fatherhood occurs in cases of anonymous sperm donation. In the mid-1980s a California appellate court said that the anonymous donor of sperm cannot even "be considered the 'natural father,' as he is no more responsible for the use of his sperm than is a donor of blood or a kidney."[33] But since the sperm donor in this case was homosexual, perhaps this is why the court was reluctant to consider him to be the "natural father."

Paternity is sometimes used as a synonym for procreation, supplying the sperm that fertilizes a woman's egg. Given that most men have the potential to create billions of sperm over a lifetime, it is easy to see why some men have so little interest in what becomes of a few of their sperm. Similarly, while procreation is something many men brag about, it is not the sort of thing that is linked in their minds to relationships and to the type of nurturing that is so important for sustaining relationships over time. On the other hand, a woman normally has the capacity to produce only several hundred ripe eggs over the course of a lifetime, and each one that is fertilized must be nurtured in her body in order to develop into a child. Men see their sperm as more like blood than like the woman's eggs. But why should this continue to be the norm?

Procreation, like pregnancy, at least when both are voluntary, should be seen as the beginning of a commitment. The act of procreation constituting paternity is not the same as fatherhood. Procreation can be the first stage in fatherhood, but only when it is conjoined with a commitment to care for the ensuing offspring. A number of courts seem to recognize as much when they ask whether the biological father has committed to undertake the responsibilities of parenthood. But it is not at all clear that the courts have worked out what would be the sufficient signs that someone has made such a commitment. In what follows I will reflect on what a commitment to fatherhood might involve, along the way considering what commitment itself involves.

The adoption cases we have surveyed present the following problem: how can a man display a commitment to be a good father before his child is born? In most cases, by continuing her pregnancy and acting in a caring way toward the fetus, a woman displays a commitment to be a good mother, a commitment that can be rebutted by her future actions, to be sure. What the biological mother does is to engage in a caring relationship that involves physical and social sacrifice for the future child.[34] Her body must literally labor in behalf of the child, her relationship to the growing child is publicly presented to all whom she meets. There is no corresponding laboring of the body, caring for the fetus, and public manifestation of a relationship with the fetus which men must experience for their children to be born. And for this reason, men must demonstrate in some other way that they are committed to these children.

Consider the case of *In Re Raquel Marie X*.[35] Miguel and Louise had a long-standing sexual relationship but had never married. When Raquel Marie was born, they were living apart. Shortly after giving birth, Louise put her daughter into foster care and eventually consented to her adoption. Miguel filed suit to block the adoption. The New York State Court of Appeals noted that Miguel "had an older daughter by Louise, named Lauren, and had failed to support her. According to Louise's allegations, Raquel Marie had been conceived during Miguel's forcible rape of Louise, in violation of a protective order. Many times before and after Raquel Marie's birth, Louise had sought court protection from Miguel's abuse."[36] Nonetheless, this appellate court found that Miguel had properly grasped his opportunity to demonstrate commitment to be a responsible parent, largely because of his timely filing of a challenge to the proposed adoption.

To be committed one must do more than merely indicate one's intentions. Commitment involves some acts which indicate that one is already "engaged" with what it is that one claims to be committed to. A person needs to indicate that his or her life plans have been directed or altered so as to encompass the commitment in question. Often this means dropping some current activity so as to make room for the tasks involved in the activity a person is committed to. At minimum, a person must not engage in those tasks that are antithetical to the activity one is committed to. It is possible to be engaged in a set of tasks and not yet to be accomplishing them, as is true of the father who takes parenting classes prior to the birth of his child, or who practices parenting skills on other children who are in the extended family. Such activities show that a person is engaged in being a caring parent even though the forthcoming child is not yet available to be cared for.

Miguel failed to demonstrate that he cared about either Raquel Marie or Louise; indeed he seems to have demonstrated just the opposite. Of course, it is possible that despite his history of abusive actions he could now show that he is ready to be a good parent. But his words alone, and his timely filing of a legal form publicly displaying those intentions are not sufficient. Miguel has to rebut the overwhelming evidence that he is likely to be at best an absent and at worst an abusive parent to Raquel Marie. Something like a complete change of character and ensuing signs thereof would have to be forthcoming, and such a change is very unlikely.

One legal commentator, Deborah Forman, maintains that the question of whether a man is fit to be a parent should be separated from the question of whether he is committed to be a parent. She says it is the latter question that should be paramount in deciding whether a man has the right to veto a proposed adoption. In considering the case of the proposed adoption of Raquel Marie discussed above, Forman writes:

> As abhorrent as Miguel's conduct is, and as harmful as it might prove to the child, it does not necessarily prevent him from demonstrating a substantial commitment to assuming the responsibilities of parenthood. Consider if Miguel had done everything possible to manifest his intent to obtain custody of Raquel Marie — he had publicly acknowledged her, filed for paternity as soon as possible, and provided substantial financial support for her. We would then be hard-pressed to conclude, based solely on his conduct toward Louise, that he had not made a substantial commitment to assuming his parental responsibilities. His violent behavior should, however, still render him unfit as a parent.[37]

Forman notes that Louise and Miguel subsequently reconciled and married. She asks, rhetorically, why courts should be less forgiving than spouses.

The major difficulty with this analysis is that it not only distinguishes fitness from commitment, but it also separates the financial responsibilities of fatherhood from the rest of the responsibilities. Miguel's rape of Louise demonstrates that he is unlikely to perform his responsibilities of caring and nurturance. If he were applying to be an adoptive father, his publicly stated intention to support the child would almost surely not be sufficient to rebut such a history.[38] Forman recognizes some of these problems but dismisses them in favor of defending fathers' rights. She concludes that it is right for courts "to consider the father's prebirth and postbirth actions regarding the child, as well as his conduct toward previous children. Surely such conduct is relevant, but it should not preclude a father from convincing the court that this time he will commit."[39] Forman seems to be urging us to be even more forgiving than most of the spouses in such cases.

While I agree that biological fathers with a history of abusive behavior should be given the opportunity to convince a court that they have changed and will be good fathers in the future, I would hope that these occurrences would be rare. For there is a strong initial case for thinking that someone like Miguel is and will be a bad father from the record of past behavior toward his other children and toward Louise, as well as his pre- and post-birth behavior toward the child in question. What could count to override this initial case would have to be something quite extraordinary (and to my mind nearly unimaginable). Courts should not close off the possibility of such demonstrations of change of heart, but they should set a very high standard of proof.[40]

v Giving Fathers Their Due

I would urge that we apply the same standard to these biological "fathers" that is applied to prospective adoptive parents.[41] The New York State Legislature recently considered a bill that would give the right to veto a biological mother's decision to place her child for adoption "only to unwed biological fathers who demonstrate that they have been and will be actively engaged in the care and upbringing of the offspring."[42] It seems to me that such a standard should be adopted throughout the country. In this section of the chapter I will offer some additional support for such a suggestion, arguing that this change in law would give fathers, not merely paternal procreators, their due.[43]

While largely supportive of a standard like the one proposed in New York, some legal scholars have worried that such a law would not sufficiently protect unwed mothers' rights.[44] For even after the father has shown commitment to be actively involved in care and upbringing, the mother may still have legitimate objections to granting custody to the father, perhaps based on his treatment of her. If the mother can show that she was coerced into sexual relations with the father, the father should be judged unfit to be a parent and hence not deserving of custody. Courts must listen to the mother's reasons based on her relationship with the father and not merely look at the relationship between father and child.

I agree that the mother's testimony about her interactions with the father can be important, especially where it indicates a disposition to violence, as is true in the case of pregnancy caused by rape. But I do not believe that biological mothers should be given so much weight in these proceedings that the mothers, simply because they are the mothers, can veto the custody claims of unwed biological fathers. It is quite possible that a father can be a very good father and yet not be able to maintain much of a relationship at all with the child's mother. Custody battles often illustrate that neither parent is a fit spouse for the other but that one or both can nonetheless be quite a good parent for the child. The fathers' rights movement should not be completely discounted. There is no initial reason to give priority to the genetically based claims of either the biological father or mother.[45]

Giving fathers their due does not mean following the path seemingly established by the string of cases culminating in the Baby Jessica and Baby Richard rulings. In the Baby Jessica case, it should have been relevant that the biological father, Daniel Schmidt, had effectively abandoned his other daughter. In the Stanley case, where the Illinois court tried to strip an unmarried father of custody of his children, it should have mattered that Stanley did not demonstrate his continued commitment to care for his children. But in addition, it should matter quite a bit in the Baby Richard case that Otaker Kirchner, the biological father, did show his commitment to be a good parent. Nevertheless, his mere paternity does not warrant much consideration at all — just as his insemination was a relatively minor act so should be the status of the ensuing mere paternity.

Other theorists have argued that fathers' rights should be much stronger than I have indicated. I will end this section with a consideration of some of these objections to a view like mine. The sort of case that is most interesting to such theorists is that in which a biological father wants a pregnancy to continue and a biological mother wants the pregnancy to end. The chief basis of the claim that biological fathers should have veto power over biological mothers' abortion decisions is that men have a morally legitimate interest in procreation, the denial of which is initially seen as an abridgment of their autonomy.[46] Based on this procreative interest, in certain special cases, men can press their claims to veto a woman's decision to have an abortion.

What is most peculiar about this argument is that it advocates interfering with a woman's autonomy by compelling her to carry a fetus to term so as to protect the autonomy and procreative interests of a man. Yet, surely it is just the woman's autonomy claim that is normally cited, and rightly so, as the basis for accepting her abortion decision. It is after all her uterus, not his, her suffering and risk, not his, which are at stake. To require the woman to carry an unwanted fetus to term is similar to enforced servitude. I may have a very strong interest that you provide various services to me that you have contractually committed yourself to perform, so that I can exercise my autonomy by making a certain product, say. But my interests are not so strong as literally to compel you to perform the service, for this compulsion would require the kind of force that is unjustified. I may be owed damages as a result of your nonperformance, but that is a different matter. If this argument shows anything, it is only that a woman may harm a man by not carrying a fetus to term; it does not show that she should be required to carry the fetus to term.

Fathers' rights should be given weight, but only when a man is a true father in the nurturant sense. As indicated earlier, it is harder to demonstrate that one is a true father before the birth of the child, but not impossible. Prospective fathers can take classes on parenting, support the pregnant woman in a variety of ways, and practice their caring skills on other children in the extended family. These are the factors that the courts should be considering, in at least as serious a manner as costly DNA testing, to determine whether a man is a true father and deserving of the rights and obligations that attach to fatherhood. Paternity should not be confused with true fatherhood. By avoiding this confusion we will stop treating men as mere inseminators, and we will also stop infantilizing men. When men show that they are committed to being good parents, then it is appropriate to give them the status that women are already afforded in contested adoption cases.

VI Positive Paternity

In an important and widely cited essay, Virginia Held argues that the "continued existence of humanity may require that we cease to turn 'mothering' into an activity filled only by mothers."[47] Expanding on Held's insights, I wish to provide a positive construal of paternity and fatherhood which shifts the burdens and benefits of nurturance and child care from the exclusive purview of women to include *male* child rearers. I do not mean to suggest that men must become like women; this is not an endorsement of androgynous parenting. Rather, it is important that men find ways to bring their aptitudes, sensitivities, and skills to bear on their paternal role. What is needed is a substantive, not merely a procedural, view of gender equality in parenting roles.

Procedural equality is the view often associated with the first phase of feminism.[48] Equality was characterized as a moral principle requiring that all people, regardless of gender, be treated the same. In the context of child rearing, it was thought that men needed to do their fair share of housework and child care, splitting jobs evenly with their female partners, so that no one was given a greater burden or benefit in the child-rearing domain. This notion of procedural equality was quite useful for combatting blatant discrimination against women, such as the expectation that women would do all the child care and men none simply because child care was "women's work." Exposing the underlying moral flaw in such a position was important in the struggle for the recognition that women are equal human beings, not essentially different from men.

The alternative to procedural equality, substantive equality, is associated with the second phase of the feminist movement. Equality is here characterized as a moral principle that calls for equal treatment when people are relevantly the same and differential treatment when people are relevantly different. Substantive equality would recognize that if men and women really are different in some respects, then these differences could serve as the basis for legitimate differences in treatment. For instance, since women can give birth, but men cannot, a policy that gives extra health benefits to "pregnant people" does not necessarily violate the principle of equality, even though such extra benefits cannot be enjoyed by men.

There are at least two ways to view parenting roles. According to the procedural account, men and women should do exactly the same work in the realm of child care. Individual differences between men and women, whatever their causes, should not enter into the determination of who does what. This view of childcare is sometimes called the androgynous view, since it treats men and women as essentially the same, assigning to each the same childcare burdens and benefits as if men and women were really the same, that is, members of the same androgynous gender group, rather than members of different gender groups. According to this view, if men do not do their fair share of early childhood nurturing they will lose any claim to equal rights in decisions about how their children are to be raised.[49]

The second way to view equality in parenting roles is to require that men and women share equally in child-care duties, while taking into account legitimate differences in aptitude or competence between them. If it turns out that men find it far more difficult to do certain child-rearing tasks, such as feeding or bathing a newborn, and women find these same tasks much easier, substantive equality will allow for these differences to be taken into account. It will not necessarily be expected that men perform the same tasks as women in order to demonstrate that they are participating equally in child care. What is required is that the tasks performed by men and women be equally burdensome or beneficial to them. Such a position at least opens the door for thinking that men can demonstrate that they have met their child-care obligations and hence deserve equal rights in decision making, without necessarily doing exactly the same jobs or doing them for the same amount of time as women.

This second way of viewing parenting roles runs the risk of slipping into a retrenchment of gender sterotypes in our society. I wish to conclude this chapter with a consideration of Virginia Held's proposal to avoid such a retrenchment. Held proposes that most differences in child-care aptitude and competence are due to differential socialization where "boys are encouraged to study and work at various jobs and girls to babysit and do housework."[50] We should try to make sure that these differences are not perpetuated by differential child-care arrangements. Indeed, Held suggests that such socialized differences probably create only temporary differences in aptitude and competence, and they should therefore be regarded skeptically.

Held's rule of thumb for determining whether duties are being assigned on the basis of stereotypes is to ask whether arrangements about task sharing would be accepted if the male and female partners were roommates of the same sex. And Held also proposes that the assessment of one partner's competence or its lack should be made by the other partner, in order to diminish the likelihood that existing social biases will influence the assessments. In addition, we need to weigh the cost of letting men participate less in early childhood care, namely, that the next generation of boys will lack a model of men doing such tasks. All in all, the various components of her strategy make it unlikely that many differences in aptitude and competence will justify long-term differences in the distribution of the tasks of child rearing for men and women. As Held points out, child rearing requires on-the-job training, and women as well as men will often feel that their past experiences did not prepare them for coping, for instance, with "the outbursts and demands of small children."[51]

A positive conception of paternity will have as its ideal that men take an interest in child rearing as active as that of most women. Men will be committed to maintaining a safe and loving home for their children, spending time with their children in ways that are mutually beneficial, but also in ways that burden men as much as they burden women. Men will be willing to "mother" their children, to provide nurturance and comfort and support, as well as to "father" them. But men need not become slightly larger and hairier versions of women in order to embrace positive paternity. What is needed, instead, is that they become committed to being equal participants in the raising of their children. When such commitment is demonstrated, then they will also be afforded equal rights in decision making concerning the welfare of their children.

I must admit that this discussion of positive paternity has a selfish as well as an altrusitic motivation. I agree with Virginia Held that men would be cheated if women were to continue to be the only ones who could be child rearers. Having participated actively in the raising of a child, I would have felt tremendously cheated to be told that by nature or nurture I was not suited to be an equally participating parent.[52] As Held has said, even if men were so foolish as not to recognize the value of such parenting, "they would still be entitled to equality, and mothers would have an obligation to help them realize it."[53] When men have a positive conception of their paternity they will demand, rather than shirk, the obligations of parenthood, and paternity will cease to be equated with mere procreation.

3

Sexuality and Confession

(with James Bohman)

This chapter is an attempt, based on our experience, to understand why male sexuality, especially coercively aggressive sexual practices by men and boys, has achieved widespread acceptability, even as it is publicly condemned. We will argue that the widespread practice of confessing about sexuality in the Catholic Church (along with similar practices in other religions) helps to legitimate coercively aggressive sexuality, which has a profound impact on what it means to be a heterosexual male or female. Because of our own experiences in the largely sex-segregated society of Catholic children, we will focus on how confessing sexuality affected our conception of masculinity. But this discussion is relevant to conceptions of female sexuality as well, since men's view of heterosexual male identity is the mainstay of a dominant view of sexuality which contributes to how women think of their own (especially heterosexual) identities.

Throughout this chapter we contend that the Catholic practice of confessing heterosexual male transgressions (along with similar practices in other religions) reinforces a conception of sexuality which fails adequately to distinguish masturbation and impure thoughts from the serious offenses of sexual coercion and rape. Like other forms of male socialization, the pre–Vatican II Catholic practice of confessing sins to a priest provided boys with mixed messages: sexual transgressions are bad but so common as to be expected; sexual transgressions, no matter how bad, can be easily forgiven so that life may go on as it had. Similar mixed messages are provided when some members of the men's movement publicly confess their patriarchal sins through their writings.

▮ The Myth of Uncontrollable Male Sexuality

As we prepared for our first confession, various categories of sins were explained to us in great detail. By far the most interesting was the category of "impure thoughts and actions." We were told that it was a sin — that is, that it was forbidden — for us to touch ourselves "down there" or to think about things that would make us want to touch ourselves. It was recommended that we go to confession once a week. As a group we were all paraded over to the church, and anyone who "wanted" to go to confession was given ample opportunity. The ones who did not avail themselves of this opportunity clearly stood out and knew that they would be criticized later for this lapse.

What were we to confess? We were initially provided with a kind of litany: "I have disobeyed my parents so many times; I have fought with other children so many times; I have lied or had impure thoughts so many times." The assumption was that we would pretty much follow this litany each week, varying the number of times we had committed each sin, but sticking pretty closely to this list. Each week we would be given a "penance" by the parish priest, which seemed to vary hardly at all. The norm was five Hail Marys and five Our Fathers and an Act of Contrition in which we promised to try harder. Hence it came to be rather routine that we all thought of ourselves as sinners, especially sexual sinners, who were dirtied by these acts and in need of cleansing once a week.

A Catholic child's first confession takes place at age seven or eight, just after achieving the "age of reason." This event also marks the first formal occasion in which sexuality is discussed openly by priests and nuns with children. Confession marked the time when sexuality was first identified and first associated with "dirtiness," with "sin." From the first confession through adolescence, as well as for some adults, the association of sex with sin was so strong that the only way it seemed one could break free of being a sinner was to stop being sexual. Hence it has become common to associate the confessional with sexual repression. Prohibition of a wide range of sexual activities certainly was (and is) the official intent of the practice of confession, especially as adolescents come to adopt their eventual social roles and sexual identities as wives and mothers, husbands and fathers.

The thing that seemed clearest to us growing up Catholic was that our male sexuality was portrayed as nearly uncontrollable. This was true from the earliest lectures on sexuality that we were exposed to in the parochial school classroom. We were urged to repress our sexual urges until a time in our lives when there would be a socially acceptable form of release for one's nearly overpowering sexual urges. Of course, the best method was to get married and have a wife who was always available to help her male partner keep his awful power in check. Since at age six or seven, even in Catholic communities, marriage was never a serious option, masturbation was the obvious answer.[1] It is curious, at least on first sight, that the Catholic Church historically took such a dim view of masturbation, sanctioning it almost as stringently as sexual violence. Both were considered forms of sexual abuse that were intrinsically evil.[2]

In an informative exposition of the Catholic confessional, a turn-of-the century peasant priest commented: "The Catholic confession, according to the intention of the Church, is not only a disclosure of sins for the sake of remittance, but also a means of directing the believers, regulating their everyday lives according to Christian principles. . . . Sexual questions are undoubtedly those most frequently raised during confession."[3] Many priests saw the confessional as a way of counteracting non-Catholic teaching about sexuality, such as that coming from physicians. Here the key was for the priest to use the powers of the confessional to overcome so-called bad habits.[4]

Our own experiences are illustrative here. The sinfulness of masturbation was emphasized over and over, but the penances were very minor. Indeed, it was expected that we would masturbate but that in feeling the obligation to confess it, we would bring it under the powers of forgiveness of the priest. Although our urges did not thereby diminish, the subsequent acts of masturbation were both "dirty" and also somehow okay, for we had every expectation that they would again and again be forgiven, and we would be cleansed. We did not feel deterred from thinking and talking about sex, especially forced sex. We were obsessed with talk about female anatomy and with viewing pornographic pictures as a stimulus to masturbation.

While there is nothing wrong with young boys thinking that masturbation is okay, what the confessional tended to do was to make us feel that all forms of sexual activity should be viewed in the same way as masturbation. It was no more sinful, or so it seemed to us, to bring oneself to sexual climax than it was to pressure and even to force a girl to bring one to climax. Both were clearly sinful and forbidden, but both would be forgiven, again and again. Most significant, both urges were by and large uncontrollable, and the best that one could hope for was that the frequency was kept to a minimum. It was in this way that the Catholic confessional both repressed and legitimated aggressive sexual behavior among males, and it was in this way that the Catholic confessional gave us a sense of our masculinity as something both sinful and not fully controllable by our own wills.

It may be objected that the Catholic Church has maintained a hierarchical ordering of sins, and that rape was considered one of the worst of the sins one could commit. Part of our response is to point out again that masturbation and rape were both considered the worst sins one could engage in. But in addition we want to point out that we are not trying to indict the Catholic Church at all. Nor is it our goal to impugn the motives of those church leaders who have constructed and reconstructed the confessional. Rather, we are interested in how the confessional worked in practice and what effects it had on male sexual socialization.[5] It is our experience, and the experience of many men we have talked to, that the confessional conveyed the message that all sexual sins were both expected and easily forgiven.

The confessional is seemingly paradoxical from the perspective of moral legitimation. On the one hand, certain sexual practices, such as masturbation or sexual violence, are condemned in the confessional. On the other hand, male sexual aggression is seen as nearly irresistible and, for this reason, forgiven and in a sense legitimated through the confessional. The paradox may be dissolved when we realize that very few institutions directly sanction the moral transgressions of dominant groups. Sociobiological justifications of men who rape[6] and neoclassical economic justifications of the mistreatment of workers can be cited as examples of direct legitimations of the acts of dominant groups. But these are exceptions to the rule, since they provide nonmoral legitimation of coercive practices of members of dominant groups. These legitimations are nonmoral to the extent that they justify practices by appealing to ineluctable causal mechanisms or to unalterable social or natural facts. Generally, harm is morally condemned, and official Catholic morality is no exception here: rape is portrayed as a serious and mortal sin. Yet, condemnation, and ultimate forgiveness, are expected by many men based on their first encounters with the confessional (and similar practices in other religions) as boys.

In the confessional, sexual transgressions by men and boys are legitimated in that they are regarded as both nearly inevitable and forgiveable. Sexual aggression is so expected that often a boy first hears about it from priests who inform the boys of this possible sin that they should confess. Once it is confessed, the priest offers forgiveness and acceptance back into the moral community, without the severe penance attached to other transgressions. As a point of contrast, consider the sin of stealing. The sin is not forgiven until restitution is made: this is part of the "firm resolution of amendment" that the priest requires. By offering forgiveness for coercive sexual behavior without requiring the moral equivalent of restitution or even apology, the confessional fails to promote moral transformation. In the sense we use the term, moral transformation demands more than contrition or even the reaffirmation of a prohibition; it requires changing the very attitudes and behaviors which the confession has socialized the male adolescent. In sexual transgressions, nothing similar to restitution, such as a public declaration of shame or a firm public resolve to change one's attitudes and behavior in the future, is required for forgiveness.[7]

Forgiveness for sexual transgressions is offered without a demand for moral transformation. This makes it quite likely that the sexual sin will be repeated, and it indicates that sexual sins are less important than other sins, such as those violating property rights. The penance for sexual sins remains a matter between the sinner and his conscience; whereas penance for "property sins" takes on a more public character, because of the requirement of restitution. In this manner, sexual transgressions come to be seen as legitimate in ways that other sins are not, setting the stage for boys to feel permitted to engage in a wider scope of sexual sins, in some cases including rape.

Officially, priests do not normally equate masturbation and rape, but the lack of any requirement of restitution tends to put rape on the same level as masturbation — serious sins that can be fairly easily, and privately, forgiven. They are both in the same class of forgivable wrongs. The legitimating role of confession is thus related to guilt. Guilt can be removed in the confessional without changing behaviors or attitudes. In addition, guilt is shifted to girls, who are portrayed as more in control of their sexual urges than boys. These two factors are at the heart of male socialization into their dominant social-sexual roles. As with many other forms of ideology, socialization into a dominant role is at odds with official doctrine. The confessional condemns sexual transgressions, and condemns rape in especially harsh terms, but male sexual aggressiveness, including coercive sexual behavior, is legitimated nonetheless.

Some members of the Catholic hierarchy have worried about the socializing effects of the confessional. In the eighteenth century, Jacques-Joseph Dugnet "cautioned his penitents against hastening to the confessional as soon as some sin troubled them. They should first reflect on their deed and consider their moral situation — not run precipitously and confess the sin merely to be free of it and forget it."[8] But this view was not very common, and in our experience just the opposite was instilled; confessing as often as possible was the greatest sign of virtue. The confessional was seen as an institution it was good to participate in frequently, where the same sins were forgiven over and over, thereby legitimating that form of behavior.[9]

Like other forms of male socialization, the Catholic confessional is situated within, and expresses, a particular set of norms. The confession clearly articulates the dominant moral vision of masculinity. For boys, the confessional practices make it clear their male sexuality is largely out of their control. For girls, the confessional stresses that it is their responsibility to try to curb the sexual aggressiveness of males. One of the worst sins for a girl is allowing herself to get pregnant, not to have resisted male aggressiveness. The boy or young man who impregnates, sins much less since his aggressiveness is seen as virtually uncontrollable by him. So, while girls are also taught to go through the confessional litany of sexual sins, there is this added dimension: they are to feel guilt or shame when they do not successfully thwart the aggressiveness of males.

▪ Legitimacy and Confession

In the Catholic confessional, the priest conveys an "official" moral viewpoint from which the penitent's actions are questioned, interpreted, judged, and punished, so that the sinner can be reconciled with the community. For the male adolescent penitent, confession is a mechanism of socialization which subjects sexuality to the moral authority of the priest and renders certain sexual acts acceptable or unaccceptable. As the Catholic pastoral writings we have quoted indicate, confession also aims to have a specific effect upon the behavior of women. In the confessional, the intimate details of a woman's life are evaluated by a religious and moral authority, the priest, and thereby brought under the control of that authority.

One effect of such subjection to authority is to enforce the standards of behavior necessary for maintaining institutions such as marriage. Authority is employed through the use of prohibitions. Indeed the prohibition against divorce is the primary vehicle of such authority since it takes away even the woman's option to leave an unacceptable marriage. But for men the confession operates quite differently. This difference represents the larger difference between the legitimating function of morality in dominant as opposed to nondominant groups.

Earlier we referred to familiar anecdotes that emphasize the role confession plays in the moral life of children. During training for one's first confession, emphasis is placed on the "dirty" things one ought not to do. Such prohibitions are consistent with the child's subordination to priest and parents. The first sexual experiences of a child are considered in this moral light through the confessional, where conscience is shaped by the internalization of the authority of the priest and the fear of his punishments. In our experience, and the experience of those we have talked to, this is true of the sexual experiences of both boys and girls, although sexual conduct of girls is more severely chastised than is sexual conduct of boys. The condemnation of certain kinds of sex by girls is consistent with their current and future subordinate roles, particularly in relation to their fathers and husbands. But boys will become fathers and husbands and hence will not remain subordinate to adult males as a group in the same way that women will. The confession comes to play quite a different role for boys than for girls, aligning their social functions with their moral roles.

It should be noted that Catholic religious leaders no doubt thought that they had good motives or at worst paternalistic motives in providing this dual standard: they saw themselves as trying to protect girls from a hostile world. Children in general were not seen as sexual beings; rather, sexuality was introduced into discussions with children to ward off problems for them later in life. Indeed, pastoral manuals counseled treating children differently from adults. It was recommended that the priest remain "roundabout and vague," whereas in the case of adults confession was to be completely revealing. As Foucault puts it, for adults "sex was taken charge of, tracked down as it were, by a discourse that aimed to allow it no obscurity, no respite."[10]

Other religious traditions, as well as some nonreligious ones, also convey mixed messages to boys and young men about their sexuality. In Orthodox Judaism, rape is condemned, but its punishment varies based on such factors as whether the woman cries out, whether she is betrothed, and whether she is a virgin. One commentator suggests that the variability of punishment sends a mixed message to young Jewish men.[11] In traditional Islamic teachings, it is justifiable for a man to kill the one who steals his daughter's virginity, but if there is even a hint that a woman did not sufficiently resist, she may justifiably be killed.[12] The mixed message here should be obvious.

In religious traditions other than Catholicism somewhat similar mixed messages about sexuality are conveyed to young boys. What is unique about the Catholic confessional is that the mixed message is often quite explicitly conveyed. Catholic boys are encouraged to admit to their sexual sins in the presence of a church leader, and these sins are relatively easily forgiven. Discussions of sexuality therefore tend to be much more "above board" in Catholicism than in many religions, and hence easier to examine and understand. The form of the socialization in the Catholic confessional also has interesting similarities to problematic socialization espoused by some men who have recently written about masculinity, as we will see in the next section.

When boys, as potential members of a dominant group, are socialized, they are afforded a greater range of permissible action than are girls. Such permissibility is, as we have argued, often contrary to publicly articulated norms. The greater range of permissible behavior of boys is purchased at the price of being inculcated into a rigid sexual identity, in which all traces of femininity must be rooted out as a sign of weakness or homosexuality.[13] To be sure, there is a range of permissible behavior: some actions are regarded as neutral, others are morally condemned, and others are officially prohibited but unofficially seen as natural and unavoidable; still others are seen as the prerogative of the dominant group. Male heterosexual activity (outside of marriage) is a case in point: it is officially prohibited, but unofficially tolerated, and this extends to include many acts of sexual coercion. Impermissible actions include homosexual activity and, at least in previous times, sexual relations with women who were married.

In general, dominant groups assert themselves not merely through prohibition, but also through permission, especially unofficial permission that is technically at odds with the official prohibitions. Prohibitions alone are not subtle enough to convey the complex and often conflicting messages about how a dominant group should act toward a nondominant one. One reason they are not is that it is important for the legitimacy of a dominant group that it not appear to be operating under a double standard. If the confessional prohibits girls and women from engaging in extramarital heterosexual relations, but not men, then the confessional is percieved as blatantly biased. But if the prohibitions apply to both gender groups, but the prohibitions are subtly different for each group, issues of fairness do not so readily arise. Unofficial permission conjoined to official prohibition does not create a crisis of legitimacy in the same way that differentiated offical prohibitions would.[14]

By employing various categories of sin and by circumscribing the proper moral behavior of women and men, the confessional can legitimate male sexual aggressiveness. The confession, in effect, circumscribes the moral space of the dominant group. Without a very narrow circumscription of acceptable sexual behavior, men's sexually aggressive behavior would be seen as threatening to disrupt their relationships with their wives, children, and others. The confessional, by circumscribing this moral space, entrenches what it means to be a real man. Thus it is reasonable to conclude that the confessional (and similar practices in other religions) is a mechanism for exerting patriarchal social power.[15]

In the confessional, nonsexual sins are not subjected to the same rigorous scrutiny as are sexual ones. The primacy afforded to sexuality reinforces the idea that the confessional is, albeit unintentionally, a vehicle of legitimacy for a certain form of sexual hegemony. For instance, priests could, but do not, insist that mine owners confess to the specific details of their complicity in the deaths of child laborers, and they could, but do not, insist on this in the same way that they demand that married men confess their infidelities. The confessional seemingly is primarily concerned with the intimate, sexual lives of those it oversees, not with the public world of overt economic and political matters. Perhaps it is so because of the intensely private nature of the confessing and penance-rendering activities, conducted behind the "veil" or "screen" of the confessional box — where a moral space is created in which there is room for only priest and penitent.[16]

The "moral space" circumscribed by the confessional is more than mere metaphor. Charles Taylor, who has written extensively about this concept, claims that there is an "essential link between identity and a kind of orientation. To know who you are is to be oriented in moral space, a space in which questions arise about what is good or bad, what is worth doing and what not, what has meaning and importance for you and what is trivial and unimportant."[17] Following Taylor, we would contend that the prohibitions and permissions of the confessional create an orientation and an identity for males and, to a more limited extent, for females.

The concept of a moral space is useful for our analysis because it reveals the way in which many interrelated moral distinctions and evaluations make up a sexual identity. In the case of a dominant male identity, the cultural and moral space of the dominant culture constructs permissions and prohibitions for both male and female heterosexuality. Thus the mapping of the moral space that takes place in confession defines and evaluates possible identitites and actions within it. These evalautions are not mere preferences; they consist of what Taylor calls "strong evaluations," which define the identities of the penitents.[18]

The apparent privacy of the confessional also hides the fact that the moral space created by the confessional reifies the moral space of public male hegemony. A moral space must be articulated and rearticulated if it is to provide a strong moral orientation. This articulation is accomplished through what Taylor calls "qualitative distinctions," that is, by dividing up the moral landscape into good and bad actions. In Catholicism the confessional accomplishes this task for sexuality. We now turn to a parallel development in the recent confessional writings by some men about their sexuality.

III Male Feminist Confessions and Patriarchy

It has become common in popular writing about masculinity for men to confess their past patriarchal sins, especially concerning their sexual practices. Robert Bly and John Stoltenberg are perhaps only the most famous members of the group of writers who have gone to great lengths to make as public a confession as possible. As in the Catholic confessional tradition we described above, these men assign themselves a kind of penance for their sins, but as is certainly true in the case of Robert Bly, they assign only a few mea culpas so that they can get a kind of affirmation of what they have done and of how they continue to behave. In this sense, confessing about one's male sexuality is a project of seeking legitimation. It is also often a project of at least implicitly conceptualizing masculine sexual aggressiveness and abusiveness as dirty, uncontrollable, and something to be regretted but not to be actively challenged and changed.

Robert Bly's image of the "wild man" is one such attempt to legitimate a form of male sexual aggressiveness. In the beginning of his book *Iron John*, Bly tries to distinguish his "wild man" from the savage man, who has historically raped and spoilt both women and nature. The wild man is different from the savage man chiefly in learning from his mistakes, from his sins. He does not allow his sins to incapacitate him, to make him soft, receptive, and caring like a woman. Instead, the wild man tries to teach other boys and men the value of being hard yet not hurtful. The wild man draws inner strength from the same source that had previously driven him to rape women and nature. Only this time he restrains himself, knowing that only at certain times is it good to be hard and wild.

What is interesting from our perspective is that Robert Bly's wild man is very much like the man who confesses his sexual sins and as a result comes to repress his aggressive tendencies in certain circumstances, but in other circumstances feels that his aggressive sexual behavior is justifiable. In both cases a fine line is drawn between the "rapist" and the man who sometimes "rapes" but learns from his sins.[19] These men are convinced that they are not the hurters, not the savage, nearly inhuman "rapists." How could they be rapists since everyone in the culture tells them that they are good and that their lives can go on? Bly says clearly that men should stop blaming themselves for women's oppression. In fact, Bly shifts the burden, arguing that women have made men feel guilty for their sexuality to such an extent that it is now men who are grieving and oppressed.[20]

In a number of other writings by men on masculinity there has also been a reference to the debilitating suffering that men have had to bear for their supposed past sins. Mark Gerzon begins his influential book, *A Choice of Heroes*, by saying that he, like many men, "resists facing much less sharing, my feelings about masculinity" because feminists, among others, have made it such a political issue.[21] William Betcher and William Pollack begin their book on masculinity by saying: "It is a difficult time to be proud of being a man." They quote a man named Carl, who says, "I have never felt fully alive or genuine."[22] Like many others, they claim that strong women and feminists have made it difficult for men to feel good about themselves.

Those writers who have been influenced by the psychoanalytic tradition use the confessional mode to speak of the fear of castration, or a "male wound," which originates in the forced separation of very young boys from their mothers. As a result of this woundedness, many psychoanalysts say, men should not be made to feel guilty for their aggressiveness, since it originates in something so deep.[23] If men cannot satisfy their need to dissipate the tension in their lives through normal sexual means, they will be driven into "promiscuity. Intimate violence and perversion may result too."[24] Jungians are especially likely to rationalize male aggression by reference to its deep-seatedness.[25]

Here we have a sampling of recent writings on masculinity, that both acknowledge the sins of men and yet attempt to explain them in a way which does not call for condemnation. In this sense, these writings provide a basis for condoning male aggressive, and even violent sexual behavior in much the same way as the Catholic confessional (and other religious practices).[26] These writers, who are often psychoanalysts or inspired by Freud and Jung, want to help men to be able to go on with their lives. And while this is obviously not a bad goal by itself, focusing on moving on has the unfortunate result that notions of responsibility are thrust to the background, if not discarded. And men are once again given two messages at once: it is bad to be sexually aggressive, but it is accepted. As long as one confesses and is penitent, guilt is inappropriate.

Traditional Catholic confession is not a good model for the men who write about masculinity, if these men wish to be progressive.[27] Confession takes place within an already articulated moral space that has historically justified male aggression. It socializes men into this space and aids them in finding their sexual identity within it. But men who are writing about masculinity, if they wish to be progressive, do not need this kind of confession since such confession will legitimate roles as they are. Rather, what is needed is consciousness raising, that is, the sort of confessional discourse that articulates a new moral framework and a new space for different qualitative evaluations and different moral identities.[28] Here men who write about masculinity could find inspiration in the women's movement, which sought to create alternative moral spaces for the formation of new identities. In this respect, the work of John Stoltenberg, as we will see, can be cited as involving the kind of confessional discourse that is aimed at the transformation rather than the legitimation of existing gender roles and norms.

IV A Positive Role for Confessing

At the very beginning of this chapter, we employed a confessional mode of writing about our own sexual experiences. Indeed, when male philosophers try to write from a progressive perspective, they are often drawn to the confessional mode, as were female philosophers, at least in the early years of the feminist movement. Perhaps this is due to the desire to be cleansed, and to be forgiven for one's past acts of which one is now ashamed. Like the members of Alcoholics Anonymous who stand up at each meeting and say "Yes, I am an alcoholic, but I don't drink anymore," some men seem to want to stand up and say, "Yes, I am a rapist, but I don't rape anymore." What is wanted is some kind of recognized ritual cleansing, but the kind of cleansing that must go on again and again. How can they do this without sending mixed signals? How can they (and we) so forthrightly confess their sins without conveying some sense of pride in their (and our) forthrightness?

If we are to hold onto the notion of a transformed, progressive confession, perhaps the first step is to express humility, instead of pride, as well as penitence. As boys we were proud of our sexual transgressions, even as we expressed our sorrow, our mea culpas. The problem with many men inspired by the psychoanalytic tradition is that they eschew guilt, shame, and humility, seeing them as signs of debilitating weakness that men should resist. But what do the pride and forthrightness convey to the next generation of boys? It seems to be too easily misconstrued as once again providing mixed signals. Oedipus himself, the ancient man most written about in the psychoanalytic tradition, is able to remain proud even as he goes on his long journey of abnegation, because his sins of incest and patricide were truly beyond his control. When the psychoanalytically oriented writers we cited above remain proud in their confessing, it is as if they are also saying "my sins were beyond my control, and while I am sorry for them, true guilt and shame are not appropriate."

To avoid the mistakes of those influenced by the psychoanalytic model, those who use the confessional mode must signal that they take responsibility for their sexual sins. If one truly takes responsibility for one's past acts of sexual aggression and coercion, pride will be out of place. But will it be possible to avoid the debilitating weakness of those who hang their heads so low in penance and humility that their backs are permanently bowed over? Our answer, which we can only begin to sketch in the remaining few paragraphs of this essay, is to express humility and responsibility in a way that leads to positive growth and is an impetus to progressive change rather than to passivity.

One way to do so might be to focus on the positive, accepting responsibility, rather than the negative, feeling guilty. In some cases, guilt is too easy to remove, it is too easy to distance oneself from one's guilty act, and therefore not to feel much motivation to change because of being perceived, or of perceiving oneself, as guilty. So, in some cases guilt is inappropriate because it is not a good basis for getting someone to change whole perspectives or attitude clusters or behavior patterns. Taking responsibility for one's sexuality involves a more encompassing transformation of the self. There is no particular penance that will make things right; there is no easy way to distance oneself from the basis of the responsibility. What is called for is a series of acts over time which demonstrate that the person has changed.

Charles Taylor talks of confession as expressing the need that some people feel to "escape from the restrictions of the unitary self,"[29] which is unconflicted but, for that reason, has few resources for liberating itself from a narrow set of strong, identity-oriented evaluations. In order to escape the restrictions of the unitary self it is not always possible to continue without major changes in one's moral identity. Our proposal pushes the one who accepts responsibility beyond the standard confessional mode of discourse: I do not address myself to an authority who will excuse me, after penance, of those moral burdens that keep me outside the moral community. I must show, instead, that I am engaged in serious self-transformation and, hence, am not now the same person as before.

The "penance" involved in progressive confession is acutely public in that it calls for a transformation of who one is before the eyes of the larger community. This transformation is successful to the extent that the discourse in which I express my responsibility no longer legitimates my past identity, and no longer gives me the permission to engage in coercive sexual behavior. Instead, what is sought is a readmission into a new moral community where people are treated with respect. There is something like a penance here, in that men must do something quite unpleasant, namely, admit that they have done wrong and indicate what steps they will take to change their behavior in the future.

In traditional Catholic confession, one speaks of one's past act as something that one regrets and that one regards as not truly of the self that one has control over. This is why the fulfilling of a simple penance, wipes the slate clean and allows the person to go on as before. If the past act is seen as emanating from a person's true self, then the self is implicated, not merely its past acts, and what must change is the whole structure of one's past evaluations of what is good and bad. Thus, public confession is not just about what one condemns but also about the contours of both old and new evaluative outlooks. In a progressive form of confession there will be no thought that simple acts of contrition will make it possible to go on as before. Rather the progressive confession involves the project of remaking the self, of beginning on a journey of changes in perspective, attitude, and behavior which will cumulatively show that a man has accepted responsibility for who he is.

One writer who employs a progressive confessional mode of writing is John Stoltenberg. In *Refusing to Be a Man*, he confesses his own past sins, but he does so in a way designed to help others transform their attitudes and behavior.[30] "So to begin with, refusing to be a man means learning a radical new ethic: determining to learn as much as one can know about the values in the acts one has done and the acts one chooses to do and their full consequences for other people — as if everyone else is absolutely as real as oneself."[31] Such a refusal is based largely on a rejection of excuses for being a man. For, according to Stoltenberg, "it is thoroughly possible to change how we act,"[32] but only if we stop lying to ourselves and accept responsibility for who we are and for what we can make of ourselves in the future. Stoltenberg ends one of his chapters with a call to action: "I invite you too to resist the lie. I invite you to become an erotic traitor to male supremacy."[33]

Stoltenberg argues, as the title of his book *(Refusing to Be a Man)* indicates, that the preferred strategy would be for men and women to become roughly the same, to become ungendered, not merely for men to give up their current patriarchal conceptions of masculinity. We agree that progressive confessions are meant to get men to take responsibility for who they are and to change some of the aspects of their masculine identities. But we do not believe that men must cease, or refuse, to be men in order to take responsibility for their sexuality.[34] Indeed, there are important resources that men can draw on, as men, that can be useful for childrearing or forming intimate friendships.[35]

It might be objected that "progressive confessions" still fall prey to the problems that have plagued both the Catholic and psychoanalytic confessional modes. Even those men who present themselves as transformed will still give voice to a legitimacy for male sexual coercion when they confess their past exploits. What other reason could be given, so this line of argument would run, for discussing these past sins except to garner for them a kind of acceptance? Why isn't it enough for the transformed man to talk of how he lives now? Why does he need to discuss the way he used to live, given its potential for tapping into the subconscious desire for cleansing that many nontransformed men feel?

What we are proposing is that the progressive confessional exploit the desire for cleansing and turn it in a positive direction. This task is easier to accomplish if men admit to their common socialization. To gain credibility, those men who urge that others transform themselves need to establish that they were once like the others, that they understand what it is like to be a traditional male, and hence that they can judge that it is indeed better to be transformed. The chief difference between progressive confession and the other two types of confession we have been exploring is that progressive confession joins accounts of past "sins" with an account of the new attitudes and behaviors, acceptance of which has now made it less likely that these past sins will be repeated.

Progressive confessions will not be so easily dismissed as potentially expressive of a double standard. It will not be acceptable for a man to say to himself "mea culpa for my action" and still to feel proud of who he is and has been. Progressive confession, since it is about the whole person, does not lend itself to the double standard. Progressive, consciousness-raising confession[36] resembles Catholic or psychoanalytic confession only superficially. My past self is not here forgiven, even by me, but transformed along with the moral space of my evaluations. Progressive confession makes it less likely that I will merely rearticulate the morality of a dominant group.

Various men who have written about masculinity have displayed a desire for public acceptance of their moral identities. Such public acceptance will only occur when men stand willing to engage in dialogue with women and men, most especially with those women who have been the victims of men's past acts of coercive sexual aggression. Men need to show that they have started on the road to becoming less coercively aggressive in their sexual encounters, that they have changed who they are, not merely that they regret what they have done. Confessional writing can be an aid in this endeavor, but only when it is understood on the model of consciousness raising, not the Catholic confession or the psychoanalytic confession favored by many in the men's movement.

Pornography and Pollution

Despite the best efforts of many social scientists and feminist theorists, few cases have been identified in which it is clear that an individual person was harmed by particular instances of the manufacture, sale, dissemination, or viewing of heterosexual pornography.[1] And when these cases have been identified, as when a rapist acts out the scenes of a pornographic book he keeps in his back pocket, existing laws seem quite capable of handling the harm. Nevertheless, there is a growing recognition that pornography has a damaging effect on the relations between men and women, and makes it increasingly difficult for men and women to think positively about their own sexuality. But even here it is quite difficult to show that any particular woman or man has had her or his interests setback, or rights violated by pornography. In this chapter I will explore various strategies for showing that pornography causes harm to groups. In the end, I argue that the best strategy is to focus on the accumulated effects on women as a group, and also men as a group, when degrading images of women are linked with erotically stimulating imagery. In this respect, the best analogy for understanding the group harm of pornography is the accumulated harm of industrial pollution on a community in a city like Gary, Indiana.

Obscenity laws are aimed at written or spoken material that offends a community's sentiments. The label "obscene" is used to condemn something as "shockingly vulgar or blatantly disgusting." Pornogaphy is different from obscenity in that it is merely a form of sexually explicit writing or pictures "designed to induce sexual excitement in the reader or viewer."[2] One of the most striking aspects of pornography is that its consumers, mainly men, are drawn to it over and over, regardless of the low literary or artistic quality of the material. Many men find an appeal in pornography which is largely missing from obscene materials. Obscene materials repel, but pornographic ones attract, at least for male viewers. The attraction of pornography to a large segment of the population means that it is unlikely to offend a community; but it is the attaction of pornography that contributes to its power to influence its viewers or readers, and, as I will argue, to its power to produce group harm.

▮ Some Facts

In this section I will briefly rehearse some relevant facts that motivate the discussion about censorship or regulation of pornography. First, a bit of autobiographical disclosure. When I was a teenager growing up in 1960s middle-American suburbia, my ideas about my own sexuality and sexual relations with women were strongly influenced by the pornographic images I was exposed to. Those images had certain common themes: the male was always in charge, and the female was at his beck and call, to produce whatever pleasures he demanded. What is interesting here is that as a teenager unexperienced with sex I had no idea what the range of sexual pleasures was, and certainly did not find any discussion or imagery of mutually consensual forms of sexuality in the pornographic materials I encountered. Later in life I came to realize how impoverished my conceptions of sexuality were, and also how hard it was to change the conceptions I had formed in those teenage years. It seemed to me that my ability to relate to women, sexually and otherwise, was hampered by my pornographic socialization.[3]

Some of the most dramatic evidence about male attitudes toward sexuality is found in a widely cited study by Seymour Feshbach and Neal Mala-muth, in which 51 percent of college men surveyed said that they might commit rape if they were assured they would not be caught. The same study found that men who viewed violent pornography were more likely to identify with the rapist and to feel unsympathetic to the victim than the control group.[4] In another study conducted by Dolf Zillman and Jennings Bryant, eighty men and eighty women were asked how long convicted rapists should be incarcerated. The subjects were then exposed to massive quantities of pornography, and their views were solicited again. The results are startling. The exposure to pornography "made rape appear a trivial offense" and "resulted in recommendations of significantly shorter terms of imprisonment" for rapists than had been given before exposure. Although this result was true for both male and female subjects, nonetheless both before and after the exposure, "females treated rape as a more serious offense and acted more punitively toward the rapist than did males."[5]

There is also evidence that men will be sexually aroused by pornography that depicts rape, and will describe themselves as more likely to commit rape. This evidence suggests that there is an increased arousal response to depictions of rape. "The increased arousal primarily occurs when the female victim shows signs of pleasure and arousal, the theme most commonly presented in aggressive pornography." Some men who have increased arousal patterns when viewing coercively aggressive pornography report that they themselves would rape, and these men display arousal patterns similar to those of known rapists. "This self-reported possibility of commit-ting rape is highly correlated with a) sexual arousal to rape stimuli, b) aggressive behavior and a desire to hurt women, and c) a belief that rape would be a sexually arousing experience for the rapist."[6]

There is plenty of evidence for thinking that pornography adversely affects the *attitudes* men have toward rape as well as toward women in general, but there is little evidence showing that pornography causes in-creases in rape or harmful *behavior* toward women. Indeed, in the Nether-lands and Denmark, where pornography has been essentially legalized, there has not been a corresponding increase in the incidence of rape or other violent crimes committed against women.[7] And while the increase in pornography correlates with an increase in violence against women in the United States, it is not clear how significant a causal role is played by pornography in these harms, especially when one focuses on individual laboratory cases.[8]

So the question of whether pornography causes such harms as rape is difficult to answer. It appears that exposure to pornography changes many men's attitude toward rape, but does not necessarily change behavior, which can be traced to harms to particular women. This fact has had a profound impact on legal disputes about pornography. It remains unclear whether viewing pornography causes harm to identifiable persons. As a result, anti-pornography statutes justifed on grounds that pornography harms women have been ruled to be unconstitutional in that they restrict free expression without a clear showing that the pornography is harmful. But is there some other way to conceptualize the harm caused by pornography which could be the legitimate interest of the law? Here is where the pornography debate becomes philosophical. I next turn to the question of how harm should be conceptualized in general, and then to the question of how it might be argued that pornography causes a form of group harm that should concern the law.

II Conceptualizing Harm

In order to engage in a philosophical analysis of pornography, one has to begin somewhere, and Joel Feinberg's account of harm is a useful, although not completely uncontroversial, place to begin. In his book *Harm to Others*, Feinberg offers the following analysis of "A harms B":

1. A acts . . .
2. in a manner which is defective or faulty in respect to the risks it creates to B . . . and
3. A's acting in that manner is morally indefensible . . . and
4. A's action is the cause of a setback to B's interests, which is also
5. a violation of B's right.[9]

The key element here is the notion of a setback to interests. The root idea Feinberg expresses, is that harm is a "relativistic notion: whether one is harmed by an event is determined by reference to where one was before, and whether his position has improved or regressed. . . . one is harmed only when one's interest is brought below the centerline."[10]

An interest is something in which an individual has a stake, but not all interests are important enough that setbacks to them call for legal or social sanction. An interest of mine in consuming oatmeal-raisin cookies is set back each time the Mallinckrodt food court fails to supply them in time for my lunch. But no one would seriously contend that society should sanction the food court for setting back my interest in consuming an oatmeal-raisin cookie. To put the matter quite plainly, my interest here is trivial, even if at the moment of cookie-attack hunger nothing much in life seems to matter as much to me. What society concerns itself with are interests that are enduring and have some connection to my sense of who I am.

The main reason for such restrictive attention to interest setbacks is that each intrusion by society risks loss of liberty to some individual. If legal or social sanctions were used to prevent the trivial interest setback of an individual member of society, the liberty of many others in society would be restricted. Yet these people also have interests, especially interests in how they conduct their lives, which would be set back by the society's sanctions. In order to minimize such loss of liberty, which is itself a setback to an interest, only nontrivial interest setbacks are considered potentially worthy of society's attention.

For my analysis, the most controversial aspect of Feinberg's analysis concerns the relativistic construal of setback of interest. To put the matter simply: interests are set back whenever they are caused to drop below an arbitrary point to which they had previously risen. On this construal there are few if any nonrelativistic setbacks of interest.[11] If a woman in Ghana never imagined that she could be a lawyer and, hence, never wanted to be one even though there were no legal impediments to doing so, it is not a setback of her interests if a new law is passed which prevents women from becoming lawyers.[12] Since in the past she had no interest in becoming a lawyer, if it now is impossible for her to become one, she is not harmed in terms of her interests, since her interests are no worse off now than they were before. Yet there is a sense in which she is harmed that is not captured by Feinberg's relativistic analysis of setback of interest.

A nonrelativistic conception of harm seems to be called for, since it seems that a person is harmed when an option is restricted, even if that person currently does not want to pursue that option. But what is the basis for nonrelativistic harms? I suggest that in any particular society there are options that a person has an interest in having unrestricted, even if the person does not want to pursue those options at the moment and cannot imagine wanting to pursue them in the future. One of the problems with stressing previous interests is that what one wants, and even what one can imagine wanting, is a function of beliefs that can themselves be quite transient.

I currently believe that the stocks on Wall Street are overvalued, and so I do not want to play the stockmarket, and cannot imagine a time when I would want to do so. In terms of the current baseline of my wants, I would not be harmed if people under five foot ten inches tall were prohibited from playing the stockmarket. Yet it is a serious matter for me to be so prohibited, since my beliefs and corresponding interests may very well change so that at some future time I want to play the stockmarket. To have this option restricted, even though I do not want to pursue it at the present time, is a constriction of my future options which is itself a setback to my longterm interests. Given what we know about people's interests in our society and what we know about the variability of wants, restricting options is harmful in the sense that it is a setback to future interests.

On my approach, the general basis of a person's non-relativistic interests, not linked to current wants of the person in question, is that there is reason to think that current wants of the person in question may change so that what is not wanted now will be wanted then. At least one sign that this could be true occurs in those societies where a significant number of people in a society, although not the person in question, want, or have wanted, to have a certain option unrestricted. When an option is restricted, there is also less likelihood that that option will be wanted in the future. Of course, there are cases where restricting an option, say prohibiting one's teenage son from staying out till midnight, might inspire the person to want to pursue the option which he had previously not wanted to pursue. But in many cases restricting options, over time, socializes people not to want the things that have been restricted as options. As we will later see, the existence of certain forms of pornography may reduce people's desire for certain forms of sexual relationships, which there is some reason to think they would, or might, want if pornography did not currently restrict and shape their wants.

▮▮▮ Group Harm and Group-Based Harm

The preceding account of *individual* harm as setback to interests is intuitively appealing just because, by design, it captures the ordinary way that people in America, and many other places, talk about, and think about, harm. Discussions of *group* harm are initially met with skepticism because, or at least many people seem to believe, there is not a corresponding intuitively appealing way to talk about harms that are not connected to specific individuals. In this section I will suggest several general strategies for discussing group harm in a way that connects with common intuitions about harm. In the following section I will critically examine three specific strategies propounded by several leading social theorists and legal philosophers, contrasting their views with my own.

Group harm can refer to harm that is merely aggregative. In standard English it is acceptable to use collective nouns such as "the corporation" or "the nation-state" or "the team" as a shorthand way to refer to the members of the group. Indeed, it is interesting that in American English, such collective nouns take a singular verb form, but in British English these nouns take a plural verb form. The British seem to regard collective nouns as aggregates; these collective nouns really refer to the members of a group not to anything like the group as a whole. Americans, on the other hand, seem to hold open the possibility that collective nouns could refer to singular entities with their own characteristics, and not merely the characteristics of the individual members. According to the aggregative conceptualization of group harm, talk of group harm makes sense only as a placeholder for individual harms.

Group harm, however, can also be conceptualized as harm to the group as a whole. It seems relatively uncontroversial that a nation-state can be harmed or that a business corporation can be harmed. These groups resemble individual human agents in that they have decision-making structures and assets and other characteristics, such as the ability to engage in actions that single individuals cannot perform, that are not easily reducible to the characteristics of the individual members of the group. Gender groups, of course, are not like nation-states or corporations in that gender groups do not have a decision-making structure, a charter, or mechanisms for acting collectively. Nevertheless, they too may be harmed. The possibility of harm rests on their capacity to suffer as a group. To suffer, one need not be an agent; instead, one can merely have one's status adversely affected. But can a relatively unorganized group be harmed in terms of setbacks to interests? Many have seen this kind of harm as unlikely. It seems to some that in order to have interests, an entity or a group must have intentions. Gender groups, however, lack any intentional structure that could generate interests.[13]

When considering groups such as women or men, I have been led to propose a model of group harm that is more than merely aggregative but not as full blown as true group harm of the sort that could befall agentlike groups such as nation-states and business corporations. My idea is that individual members of the group "women" are vulnerable to harm that is based on their group membership. In such cases, group membership is the key basis for identifying and adversely affecting the person. When a woman is raped, in most cases it is largely irrelevant what her particular characteristics are; what is salient is only that she is a woman. If some other woman had been in the same place at the same time, the rapist would have assaulted her. When a woman is discriminated against by being denied a job because of her gender, she is not being treated on the basis of her particular characteristics, but only on the basis of one characteristic namely her female gender, and anyone else who had that characteristic would have been treated the same. I have previously called this group-based harm.[14]

Group-based harm is harm in that when a member of a group is disadvantaged simply because he or she is a group member, there is a diminution of the status of the group that then adversely affects all of the members of the group. There are a variety of types of group-based harms. For our purposes one of the most interesting group-based harms is status harm. Some groups could be harmed in terms of their relative status, vis-à-vis other groups, that is, the group's reputation or the options that the group has open to it or, in some cases of organized groups, the assets of the group,[15] etc. In all these cases, it would be prima facie harmful to a group for its relative status to drop. On this view, a group has a non-trivial interest in preserving its status.

Interests can be quite trivial, as is true of my interest in getting an oatmeal-raisin cookie, but the interests that are morally important are interests that (a) are enduring, and (b) have some connection to one's identity. Many harms to the status of a group can be seen as harms to the interests of the group which implicate these two criteria by adversely affecting something in which the group has a stake that is intimately connected to the group identity of its members. Many groups have a nontrivial, enduring interest in having their status not be lowered. This is because the members of many groups derive much of their sense of identity from the identity of the group, especially in the case of those primary identification categories in contemporary American society such as race, ethnicity, and gender. This is at least one reason why the United States Supreme Court is especially suspicious of classifications drawn on the basis of these categories.[16] I will say more about my conception of group-based harm, in contrast to other views of this subject, in the next two sections.

IV Does Pornography Harm Women?

As we will see, a number of theorists have discussed various sorts of group harms caused by pornography. This discussion has focused on three types of harm (a) group defamation, (b) group subordination, and (c) castelike discrimination. In what follows I will set out each of these views, criticizing aspects of each. In the section following the current one, I will then sketch my alternative account, according to which pornography is a form of accumulative sex discrimination which creates a climate of opinion and attitude that restricts options for the members of the group. This restricting of options is analogous to industrial pollution that changes the environmental climate in, say, Gary, Indiana. In both cases, accumulative harm occurs when options are restricted for members of a group.

The simplest and most straightforward way to characterize the harm of pornography is in terms of group defamation, that is, in terms of its damaging effects on the reputation of the group "women." If one recognizes the existence of groups at all, it is perhaps least controversial to say that the group has a reputation, and like individuals, the group has an interest in protecting that reputation from being tarnished. In Anglo-American law, group defamation is considered actionable only if a particular member of the group is likely to have his or her reputation impaired or injured by the generally condemnatory remarks directed at the group as a whole. If someone says that all lawyers are liars, no particular lawyer's reputation is harmed clearly enough for him or her to seek redress. If the group is much smaller, such as the group of twenty-five engineers who work for a particular company or the group of sixty players on a particular school's football team, courts have allowed individual members to seek redress for the likely harm to their own reputation when, for example, the company's engineering division or the school's team was maligned.[17]

Much of contemporary pornography depicts women in very degrading or insulting ways. Women's breasts, buttocks, and vulvas are displayed in a way that makes them appear available for any male to fondle or ogle for his own sexual gratification. Women's bodies are put on display as if they were somehow not connected to people with thoughts and feelings. And when pornography concerns whole women, they are often portrayed as servile or abused, raped or tortured for the gratification of the male viewer. Since it is the depiction of the female form or female body parts, rather than the depiction of particular whole women, which is so degrading or insulting, it can be argued that pornography degrades or insults women as a group and thereby hurts the reputation of the group "women." But is the harm to women occasioned by pornography best captured as a harm to the reputation of women? Such a claim seems in some ways too weak and in other ways too strong. It is too weak in that the harm done to women by pornography is not merely, or even primarily, that the reputation of women is harmed.

The degrading aspect of pornography is not well captured by focusing on the group's reputation, for the group has suffered a loss to its overall status or standing in the society, and its reputation is only one small part of it. As I have indicated, a group's status can be harmed when options are restricted for the group's members by virtue of their group membership. The status harm involved in pornography includes the restriction of important options about sexuality, discussed in the next section, that go beyond reputation. It is in another sense too strong to say that it is the group's reputation that is harmed, especially if one is looking for a legally actionable basis for redress. A woman's reputation is no doubt somewhat tarnished when her group's reputation is tarnished. But what specific harm, and how much of it, is any particular woman likely to experience to her own reputation? The extreme difficulty of answering this question casts doubt on this strategy.

The second strategy is to argue that pornography contributes to the subordination of women. While related to the group-libel strategy, this view is more controversial in two respects: it makes pornography responsible for casting women into second-class status, and some of its advocates argue that pornography is not merely the proximal cause of subordination but subordination itself. This latter view is most prominently espoused by Catharine MacKinnon, and given an able philosophical defense by Rae Langton.[18] I agree with them that subordination is a more significant form of harm than defamation, I also agree that subordination better picks out the kind of group harm that pornography causes than does group defamation.

Rae Langton makes good use of the variety of speech acts to explain how pornography could not only cause but constitute subordination, just as uttering the words "I hereby declare you married" constitutes marriage and does not merely cause it. In order for the mere utterance of certain words to constitute something, not merely cause it, various conditions, called "felicity conditions," must be met. In the case of uttering "I hereby declare you married" the chief felicity condition is "that the speaker occupy a position of authority in a relevant domain."[19] The justice of the peace occupies a position of authority over matrimonial matters, just as the legislature occupies a position of authority over legal matters in a particular jurisdiction. According to Langton, pornographers occupy a similarly authoritative position on matters of sexuality.

The main problem with this analysis is that pornographers do not seem to have authority over sexual matters in the same way that judges have authority over matrimonial matters. Indeed, it is unclear that pornographers have much authority at all. Langton admits that pornographers generally are held in disrepute by our society, but she contends that males, especially teenage males, regard pornography as authoritative nonetheless. According to Langton, "Pornography's voice is the voice of the ruling power."[20] Langton allies herself with MacKinnon in claiming that "pornography represents degrading and abusive sexual behavior 'in such a way as to endorse the degradation.'"[21] The main evidence that it constitutes this subordination is seen in the overwhelming number of boys who think that rape is acceptable conduct. As Langton puts it:

> What is important is whether it is authoritative for those hearers who — one way or another — do seem to learn that violence is sexy and coercion legitimate: the fifty percent of boys who "think it is okay for a man to rape a woman if he is sexually aroused by her," the fifteen percent of male college students who say they have raped a woman on a date, the eighty-six percent who say that they enjoy the conquest part of sex, the thirty percent who rank faces of women displaying pain and fear to be more sexually attractive than faces showing pleasure. In this domain, and for these hearers, it may be that pornography has all the authority of a monopoly."[22]

I agree with Langton that there is overwhelming evidence that many teenage boys hold women in low esteem and believe that in at least some circumstances it would be morally acceptable to rape. And I agree that pornography plays a significant role in causing many boys, and men, to hold sexist attitudes and to be disposed to act in sexually aggressive ways to the detriment of women. But I do not think that the evidence MacKinnon and Langton cite establishes that pornography is authoritative in matters of sexuality in such a way as to constitute female subordination. There are too many other influences in the society to think that pornography alone constitutes female subordination. While being quite sympathetic to many of the claims of MacKinnon and Langton, I nonetheless feel that the group subordination arguments fail to show that pornography *constitutes* subordination. As will become clear in the next section, I certainly agree that pornography *contributes* to female subordination. What I am here objecting to is the claim that pornography alone is, or constitutes, female subordination.

The third strategy, advocated most prominently by Cass Sunstein, contends that pornography contributes to a castelike discrimination that is in some important respects analogous to nineteenth-century American slavery, and which the Fourteenth Amendment to the United States Constitution was designed to eliminate.[23] According to Sunstein, sex discrimination occurs because of the "existence of a caste-like system, based on gender and often operating through law," which creates a system of irrational and unjust distinctions based on sex. The right of free speech is interpreted and enforced in a way that deprives women of forms of redress against the assaults of pornography. But pornography is not merely offensive. Women become second-class citizens because of the disparate way that law-sanctioned hierarchies discriminate against them, especially through the perpetuation of eroticized violent images of women.

But while pornography may contribute to systematic sex discrimination, it is unclear that the law is implicated in this discrimination in a way that creates anything approximating a gender caste, that is, a legally sanctioned class hierarchy based on gender. While it is true that pornography exists because pornographers are not prosecuted at law, failure to prosecute should not lead us to think that the law plays a role in the perpetuation of pornography that is analogous to the role the law played in nineteenth-century American slavery. Slaves were returned to masters, and those who tried to free slaves were executed at law. Unlike laws protecting slaveholders, there are no specific laws that protect pornographers. The laws that do protect pornography protect most other forms of speech or expression. The role of law in allowing discrimination against women to occur based on pornography is not sufficiently like the role of law in the perpetuation of slavery to support the claim that pornography is a form of castelike discrimination. The law played a constitutive role in slavery by defining slaves as chattel and protecting the ownership claims of slaveholders according to the laws of property, but it does not play such a role in pornography.[24]

This last strategy is on the right track when it links pornography to sex discrimination, but the links are less clear-cut than the proponents of this strategy seem to realize. Most of the writing about pornography in the 1990s focused on violent pornography. Theorists as different as MacKinnon and Sunstein have agreed that violent pornography is the most egregious and most clearly sanctionable at law. It seems to me undeniable that violent pornography contributes to an increasingly pervasive rape culture.[25] But other forms of pornography may also play a role in the creation of the rape culture as well, and the mechanism through which socialization into the rape culture is conveyed is not the same as that of violent pornography. Certain forms of nonviolent pornography are at least as important a source of misogynist male bonding and of male socialization into practices of non-egalitarian sexual relationships, as is violent pornography, as I will indicate later.[26]

In summary, group defamation focuses on reputation, which is only one small aspect of the harm that women experience as a result of pornography. Group subordination comes closer to the mark, but it is hard to see that any particular instance of pornography causes, let alone constitutes, such subordination. Castelike discrimination puts too much emphasis on the role of the law and too little emphasis on the sociological contribution of pornography to a rape culure that perpetuates sex discrimination. In each strategy there are good ideas that can be salvaged. Women as a group are degraded by pornography, and such degradation does contribute to the subordination of women, which creates a kind of second-class citizenship for women. We are still in need, though, of a model for understanding how pornography creates these effects.

v The Effects of Pornography

On my view, the harm of pornography is best understood as a group-based harm, specifically, a harm to the status of women. Only in very rare cases does one particular piece of pornography cause nontrivial harm. And since the main harm is group-based rather than individual anyway, it is rare, if ever, that a single piece of pornography causes nontrivial harm to women as a group. I make this claim without at all wishing to diminish the seriousness of the harm of pornography. But on my view, the nontrivial harm of pornography normally occurs cumulatively, that is, as the accumulated effect of many individual acts, each of which is not clearly more than trivially harmful. Some women, and even some men, may take offense at some particular instance of pornography, but no individual instance of pornography brings about the subordination of women or the rape culture.

Individual instances of non-egalitarian pornography, accumulated together, cause a status harm to women that needs to be addressed.[27] As I indicated earlier, a status harm is a type of group-based harm in that the harm occurs to the members of a group due to their group membership. In the case of non-egalitarian pornography, women's status is harmed in that their options are restricted concerning things which are of enduring interest to all of the members of the group, namely options to engage in certain forms of sexuality, or to consider themselves certain forms of sexual beings.[28] Both of these options are adversely affected by the changes in attitudes that men have toward women and the attitudes that women (and men) have toward themselves, because of the prevalence of pornography.[29] While it is unlikely that any particular instance of pornography itself restricts women's options, the climate of attitudes toward women's sexuality created by accumulated instances of nonegalitarian pornography will, in many communities, have a negative impact on these options. For example, think of the emphasis on coerced sex in nonegalitarian pornography. Women who wish to have a trusting relationship with a man find it difficult in many cases because of the prevalent male attitudes about the need for overpowering and coercing women into having sex on their terms.

Women are harmed as a group when their sexual options and how they think of themselves sexually are restricted, merely because of group membership. This is because women as well as men have an enduring interest in a multiplicity of forms of unrestricted "healthy" interactions between men and women. When a person's options are curtailed merely by virtue of being a member of a certain group, then group-based harm has occurred. When women see their options for sexuality diminished by the nonegalitarian roles to which they are consigned,[30] roles that make them the objects of coercion, debasement, and even rape, or when women have difficulty thinking of themselves sexually except through the lens of a camera that depicts them as servile and softly out of focus while men are in charge and in focus, then the status of women has been harmed. Insofar as men also have their options restricted, because of the prevailing pornographic image of the real man with his ever erect, rock-hard penis seeking penetration as the only acceptable proof of masculinity,[31] then men are also harmed. In both cases, pornography affects attitudes that shape the sexual self-conceptions of men and women and thereby limit the options that men and women have. These are the group-based harms that need to be, in some fashion, redressed.[32]

In order to understand the possible group-based harms that pornography causes to women, and also to men, it is important to understand the peculiar way pornography affects the reader or viewer. The crucial dimension is erotic stimulation. Pornography captivates its viewers in ways inconceivable if the literature or films lacked this dimension. Indeed, many have noted that pornographic books and films are maddeningly the same. After all, so it is often said, there are only so many combinations and permutations of the sex act. The attraction of pornography is not primarily aesthetic or intellectual or emotional; rather the primary appeal is in genital stimulation. The appeal is primarily not to head or heart but to groin. As a result the attraction is more visceral than intellectual or emotional, and more difficult to control or counteract.

The linking of written or pictorial accounts of sexual relations with erotic stimulation has a profound impact on the reader or viewer, much like subliminal forms of advertising. Various social-psychological studies have found, not surprisingly, that both males and females retain information longer and can recall it in more detail if the information is presented in a sexually arousing manner than when it is not.[33] Pornography attracts the reader or viewer, and it attracts in ways that are difficult if not impossible to replicate without the erotic dimension. One critic of the subordination approach to pornography, nonetheless puts the point about subliminal effects of pornography well when he says:

> One who opposes ideas expressed candidly in public may try to counter-act them with candid public counter-speech. On the other hand, one who is exposed to a subliminal message is unprepared to defend himself against undue influence. The "marketplace of ideas" concept is founded on the premise that the correct retaliation to speech is counter-speech. When one hears both sides (or many sides) of an issue the truth has a chance to prevail. However, if one is exposed to subliminal speech how can one know to investigate the contrary position before formulating an opinion? If there is such a thing as subliminal speech how does one argue with it?[34]

While the erotic character of nonegalitarian pornography is in some sense quite apparent and obvious, the way that the erotic dimension rein-forces the nonegalitarian message is what is subliminal. The harmfulness of nonegalitarian pornography is especially difficult to redress by conventional means, because of the way its subliminal message defies confrontation by normal forms of counter-speech.

From a group-oriented perspective, one of the most fascinating puzzles is how pornography acts as a basis for male sexual education and socializa-tion. Male sexual socialization is effected not through single instances of pornography but through the accumulated effects reinforced by the sublim-inal way that pornography communicates. The changes in attitude that affect a person's self-conception are rarely if ever accomplished by one event, such as reading an issue of *Playboy*. As with most changes in habit and attitude, accumulated experiences produce the change. Pornography resembles industrial pollution in that each single instance contributes to a larger and much more serious problem than can be seen by examining the individual instance.[35] Also like industrial pollution or, perhaps better, like auto emission pollution, pornography seems relatively trivial at the individual level; indeed, it may be part of a useful process.

Many types of industrial pollution cause some risk of cancer even in small doses, but so do many things in the environment. As the amount of pollution increases, so does the incidence of cancer in the surrounding area. Societies must decide how much pollution is acceptable, perhaps because it allows for businesses to operate which employ members of the society, and what rate of cancer is too great to be tolerated. It may be that even small doses of pornography have a negative effect on the relations among the sexes in a given society, although this has not been proved. But there are also positive effects of pornography, which need to be weighed. Just as auto emmissions are the by-product of fossil fuel consumption that powers the engines of cars, boats, trucks, and buses, so there is a sense in which the harmful effects of pornography are a by-product of sexual pleasure and release for many men, and also some women, who read or observe it.

Because individual instances of pornography cannot be shown to cause harm to identifiable individuals, pornography should not be outlawed. But this does not mean that the law should play no role. Like pollution, pornography needs to be regulated so as to minimize the harmful cumulative effects. The main function of regulation will be to fix a ceiling above which the society finds the prevalence or type of pornography unacceptable in terms of its adverse effects on male attitudes toward rape and other forms of aggressive sexuality, and female conceptions of their options of sexuality. Pornography's chief polluting effect is on the attitudes and dispositions of men, and women, who read or observe it. Industrial pollution in Gary, Indiana, created, over time, a climate where people were much more likely to get cancer than in other cities or regions of the country. Pornographic pollution in the United States has contributed significantly, over time, to a climate of habits and attitudes in which women, and men, find their sexual options restricted.

Defenders of pornography would no doubt point out that in some countries, such as Denmark and the Netherlands, there is a greater variety of especially violent pornography and yet less incidence of rape than in the United States.[36] I find this a potentially compelling argument. Pornography alone does not cause the rape culture. It does so only, as I would interpret the empirical studies, in combination with other influences. This is yet another reason for not banning pornography wholesale. The group-based harm of pornography is also linked to various other aspects of American culture, not the least of which is the prevalence of nonpornographic, yet nonetheless sexist advertising of products from toothpaste and cigarettes to automobiles and vacation cruises.

The overall effect of pornography, at least in some communities, is that the options of women, and men, are being narrowed in a way that sets back their interests. A woman comes to think of herself as primarily needing to please a man in order to have a satisfying sexual relationship with him. A man comes to think of himself as primarily needing to dominate and control a woman in order to have a satisfying sexual relationship with her. This is at least what my own anecdotal experience would lead me to think. Starting as a teenager, and extending well into middle age, my view and the views of sexuality of many of the men and women I knew were not conducive to healthy egalitarian sexual relationships. Our interest in having a wide range of healthy sexual options was set back.

At a certain point, the accumulated effects of nonegalitarian pornography are such that these setbacks are serious rather than trivial because certain options for sexuality are restricted for women, and for men as well. At that point, the society should regulate the dissemination and production of pornography just as it regulates industrial and auto emission pollution. I will not here speculate on where this line should be drawn. Just as we have mainly left it up to individual communities to set the limits of acceptable industrial pollution, so, perhaps, we should let individual communities set the limits for acceptable pornography.[37]

VI The Metaphor of Pollution

I wish to defend the use of the pollution metaphor in describing the harm of pornography. To do so I will draw on, and criticize, various communitarian themes originally put forth by Patrick Devlin in the 1950s. I will attempt to defend a use of the metaphor of pollution that is more in keeping with recent progressive and feminist views than conservative and neoconservative views on pornography. But I cannot deny that the argument forms are often very similar, as has been seen in the strange coalitions of feminists and religious conservatives who joined forces against pornography in several midwestern cities.[38]

A number of premodern societies have employed the notion of pollution to characterize the harm to a community when one of its members has done something displeasing to the gods. According to Arthur Adkins, "a belief in 'pollution' in one form or another seems to be common to the whole

Indo-European stock."[39] In its Homeric usage, the Greek term for pollution meant "dirt, real, physical dirt, which must be removed before a man may pray to the gods with any expectation that they will listen to him . . . [since] the gods seem unlikely to accept the prayers of a man with dirty hands." In fifth century B.C. Greece, pollution came to be associated with taint, with a kind of indelible metaphysical stain that attaches to those who do evil.[40] Sophocles speaks of Oedipus as one polluted by his acts of patricide and incest, and this taint extended to the residents of whatever city he wandered into. The dirt on his hands polluted their hands, even though Oedipus's acts were unintentional, and he did not know them to be evil when he committed them.

In more modern times, the pollution metaphor takes on a more active cast. In its most significant forms, pollution refers to the effects of one's acts on either the moral character or the attitudinal environment of a community. The first of these bases is addressed by those who support the legal enforcement of morality, especially Patrick Devlin.[41] The second basis of moral pollution is the one I will defend. The two have this in common: they both rely on the cumulative effects of morally debasing acts on the entire society where these acts occur. The individual acts may be morally suspect, but insufficient in themselves to warrant societal interference. Rather, it is the cumulative polluting effects on the attitudinal environment of the community which ought to make pornography subject to societal interference through proscription or regulation.

Over thirty years ago, Devlin argued that pornography, prostitution, and homosexuality weakened the moral fiber of the society. His most straightforward claim comes toward the end of *The Enforcement of Morals:* "Let me consider first the tangible harm. It is obvious that an individual may by unrestricted indulgence in vice so weaken himself that he ceases to be a useful member of society. It is obvious also that if a sufficient number of individuals so weaken themselves society will thereby be weakened."[42] In addition, there is an intangible harm by which morally weak acts weaken the seamless web of morality in a society. The sense of right and wrong in a community has a certain fragility, according to Devlin. There is "a special difficulty due to the nature of moral belief. It is not for most men based on a number of separate rational judgments arrived at after weighing the arguments for and against chastity, for and against honesty, for and against homosexuality, and so on. Most men take their morality as a whole."[43] A successful assault on one part of a community's moral code has intangible effects on the rest. For this reason, Devlin argued, prostitution, pornography, or homosexuality, all of which he regarded as immoral, should be criminalized.

It is by now well recognized that Devlin's arguments, contrary to what he believed, could be used *to support*, not oppose, the legalization of prostitution, pornography, or homosexuality in a society where these practices are an accepted part of the moral fiber. But Devlin has put his finger on something important nonetheless. There are indeed both tangible and intangible harms that can result from the accumulation of seemingly trivial individual harms in a community. Not the least of the problems here is that it is often hard to see what has been harmed and how much by each individual act of seemingly trivial harm. Nonetheless, trivial harms can add up to non-trivial harms.

What Devlin is striving to identify is a kind of pollution of the moral climate. But where this analysis goes wrong is in thinking that there is such a thing as a fixed moral fiber or character of a given society. The moral environment is much more fluid in most societies, as H. L. A. Hart and others have lucidly explained:

> Hence if by the preservation of morality is meant the preservation of the moral attitude of conduct and its formal values, it is certainly true that it is a value. But, though true, this is really irrelevant to the issue before us; for the preservation of morality in this sense is not identical with and does not require the preservation from change of society's moral code as it is at any given moment of that society's existence. . . . From the preservation of morality in this sense which is so clearly a value we must distinguish mere moral conservatism.[44]

Devlin wrongly assumes that any change in a moral environment is a bad thing. But Hart also argues against those changes that might affect our attitudes toward what he calls "such univeral values as individual freedom, safety of life, and protection from deliberately inflicted harm."[45] Such changes as these, but not the broader set of changes identitifed by Devlin, should be resisted because they would have a negative effffect on any society. I would endorse Hart's line of argumentation if it is reformulated in terms of "enduring interests" as discussed earlier in this chapter.

Moral pollution, stripped of its conservative garb, is a useful metaphor for discussing cumulative assaults on the enduring interests of a society. It is important to note once again, though, that a society can be polluted by accumulated assaults on individual liberty, just as it can be polluted by assaults on egalitarian relations between the sexes, since both individual liberty and equality among the sexes are enduring interests. The pollution metaphor is useful, even given this fact, since it helps us focus our attention better on what is happening at the level of prevalent attitudes which restrict options in a community, as a result of seemingly trivial events at the individual level.

The metaphor of pollution is especially apt in the case of pornography since, as the interminable debates on pornography in the 1980s illustrated, the individual instances of pornographic production, dissemination, or consumption were in most cases only trivially harmful, and yet many people have felt that the relations among the sexes have deteriorated due to the way that pornography has adversely affected male and female conceptions of their own sexuality. As in the case of most industrial pollution, it is hard to put one's finger on the particular instances of pollution that are the cause of the decline in the quality of air in the environment; so in the case of pornography it is hard to put one's finger on the individual instances of pornography that are the cause of the decline in the quality of attitudes toward sexuality in a given community. Yet, in both cases a kind of pollution may have occurred which requires some regulation to correct.

VII Regulating Pornography

Not all forms of pornography are equally harmful; indeed, some pornography is not harmful to women, or men, as a group at all. There has been a tendency to treat pornography as all pretty much the same, with the exception of violent pornography, which was singled out as especially harmful. I have been arguing that harm can result from a wider range of nonegalitarian pornography than merely that which is violent in nature. But increasingly, there are forms of pornography, both homosexual and heterosexual, that are not necessarily harmful at all, since their images of sexuality are relatively egalitarian. Indeed, linking egalitarian sexual relationships with erotic stimulation may have an overall positive influence on the relations between women and men. This is, in part, the message of the defenders of some forms of gay and lesbian pornography.[46]

Most people have an enduring interest in a range of options for sexual relationships between men and women. When either men or women find it difficult to relate to one another, or find that their senses of self-worth are diminished, a clear setback has occurred not only to their own enduring interests but also to the enduring interests of the community. Some forms of pornography have a negative effect on the relations among the sexes by restricting options for healthy sexual interaction. Of course what counts as "healthy" may vary from time to time and place to place. On my view, women, and also men, currently have their options narrowed in that they find it increasingly difficult to respect themselves sexually since they either cannot or do not want to conform to the image of a sexual being presented by a largely nonegalitarian pornography industry.

My proposal is to allow individual communities to regulate pornography but not legally to ban it outright. That is, individual communities could follow the lead of the motion picture industry and restrict type of consumer (the age, etc.), or the mode of advertising (the size or placement of advertisements, etc.), or the presentation of the images (the subliminality, the degree of violence, etc.). In each case the restrictions would be based on the overall climate of attitudes toward sexuality within a community. A community, or group of communities, might encourage less violent and more egalitarian forms of pornography by imposing fewer restrictions on them than on more violent and less egalitarian forms. It would be important though to have various procedural safeguards in place, so that vocal conservative groups could not force restrictions on a largely unwilling majority.

In many ways what I am proposing here is not significantly different from what is already occurring in many communities. I am adding a new line of defense for certain forms of egalitarian pornography and a more sophisticated theoretical framework for seeing the regulation of nonegalitarian pornography as morally justified. One of the chief theoretical difficulties has been to isolate a type of harm that is deserving of redress. Individual instances of the production, dissemination, and consumption of pornography seemingly create only trivial harms that courts, legislatures, and municipalities have historically not been willing to regulate. If we turn away from individual harm to group-based harm, and if we turn away from the effects of individual instances of pornography to the accumulated effects of pornography, the job of justifying the regulation of some forms of pornography should get easier.

5

Rape and Collective Responsibility

(with Robert Strikwerda)

      As a teenager, I ran in a crowd that talked incessantly about sex. Since most of us were quite afraid of discovering our own sexual inadequacies, we were quite afraid of women's sexuality. To mask our fear, of which we were quite ashamed, we maintained a posture of bravado, which we were able to sustain through mutual reinforcement when in small groups or packs. Riding from shopping mall to fast food establishment, we would tell each other stories about our sexual exploits, stories we all secretly believed to be pure fiction. We drew strength from the camaraderie we felt during these experiences. Some members of our group would yell obscenities at women on the street as we drove by. Over time, conversation turned more and more to group sex, especially forced sex with women we passed on the road. To give it its proper name, our conversation turned increasingly to rape. At a certain stage, I tired of it all and stopped associating with this group of men, or perhaps they were in most ways still boys. The reason I left was not that I disagreed with what was going on but, if this decision to leave was reasoned at all, it was that the posturing (the endless attempts to impress one another by our daring ways) simply became very tiresome. Only much later in life did I think that there was anything wrong — morally, socially, or politically — with what went on in that group of adolescents who seemed so ready to engage in rape. Only later still did I wonder whether I shared in responsibility for the rapes that are perpetrated by those men who had similar experiences to mine.[1]

The link between violence and rape has been documented in the war in Bosnia. Young Serbian soldiers, some with no previous sexual experience, seemed quite willing to rape Muslim and Croatian women as their reward for "winning" the war. These young men were often encouraged by their fellow soldiers and sometimes even their commanding officers. Indeed, gang rape in concentration camps, at least at the beginning of the war, seems to have been common.[2] The situation in Bosnia is by no means unique in the history of war.[3] Historically, rape has never been considered a war crime. Rather, Catharine MacKinnon suggests, "rape in war has so often been treated as extracurricular, as just something men do, as a product rather than a policy of war."[4]

War crimes are collective acts taken against humanity; whereas rape has almost always been viewed as a despicable "private" act. In this chapter we wish to challenge the view that rape is the responsibility only of the rapists by challenging the notion that rape is best understood as an individual, private act. We are interested in the relationship between the shared experiences of men in groups, especially experiences that make rape more likely in Western culture, and the shared responsibility of men for the prevalence of rape in that culture. The thesis of this chapter is that in some societies men are collectively responsible for rape because most, if not all, men contribute in various ways to, and benefit from, the prevalence of rape. As a result, these men should share in responsibility for rape.

Most men do very little at all to oppose rape in their societies. Does this make them something like conspirators with the men who rape? In Canada, a number of men have founded the "White Ribbon Campaign." This is a program of fund-raising, consciousness-raising, and symbolic wearing of white ribbons during the week ending on December 6, the anniversary of the murder of fourteen women at a Montreal engineering school by a man shouting, "I hate feminists." Should men in U.S. society start a similar campaign? If they do not, do they deserve the "conspirator" label? If they do, is this symbolic act enough to diminish their responsibility? Should men have spoken out against the program of rape in the war in Bosnia? What should they tell their sons about such rapes and about rapes that occur in their hometowns? If men remain silent, are they not complicitous with the rapists?

We will argue that insofar as male bonding and socialization in groups contributes to the prevalence of rape in Western societies, men in those societies should feel responsible for the prevalence of rape and should feel motivated to counteract such violence and rape. In addition, we will argue that rape should be seen as something that a given society's men, as a group, are collectively responsible for, in a way which somewhat parallels the collective responsibility of a particular society for war crimes, crimes against humanity, perpetrated by some members of their society. Rape is indeed a crime against humanity, not merely a crime against a particular woman, and rape is a crime perpetrated by men as a group, not merely by the individual rapist.

To support our claims we will criticize four other ways to understand responsibility for rape. First, it is sometimes said that only the rapist is responsible since he alone committed the act. Second, it is sometimes said that no one is responsible since rape is merely a biologically oriented response to stimuli, and that men have little or no control over these responses. Third, it is sometimes said that everyone, women and men equally, contributes to the violent environment that produces rape; so both women and men are equally responsible for rape, and hence it is a mistake to single men out. Fourth, it is sometimes said that "patriarchy," rather than individual men or men as a group, is responsible for rape.[5] After examining each of these views we will conclude by briefly offering our own positive reasons for thinking that men are collectively responsible for the prevalence of rape in Western society.

▪ The Rapist as Loner or Demon

Joyce Carol Oates has described the sport of boxing, in which men are encouraged to violate the social rule against harming one another, as "a highly organized ritual that violates taboo." According to Oates, "The paradox of the boxer is that, in the ring, he experiences himself as a living conduit for the inchoate, demonic will of the crowd: the expression of their collective desire, which is to pound another human being into absolute submission."[6] Oates makes the connection here between boxing and rape. The former heavyweight champion of the world, Mike Tyson, epitomizes this connection, both because he is a convicted rapist and also because, according to Oates, before his fights he regularly used the taunt "I'll make you into my girlfriend," clearly the "boast of a rapist."[7]

Just after being convicted of rape, Mike Tyson made a twisted declaration of innocence: "I didn't rape anyone. I didn't hurt anyone — no black eyes, no broken ribs. When I'm in the ring, I break their ribs, I break their jaws. To me, that's hurting someone."[8] In the ring, Tyson had a license to break ribs and jaws, and interestingly, he understood that this was a case of hurting another person. It was just that in the ring it was considered acceptable. He knew that he was not supposed to hurt people outside the ring, but since he didn't break any ribs or jaws, how could anyone say that he hurt his accuser, Desiree Washington? Apparently, in Tyson's view, having sex with a woman could not be construed as having hurt her unless bones were broken.

Tyson's lawyer, attempting to excuse Tyson's behavior, said that the boxer grew up in a "male-dominated world." And this is surely true. He was plucked from a home for male juvenile delinquents and raised by boxing promoters. Few American males had been so richly imbued with male tradition or more richly rewarded for living up to the male stereotype of the aggressive, indomitable fighter. Whether or not he recognized it as a genuine insight, Tyson's lawyer points us toward the heart of the matter in American culture: misbehavior, especially sexual misbehavior of males toward females, is something which is publicly condemned but which many men condone.[9] This has given rise to the use of the term "the rape culture" to describe the climate of attitudes that exists in the contemporary American male-dominated world.[10]

While noting all of this, Joyce Carol Oates ends her *Newsweek* essay on Tyson's rape trial by concluding that "no one is to blame except the perpetrator himself," absolving the "culture" at large of any blame for Tyson's behavior. Oates regards Tyson as a sadist who took pleasure in inflicting pain both in and out of the boxing ring. She comes very close to demonizing him when, at the end of her essay, she suggests that Tyson is an outlaw or even a sociopath. And while she is surely right to paint his deed in the most horrific colors, she is less convincing when she suggests that Tyson is very different from other males in our society. In one telling statement, however, Oates opens the door to a less individualistic view of rape by acknowledging that the boxing community had built up in Tyson a "grandiose sense of entitlement, fueled by the insecurities and emotions of adolescence."[11]

Rape is normally committed by individual men, but in our view, rape is not best understood in purely individualistic terms. The chief reasons why it is not are that individual men are more likely to engage in rape when they are in groups and men receive strong encouragement to rape from the way they are socialized as men,[12] that is, in the way they come to see themselves as instantiations of what it means to be a man. Both the "climate" that encourages rape and the "socialization" patterns that instill negative attitudes about women are difficult to understand or assess when one focuses on the isolated individual rapist. There are significant social dimensions to rape which are best understood as group oriented.[13]

As parents, we have observed that male schoolchildren are much more likely to misbehave (and subsequently to be punished by being sent to "time out") than are female schoolchildren. This fact is not particularly remarkable, for boys are widely believed to be more active than girls. What is remarkable is that schoolteachers, in our experience, are much more likely to condone the misbehavior of boys than the misbehavior of girls. "Boys will be boys" is heard as often today as it ever was.[14] From their earliest experience with authority figures, little boys are given mixed signals about misbehavior. Yes, they are punished, but they are also treated as if their misbehavior is expected, even readily excusable. For some boys, as it was for us, it is a "badge of honor" to be sent to detention or "time out." From older boys and from their peers, boys learn that they can be ostracized for being "too goody-goody." It is as if part of the mixed message is that boys are given a license to misbehave.[15]

And which of these boys will turn out to be rapists is often as much a matter of luck as a matter of choice. It is estimated that in the first few months of the Bosnian war "30,000 to 50,000 women, most of them Muslim," were raped by Serbian soldiers.[16] The data on date rape suggest that young men in our society engage in much more rape that anyone previously anticipated.[17] It is a serious mistake in psychological categorization to think that all these rapes are committed by sadists.[18] Given our own experiences and similar reports from others, it is also a serious mistake to think that those who rape are significantly different from the rest of the male population.[19] Our conclusion is that typical rapists are not demons or sadists, but, in some sense, could have been many men.

Most of those who engage in rape are primarily responsible for these rapes, but the question we have posed is this: are those who perpetrate rape the *only* ones who are responsible for rape? Contrary to what Joyce Carol Oates contends, we believe that it is a serious mistake to think that only the perpetrators are responsible. The interactions of men, especially in all-male groups, contribute to a pattern of socialization that also plays a major role in the incidence of rape. In urging that more than the individual perpetrators be seen as responsible for rape, we do not necessarily mean to suggest that the responsibility of the perpetrator be diminished. When responsibility for harm is shared, it need not be true that the perpetrators of harm find their responsibility relieved or even diminished. Rather, shared responsibility for harm merely extends the range of people who are implicated in these harms. (More will be said on this point in the final section of this chapter.)

▌▌ The Rapist as Victim of Biology

Randy Thornhill and Nancy Wilmsen Thornhill have provided a recent psychological study of rape that has received significant scholarly attention.[20] In this work, any contention that coercion or rape may be socially or culturally learned is derisively dismissed, as is any argument for changing men's attitudes through changing especially group-based socialization. The general hypothesis is that "sexual coercion by men reflects a sex-specific, species-typical psychological adaptation to rape: Men have certain psychological traits that evolved by natural selection specifically in the context of coercive sex and made rape adaptive during human evolution."[21] They claim that rape is an adaptive response to biological differences between men and women.

The Thornhills contend that the costs of sex for women ("nine months of pregnancy") greatly exceed the costs for men ("a few minutes of time and an energetically cheap ejaculate"). As a result women and men very early in evolution adapted quite differently sexually. "Because women are more selective about mates and more interested in evaluating them and delaying copulation, men, to get sexual access, must often break through feminine barriers of hesitation, equivocation, and resistance."[22] Males who adapted by developing a proclivity to rape and thus who "solved the problem" by forcing sex on a partner were able to "out-reproduce" other more passive males and gain an evolutionary advantage.

In one paragraph, the Thornhills dismiss feminists who support a "social learning theory of rape" by pointing out that males of several "species with an evolutionary history of polygyny" are also "more aggressive, sexually assertive and eager to copulate." Yet, in "the vast majority of these species there is no sexual training of juveniles by other members of the group." This evidence, they conclude, thoroughly discredits the social learning theory and means that such theories "are never alternatives to evolutionary hypotheses about psychological adaptation."[23] In response to their critics, the Thornhills go so far as to say that the feminist project of changing socialization patterns is pernicious.

> The sociocultural view does seem to offer hope and a simple remedy in that it implies that we need only fix the way that boys are socialized and rape will disappear. This naive solution is widespread. . . . As Hartung points out, those who feel that the social problem of rape can be solved by changing the nature of men through naive and arbitrary social adjustments should "get real about rape" because their perspective is a danger to us all.[24]

According to the Thornhills, feminists and other social theorists need to focus instead on what are called the "cues that affect the use of rape by adult males."[25]

This evolutionary biological account would seem to suggest that no one is responsible for rape. After all, if rape is an adaptive response to differential sexual development in males and females, individual males who engage in rape are merely doing what they are naturally adapted to do. Rape is something to be controlled by those who control the "cues" that stimulate the natural rapist instincts in all men. It is for this reason that the Thornhills urge that more attention be given to male arousal and female stimulation patterns in laboratory settings.[26] Notice that on the Thornhills' terms, those who provide the cues may be responsible for the prevalence of rape, even if the perpetrators are not. But the Thornhills deny that there are any normative conclusions that follow from their research and criticize those who wish to draw out such implications as committing the "naturalistic fallacy."[27]

Lionel Tiger, who gives a more plausible sociobiological account, is often cited as someone who attempted to excuse male aggression. In his important study he distinguishes aggression from violence but nonetheless sees violence as one possible outcome of natural aggressive tendencies, especially in men: "Aggression occurs when an individual or group see their interest, their honor, or their job bound up with coercing the animal, human, or physical environment to achieve their own ends rather than (or in spite of) the goals of the object of their action. Violence may occur in the process of interaction."[28] For Tiger, aggression is intentional behavior which is goal-directed and based on procuring something that is necessary for survival. Aggression is a " 'normal' feature of the human biologically based repertoire."[29] Violence, "coercion involving physical force to resolve conflict,"[30] on the other hand, is not necessarily a normal response to one's environment, although in some circumstances it may be. Thus, whereas human males are evolutionarily adapted to be aggressive, they are not necessarily adapted to be violent.

Tiger traces aggression in males to their biological evolution.

> Human aggression is in part a function of the fact that hunting was vitally important to human evolution and that aggression is typically undertaken by males in the framework of a unisexual social bond of which participants are aware and with which they are concerned. It is implied, therefore, that aggression is "instinctive" but also must occur within an explicit social context varying from culture to culture and to be learned by members of any community. . . . Men in continuous association aggress against the environment in much the same way as men and women in continuous association have sexual relations.[31]

Whereas men are thus predisposed to engage in aggression, in ways that women are not, it is not true, in Tiger's view, that a predisposition to violence is a normal part of this difference.

The Thornhills fail to consider Tiger's contention that men are evolutionarily adapted to be aggressive but not necessarily violent. With Tiger's distinction in mind, it may be said that human males, especially in association with other males, are adapted to aggress against women in certain social environments. But this aggressive response need not lead to violence or the threat of violence of the sort epitomized by rape; rather, it may merely affect noncoercive mating rituals. On a related point, Tiger argues that the fact that war has historically been "virtually a male monopoly" is due to both male bonding patterns and evolutionary adaptation.[32] Evolutionary biology provides only part of the story since male aggressiveness need not result in such violent encounters as occur in war or rape. After all, many men do not rape or go to war; the social or cultural cues provided by socialization must be considered at least as important as evolutionary adaptation.

We side with Tiger against the Thornhills in focusing on the way that all-male groups socialize their members and provide "cues" for violence.

Tiger has allied himself with feminists such as Catharine MacKinnon and others who have suggested that male attitudes need to be radically altered if the incidence of rape is to be significantly decreased.[33] One of the implications of Tiger's research is that rape and other forms of male aggressive behavior are not best understood as isolated individual acts. Rather than simply seeing violent aggression as merely a biologically predetermined response, Tiger places violent aggressiveness squarely into the group dynamics of men's interactions — a result of his research not well appreciated.

In a preface to the second edition of his book, Tiger corrects an unfortunate misinterpretation of his work.

> One of the stigmas which burdened this book was an interpretation of it as an apology for male aggression and even a potential stimulus of it — after all, boys will be boys. However I clearly said the opposite: "This is not to say that . . . hurtful and destructive relations between groups of men are inevitable. . . . It may be possible, as many writers have suggested, to alter social conceptions of maleness so that gentility and equivocation rather than toughness and more or less arbitrary decisiveness are highly valued."[34]

Tiger also contends that the most important "cues" are those which young boys and men get while in the company of other boys and men.[35] If Tiger is right, then the feminist project of changing male socialization patterns may be seen as consistent with, rather than opposed to, the sociobiological hypotheses. Indeed, other evidence may be cited to buttress the feminist social-learning perspective against the Thornhills' view. Different human societies have quite different rates of rape. In her anthropological research among the Minangkabau of West Sumatra, Peggy Reeves Sanday has found that this society is relatively rape-free. Rape does occur, but at such a low rate — 28 cases of rape reported in 1981–1982 in a population of 3 million, for example — as to be virtually nonexistent.[36] In light of such research, men, rather than women, are the ones who would need to change their behavior. This is because, as we will next see, it is the socialization of men by men in their bonding-groups, and the view of women that is engendered, that provides the strongest cues toward rape. Since there may indeed be something that males could and should be doing differently that would affect the prevalence of rape, it does not seem unreasonable to continue to investigate the claim that men are collectively responsible for the prevalence of rape.

▐▐ The Rapist as Victim of Society

It is also possible to acknowledge that men are responsible for the prevalence of rape in our society but nonetheless to argue that women are equally responsible, since both men and women contribute to the socialization patterns of young boys. Rape is often portrayed as a sex crime perpetrated largely by men against women. But it is important to bear in mind that rape is also a crime of violence, and many factors in our society have increased the prevalence of violence. This prevalence of violence is the cause of both rape and war in western societies. Our view, that the likelihood of violence of both sorts is increased by patterns of socialization of boys and men by other men, which then creates collective moral responsibility for men, may be countered by pointing out that socialization patterns are created by both men and women, which thereby seems to implicate both men and women in collective responsibility for rape and war.

Sam Keen contends that it is violence on which we should be focusing, rather than sex or gender, in order to understand the causes and remedies for the prevalence of rape. According to Keen, "Men are violent because of the systematic violence done to their bodies and spirits. Being hurt they become hurters. In the overall picture, male violence toward women is far less than male violence toward other males. . . . these outrages are a structural part of a warfare system that victimizes both men and women."[37] Keen sees both men and women as conspiring to perpetuate this system of violence, especially in the acceptance of violence they impart to their male children.

Keen singles out women as having failed to come to terms with their share of responsibility for our violent culture. Men, he says, have been assigned guilt for rape so often that they have become desensitized to it. Keen thinks it is a mistake to single out men, and not women also, as responsible for rape. "Until women are willing to weep for and accept equal responsibility for the systematic violence done to the male body and spirit by the war system, it is not likely that men will lose enough of their guilt and regain enough of their sensitivity to accept responsibility for women who are raped."[38] Even though women are equally responsible for the rape culture, in Keen's view, women should be singled out because they have not previously accepted their share of responsibility for the creation of a violent society.

Keen is at least partially right, insofar as he insists that issues of rape and war be understood as arising from the same source, namely, the socialization of men to be violent in Western cultures.[39] We agree with Keen that rape is part of a larger set of violent practices that injure both men and women. He is right to point out that men are murdering other men in our society in increasing numbers and that this incidence of violence probably has something to do with the society's general condoning, even celebrating, of violence, especially in war. We took note of this fact when we began this chapter discussing the role that rape plays in war.

Keen fails to note, though, that it is men, not women, who are the vast majority of both rapists and murderers in our society. And even if some women do act in ways which contribute to the socialization of men to be violent, nevertheless, this pales in comparison with the way that men socialize each other to be open to violence. As Tiger and others have suggested, aggressive violence often results from male-bonding experiences. Men influence the rape culture both through early childhood socialization and through male-bonding socialization of older male children. But when women contribute to the perpetuation of rape, it is mainly through early childhood socialization.[40] For this reason, Keen is surely wrong to think that women share responsibility *equally* with men for our rape culture. Of course, when women share in the perpetuation of the rape culture, they are at least partially responsible for it, even though their share in responsibility is not normally equal to that of men.

In our view, some women could prevent some rapes, and some women do contribute to the patterns of socialization of both men and women which increase the incidence of rape. For these reasons, it would not be inappropriate to say that women share responsibility for rape. But we believe that it is a mistake to think that women share equally in this responsibility with men. For one thing, women are different from men in that they are, in general, made worse off by the prevalence of rape in our society. As we will next see, there is a sense in which men, but not women, benefit from the prevalence of rape, and this fact means that men have more of a stake in the rape culture, and hence have more to gain by its continued existence.[41]

In general, our conclusion is that women share responsibility, but to a far lesser extent than men, for the prevalence of rape. We do not support those[42] who try to "blame the victim" by holding women responsible for rape because of not taking adequate precautions, or dressing seductively, etc. Instead, the key for us is the role that women, as mothers, friends, and lovers, play in the overall process of male socialization that creates the rape culture. It should come as no surprise that few members of Western society can be relieved of responsibility for this rape culture given the overwhelming pervasiveness of that culture. But such considerations should not deter us from looking to men, first and foremost, as being collectively responsible for the prevalence of rape.

IV The Rapist as Group Member

Popular literature tends to portray the rapist as a demonic character, as the "Other." What we find interesting about the Thornhills' research is that it operates unwittingly to support the feminist slogan that "all men are rapists," that the rapist is not male "Other" but male "Self." What is so unsettling about the tens of thousands of rapes in Bosnia is that ordinary men perpetrated these crimes and that the attitudes of ordinary men in many cultures are not significantly different from the attitudes of the "sex fiends." The thesis that men are predisposed to be rapists regardless of what else we think of the thesis, should give us pause and make us less rather than more likely to reject the feminist slogan. From this vantage point, the work of Tiger as well as the Thornhills sets the stage for serious reconsideration of the view that men are collectively responsible for rape.

Two things might be meant by saying that men are collectively responsible for the prevalence of rape in Western culture. First, seeing men as collectively responsible may mean that men as a group are responsible in that they form some sort of superentity that causes, or at least supports, the prevalence of rape. When some progressives and feminists talk of "patriarchy," what they seem to mean is a kind of institution that operates through, but also behind the backs of, individual men to oppress women. Thus it may be that men are collectively responsible for the prevalence of rape and yet no men are individually responsible. We call this nondistributional collective responsibility.[43]

Second, seeing men as collectively responsible may mean that men form a group in which there are so many features that the members share in common, such as attitudes or dispositions to engage in harm, that what holds true for one man also holds true for all other men. Because of the common features of the members of the group "men," when one man is responsible for a particular harm, other men are implicated. Each member of the group has a share in the responsibililty for a harm such as rape. We call this distributional collective responsibility.[44] In what follows we will criticize the first way of understanding men's collective responsibility, and offer reasons to support the second.

When collective responsibility is understood in the first nondistributional sense, responsibility is assigned to those groups that have the capacity to act. Here there are two paradigmatic examples: the corporation and the mob.[45] The corporation has the kind of organizational structure that enables the group to form intentions and carry them out, almost as if the corporation were a person. Since men, qua men, are too amorphous a group to be able to act in an organized fashion, we will not be interested in whether they are collectively responsible in this way. But it may be that men can act in the way that mobs act, that is, not through a highly organized structure but through something such as like-mindedness. If there is enough commonality of belief, disposition, and interest among all men, or at least all men in a particular culture, then the group may be able to act in somewhat the same way as a mob responds to a commonly perceived enemy.

Some feminists have contended that patriarchy is the cause of rape. Patriarchy here refers to the oppressive practices of men coordinated by the common interests of men but not organized intentionally. If there is a "collective" supporting or creating the prevalence of rape, it is not a highly organized one, since there is nothing like a corporation that intentionally plans the rape of women in Western societies. If the Serbian army engaged in the systematic and organized rape of Muslim women as a strategy of war, then this would be an example of nondistributional collective responsibility for rape. But the kind of oppression characterized by the prevalence of rape in most cultures appears to be systematic but not organized. How does this recognition affect our understanding of whether men are collectively responsible for rape?

If patriarchy is understood merely as a system of coordination that operates behind the backs of individual men, then it may be that no single man is responsible for any harms that are caused by patriarchy. But if patriarchy is understood as something that is based on common interests, as well as common benefits, extended to all or most men in a particular culture, then it may be that men are collectively responsible for the harms of patriarchy in a way that distributes out to all men, making each man in a particular culture at least partially responsible for the harms attributable to patriarchy. This latter strategy is consistent with our own view of men's responsibility for rape. In the remainder of this chapter we will offer support for this conceptualization of the collective responsibility of men for the prevalence of rape.

Our positive assessment, going beyond our criticism of the faulty responses analyzed in earlier sections of this chapter, is that men in Western culture are collectively responsible in the distributional sense. That is, each man shares responsibility for the prevalence of rape. This claim rests on five points. (1) Insofar as most rapes are committed by men, then, in most cases, men are responsible as perpetrators for the rapes they committed. (2) Insofar as many men, by the way they interact with other (especially younger) men, contribute to a climate in our society which makes rape more prevalent, then they are collaborators in the rape culture and for this reason share in responsibility for rapes committed in that culture. (3) Also, insofar as many men in our culture are not unlike the rapist, since they would be rapists if they were placed in a situation where their inhibitions against rape were removed, then these men share responsibility with actual rapists for the harms of rape.[46] (4) In addition, insofar as most other men in our culture could have prevented fellow men from raping, but did not act to prevent these actual rapes, then these men also share responsibility along with the rapists. (5) Finally, insofar as most men in our culture benefit from the existence of rape in our society, these men also share responsibility along with the rapists.

It seems to us unlikely that many, if any, men in our society fail to fit into one or another of these categories. Hence, we think that it is not unreasonable to say that men in our society are collectively responsible (in the distributional sense) for rape. We expect some male readers to respond as follows:

> I am adamantly opposed to rape, and though when I was younger I might have tolerated rape-conducive comments from friends of mine, I don't now, so I'm not a collaborator in the rape culture. And I would never be a rapist whatever the situation, and I would certainly act to prevent any rape that I could. I'm pretty sure I don't benefit from rape. So how can I be responsible for the prevalence of rape?

In reply we would point out that nearly all men in a given Western society meet the third and fifth conditions (concerning similarity and benefit). But women generally fail to meet either of these conditions, or the first. So, the involvement of women in the rape culture is much less than is true for men. In what follows we will concentrate on the similarity and benefit issues.

In our discussion above, we questioned the view that rapists are "Other," that is, significantly different from normal men. Diane Scully, in her study of convicted rapists, turns the view around, suggesting that it is women who are "other." She argues that rapists in America are not pathological but, instead, that men who rape have something to tell us about the cultural roots of sexual violence. . . . They tell us that some men use rape as a means of revenge and punishment. Implicit in revenge rape is the collective liability of women. In some cases, victims are substitutes for significant women on whom men desire to take revenge. In other cases, victims represent all women. . . . In either case, women are seen as objects, a category, but not as individuals with rights. For some men, rape is an afterthought or bonus they add to burglary or robbery. In other words, rape is "no big deal.". . . Some men rape in groups as a male bonding activity — for them it's just something to do. . . . Convicted rapists tell us that in this culture, sexual violence is rewarding. . . . these men perceived rape as a rewarding, low-risk act.[47]

It is the prevalent perception of women as "other" by men in our culture which fuels the prevalence of rape in American society. As was indicated in the last chapter, 50 percent of teenage boys surveyed said they would commit rape if they thought they could get away with it. Insofar as teenage boys and men have attitudes similar to those of rapists, then there is a sense in which it is true that many men could have been rapists but for circumstances largely not under their control. Responsibility for what one of these men does, but which the other would have done in somewhat different circumstances, is plausibly shared by both men.[48]

Turning to the issue of benefit, we believe that Lionel Tiger's work illustrates the important source of strength that men derive from the all-male groups they form. And it is also true that men benefit from the all-male groups that they form in our culture. Male bonding is made easier because there is an "Other" that males can bond "against." And this other is the highly sexualized stereotype of the "female." Some men benefit from the rape culture by finding it easier to engage in male bonding; but there is a social cost: from the evidence we have examined there is an increased prevalence of rape. Men need to consider this in reviewing their own role in a culture where there is so much rape.

There is another sense in which benefit is related to the issue of responsibility for rape. There is a sense in which many men in our society benefit from the prevalence of rape in ways of which many of us are quite unaware. Consider this example:

Several years ago, at a social occasion in which male and female professors were present, I asked off-handedly whether people agreed with me that the campus was looking especially pretty at night these days. Many of the men responded positively. But all of the women responded that this was not something that they had even thought about, since they were normally too anxious about being on campus at night, especially given the increase in reported rapes recently.[49]

We men benefited in that, relative to our female colleagues, we were in an advantageous position vis-à-vis travel around campus. And there were surely other comparative benefits that accrued to us as a result of this advantage concerning travel, such as our ability to gain academically by being able to use the library at any hour we chose.

In a larger sense, men benefit from the prevalence of rape in that many women are made to feel dependent on men for protection against potential rapists. It is hard to overestimate the benefit here, for it potentially affects all aspects of one's life. One study found that 87 percent of women in a borough of London felt that they had to take precautions against rape, with a large number reporting that they never went out at night alone.[50] Whenever one group is made to feel dependent on another group, and this dependency is not reciprocal, then there is a strong comparative benefit to the group that is not in the dependent position. Such a benefit, along with the specific benefits already mentioned, supports the view that men as a group have a stake in perpetuating the rape culture in ways that women do not. When men do not act so as to distance themselves from the rape culture and the advantages they accrue from it, these men become complicitous in that rape culture. Just as the benefit to men distributes throughout the male population in a given society, so at least a small share in the responsibility should distribute as well.[51]

V Collective Responses

When people coerce one another they fail to treat one another with respect as fellow autonomous beings. Rape and murder in wartime situations victimize members of various groups simply because they are group members. These two factors combine to create a form of dehumanization that can warrant the charge of crime against humanity. What makes an act of violence more than just a private individual act in wartime, or in other situations, is that killing and rape are perpetrated not against the individual for his or her unique characteristics but solely because the individual instantiates a group characteristic, for example, being Jewish, or Muslim, or being a woman.[52] Such identification fails to respect what is unique about each of us.

Our point is not that all men everywhere are responsible for the prevalence of rape. Rather, we have been arguing that in Western societies, rape is deeply embedded in a wider culture of male socialization. Those who have the most to do with sustaining that culture must also recognize that they are responsible for the harmful aspects of that culture.[53] And when rape is conjoined with war, especially as an organized strategy, then there is a sense that men are collectively responsible for the rapes that occur in that war,[54] just as groups of people are held responsible for the crimes of genocide, where the victims are persecuted simply because they fall into a certain category of people who are ripe for assault.[55]

Rape is normally an act of violence perpetrated by a man against a woman merely for being an instantiation of the type "woman." Insofar as rape in times of war is a systematically organized form of terror, it is not inappropriate to call rape a war crime, a crime against humanity. Insofar as rape in times of peace is also part of a pattern of terror against women, then such rape is also a crime against humanity.[56] Rape, in war or in peace, is rarely only one person's act of aggression against another person. It is an act of hostility and terrorism that manifests a complete failure to show basic human respect.[57] And more than this, rape is made more likely by the collective actions, or inactions, of men in a particular society. Insofar as men in a particular society contribute to the prevalence of rape, they participate in a crime against humanity for which they are collectively responsible.[58]

We have argued for the view that all men contribute to the prevalence of rape. How is this view related to the feminist slogan "All men are rapists?" Is the feminist slogan mere hyperbole? It is if what is meant is that each time a rape occurs, every man did it, or that only men are ever responsible for rape. But as we have seen, each time a rape occurs, there is a sense in which many men could have done it, or made it less likely to occur, or benefited from it. By direct contribution or by negligence or by similarity of disposition or by benefiting, most, if not all, men in a particular society do share in each rape in that society. This is the link between being responsible for the prevalence of rape and being responsible, at least to some extent, for the harms of each rape.

The purpose of these arguments has been to make men aware of the various ways they are implicated in the rape culture in general as well as in particular rapes. And while we believe that men should feel some shame for their group's complicity in the prevalence of rape, our aim is not to shame men but to prompt men to take responsibility for resocializing themselves and their fellow men. We see resocialization as required for the development of morally capable and responsible people. Most of us can to some extent change the effects of our past socialization. The main point of this chapter is to render plausible the view that men in our society contribute to the prevalence of rape. We hope that such a view would begin to inspire men to change the rape culture.

How much should any particular man do? Men must find ways of behaving which distance them from the dominant forms of socialization which perpetuate the rape culture. In each society different opportunities will be available for men to display that they are not, at least in some significant senses, like the traditional men we have been discussing in this chapter. Participating in the Canadian White Ribbon Campaign or in antisexism education programs would be two such efforts.[59] Suffice it to say that the status quo, namely, doing nothing, individually or as a group, is not satisfactory and will further compound our collective and shared responsibility for the harms caused by our fellow men who commit rape.

Discussions of collective responsibility often elicit extreme responses. Many people, especially in Western cultures, are simply not prepared to admit collective responsibility onto the same moral level as individual responsibility. Talk of collective responsibility seems to get individual men off the hook too easily. In discussions of rape this objection is especially troubling. Joyce Carol Oates is not off base when she worries that talk of how Mike Tyson could be any man diminishes the truly horrible character of what he individually did. We do not view male socialization patterns as the basis of an excuse for the behavior of individual men. Such patterns of socialization may diminish but would rarely eliminate individual responsibility.

It has been difficult for us to discuss our own complicity as participants and even as perpetrators of rape. We assume that it is even more difficult for women to discuss what it is like to be a potential victim of rape. One reason for the difficulty men have with this issue is that admitting their complicity in the rape culture means that they are not fully trustworthy. The difficulty that many women have with this topic is that it implicates men who may be significant companions in their lives. And while it was not our intent to argue that women should not trust men, our analysis of rape does set the stage for the view that the burden of proof is on men to show that they deserve the trust of the women in their lives. Until socialization patterns are changed, it is not absurd for women to view every man as a potential rapist. Individual men in relationships with individual women may deserve and come to win that trust, but it is not unfair — though it may be a burden — for those men to have to start over again, in each new relationship, to show that they deserve to be trusted. It is up to each of us men to show that we are not contributing to the rape culture and that we are attempting to change ourselves and our society to diminish the incidence of rape.

Sexual Harassment and Solidarity

Sexual harassment, like rape, seems obviously wrong. Yet, many men are not as willing to condemn it as they are willing to condemn rape. In part, this is no doubt due to the fact that it is less clear what are the boundaries of the concept of harassment, where some putative forms of harassment are not easily distinguished from "horse play" or pranksterism.[1] But it may also be due to the fact that men are reluctant to condemn practices which have for so long functioned to build solidarity among men.[2] The *Playboy* centerfold pinned to the bulletin board at a workplace has at least two functions. It is a constant source of erotic stimulation for the men who work there; and it is a constant source of embarrassment and annoyance for many of the women, a clear sign that this is not the kind of place for them, but that it is a place for men.

In this chapter I wish to examine sexual harassment in its various forms, seeking a basis for moral criticism of it. In addition to more standard criticisms, largely parallel to those developed in law, I offer a new critique that calls attention to the way that sexual harassment promotes male solidarity and also thereby often excludes women from full and equal participation in various practices and contexts. At the end of the chapter I discuss positive aspects of male solidarity and indicate why sexual harassment is not a good basis for such solidarity. Men need to feel good about who they are as men, not on the model of little boys retreating to a clubhouse with a "no girls allowed" sign on the door, but on the model of reformed alcoholics who are now so changed that they are not afraid to discuss their past problems with others as well as among themselves.

▎ Sexual Intimidation

The case of *Alexander v. Yale University* was the first sexual harassment lawsuit to concern an educational rather than a workplace setting.[3] The case concerned a female student at Yale University who alleged that one of her male political science professors threatened to *lower* her grade on a term paper (from a B to a C) unless she slept with him. The student, who was hoping to go to law school, felt intimidated by the proposal but did not capitulate. After her initial accusation, other women came forward with similar stories about this particular political science professor. The professor denied these other charges but admitted discussing grades with the student who sued. He claimed that he had offered to *raise* the student's grade (from a C to a B) if she slept with him, but that she had simply declined his offer. Since, on his view, the grade had remained what the student had earned, no harm had been done to the student. No foul, no harm.

This case raised difficulties with the way that sexual harassment had been previously understood. Previously, sexual harassment was thought by the courts to involve five elements:

(1) a sexual advance
(2) by a person in a more powerful position
(3) made to a person in a less powerful position
(4) against the second person's will
(5) which adversely affected
     (a) retention of job
     (b) evaluation
   or (c) promotion.

At least according to the version of the story told by the political science professor, the student had not been adversely affected, and so the fifth element of sexual harassment was not present.

Sexual harassment was understood to be harmful in that it constituted an unjustified form of intimidation, much like blackmail. But the attorneys who defended the Yale student felt that a different model was needed given the group-oriented nature of the offense. So they seized on the idea that sexual harassment like that directed at the student was a form of sex discrimination and thus harmful as a form of degradation. But what if the facts were as alleged by the professor, was there any discrimination against or degradation of the student? This seemed not to be like blackmail, since there was no clear indication that she would be rendered worse off if she turned down the professor's proposal.

If the facts were as the student alleged, then this was an egregious case of sexual intimidation. No one who understands the purpose of educational institutions would countenance the idea of a male professor threatening to give a student less than she deserved unless the student did something so utterly outside the realm of academic achievement as providing sexual favors. Worse than this is the idea of a male professor abusing his power and authority over often naive students for his own personal gain. And worse yet is the idea that a man could extort sex from an otherwise unwilling female by threatening to do something undeserved to harm her career prospects. For all these reasons, sexual harassment of the sort alleged by the student is clearly morally wrong.

If we believe the male political science professor, something morally wrong has occurred as well, although somewhat less clearly so. On his version he offered to give the student a grade better than she deserves, and so he seemingly did not threaten to harm her undeservedly. But there was an indication that the female student may have been harmed which can be seen in that she would not have wanted to have such proposals made in the first place. The student was put in the position of having her sexuality count as a basis of academic achievement. This had a negative impact on the educational environment in which the student resided.[4] I have elsewhere argued that this was indeed a form of sex discrimination which effectively coerced the student, even though there was no direct threat to her, at least if we believe the professor's story.[5]

The professor's "offer" changes the range of options that the student previously had in a way which makes her post-offer situation worse than it was in the pre-offer state. The student could no longer proceed as before, thinking of her options in a purely academic way. And in this sense she is disadvantaged, perhaps even coerced, in that she is made to accept a set of options that she would not otherwise choose. When such proposals get made, the well is poisoned, and it is no longer possible for the student to think of herself as merely a student and not also as a sex object.[6] In the case of sexual harassment, seen as either a direct threat or as a seemingly innocent sexual offer, harm has occurred.

Laurence Thomas has challenged my analysis of sexual harassment in offer situations. He contends that not all examples of sexual offers contain veiled threats or can be characterized as situations that the woman would prefer not to be in. He gives an example: "Deborah is Peter's secretary. Peter offers to pay Deborah so many dollars per week, in addition to her present salary, if she would be his exclusive sexual partner. The money would come out of his own pocket."[7] Thomas stipulates that there is no veiled threat here, and no one is under psychological duress. In the case in question, Thomas "is not inclined to think that there is a moral wrong here."[8] His rationale is expressed in this blunt statement: "It simply cannot be the case that we should not enter into any interaction if there is the possibility that it might become morally explosive."[9]

It seems to me, however, that Peter has done something morally suspect by introducing sex into the workplace. Even though Deborah can take the offer or leave it, she cannot, on her own, return to a situation where her relationship with Peter was strictly professional. By turning the offer down, she does not return to the previous state of affairs because of the way that Peter's offer has changed the relationship between them and set the stage for abuses of Peter's authority.[10] This much Thomas admits; yet he claims that we cannot stop acting just because it might turn out that abuse could occur. But he has focused on only one aspect of the problem, the possibility that things might turn ugly. What he has missed is that the relationship has changed, nearly irrevocably, in a way that is out of Deborah's control.

In some cases of sexual offers, or sexual innuendos, nothing straightforwardly coercive occurs, but there may be reason nonetheless to think that a moral wrong has occurred. The moral wrong concerns the way that a person's options are restricted against that person's will. It is morally wrong not only to make a person's options worse than they were before, but also to limit them undeservedly if this is against the person's will. In this latter case, it is not the worsening of the situation but rather the way that it is undeservedly taken out of the control of the woman which makes it morally suspect. To put the point starkly, sexual harassment normally involves a

restriction of options which also restricts autonomy.[11] In the straightforwardly coercive cases of sexual harassment, autonomy is restricted because
a woman is forced to accede to a man's wishes or risk harm to herself. In
some subtler cases of sexual harassment, autonomy is restricted in that a
change in relationship is effected against the wishes of the woman, possibly
to her detriment. But even if it is not to her detriment, she has been
undeservedly forced into a situation that she has not chosen. In the next
sections I will explore in more detail the moral harms of some of the subtle
cases of sexual harassment.

‖ Hostile Environments

In 1993 the United States Supreme Court gave its clearest support to a
relatively new basis for understanding the harm of sexual harassment which
is closer to the basis I have just suggested than is the intimidation model,
although with several important differences. The Court carefully enunci-
ated a doctrine that held that sexual harassment can be harmful in that it
produces a hostile or abusive work environment for a person because of her
gender.[12] I want to explore various theoretical issues that are implicated in
this new approach to sexual harassment, where the older model of intimidation and blackmail is by and large abandoned. I am especially interested in
how this new model affects our understanding of male behavior in educational and workplace settings.

Here are some of the relevant facts of the case of *Harris v. Forklift
Systems, Inc.*

> Teresa Harris worked as a manager at Forklift Systems, Inc., an equip-
> ment rental company, from April 1985 until 1987. Charles Hardy was
> Forklift's president. The magistrate found that, throughout Harris's time
> at Forklift, Hardy often insulted her because of her gender and often
> made her the target of unwanted sexual innuendos. Hardy told Harris
> on several occasions, in the presence of other employees, "You're a
> woman, what do you know" and "We need a man as the rental manager";
> at least once, he told her she was "a dumb ass woman." Again, in front
> of others, he suggested that the two of them "go to the Holiday Inn to
> negotiate [Harris's] raise." Hardy occasionally asked Harris and other
> female employees to get coins from his front pants pocket. He threw
> objects on the ground in front of Harris and other women, and asked

them to pick them up. He made sexual innuendos about Harris's and other women's clothing.[13]

This pattern of harassment was not aimed at extracting a particular form of behavior, such as a sexual favor. It was not straightforwardly coercive, but nonetheless something seems morally wrong about Hardy's actions.

What Hardy did was to create an environment in which it was very difficult for his female employees to be taken seriously as equals to their male counterparts. Justice Sandra Day O'Connor, delivering the opinion of the court, considered this case an example of a "discriminatorily abusive work environment." This new standard "takes a middle path between making actionable any conduct that is merely offensive, and requiring the conduct to cause a tangible psychological injury." A hostile environment is, according to O'Connor, not something that can be defined with mathematical precision, but it can be determined by "looking at . . . the frequency of the discriminatory conduct; its severity; whether it is physically threatening or humiliating, or a mere offensive utterance; and whether it unreasonably interferes with an employee's work performance."

The harm of a hostile work environment is relatively clear. Again, according to O'Connor, a "discriminatorily abusive work environment, even one that does not seriously affect employees' psychological well-being, can and often will detract from employees' job performance, discourage employees from remaining on the job, or keep them from advancing in their careers." Even without a showing of these specific harms, O'Connor rightly pointed to the denial of "workplace equality" which is broadly guaranteed by Title VII of the Civil Rights Act of 1964.[14] The key here is that this form of behavior treats men differently from women, subjecting only the women to these risks.

The chief harm of sexual harassment is indeed that it discriminates against women by subjecting women to "run a gauntlet of sexual abuse in return for the privilege of being allowed to work and make a living"[15] and thereby demeans them. Sexual harassment, even of the more subtle variety, normally changes the work environment against the wishes of the women. And this creates a difference between male and female employees. Women are forced to be seen as both workers and sexual objects, while men are free either to be seen as only workers or to be seen as workers and sexual objects. The environmental change effected by sexual harassment discriminates against women, generally to their detriment.

What if the changes in the work environment are welcome? What if a particular woman wishes to be able to advance by the use of sexual favors? To go back to Thomas's example, what if Deborah wishes to be able to supplement her income by doing sexual favors, on the side, for her boss? Does it still make sense to say that the environment is discriminatory? I believe the answer to this question is yes. But I'm not so sure that the environment is always hostile or abusive. In order to see this one needs to think about the way that women in the workplace, or in an educational setting, will be affected as a group. The environment is discriminatory because of the way that only women have had their options restricted in respect to the kind of relationships they can have with their male bosses. Normally only women, not men, are the ones whose appearance and sexual characteristics matter and who will be judged according to non-work-related, sexual criteria.

In my view the court has done well to focus on the discriminatory environment, rather than intimidation, created by even subtle examples of sexual harassment. But it has potentially led us astray by calling that environment hostile or abusive. Surely in the most egregious cases, such as that of Charles Hardy and Teresa Harris at Forklift Systems, Inc., the discriminatory work environment does become abusive. But in the more subtle cases, this is not necessarily so, and yet the environment is still discriminatory, and morally suspect for that reason. When more subtle forms of sexual harassment occur, such as when a *Playboy* centerfold is displayed in a common room, women are treated in a way that men are not, and even if some women find this to be welcome it still puts them at a competitive disadvantage in terms of being taken as seriously as their male counterparts with regard to job performance. Their sexuality is considered, illegitimately, to be relevant to job performance, and other, legitimate, bases of job performance are put on the same level as this illegitimate basis, thereby tainting the legitimate bases. This situation has been forced upon them and is, generally speaking, contrary to the autonomy of the women in question.

Sex discrimination can be morally wrong on at least three counts: women are degraded; they are treated unfairly; or they are denied a certain amount of autonomy over their lives. When women seem to welcome differential status in a given context, as in the case of Deborah welcoming the opportunity to make more money by sleeping with her boss, it can appear that women are gaining autonomy rather than losing it. But this is not the case. For what is being lost is the choice of whether to be treated only as a worker and not also as a sex object. In most contexts this loss of control brings more harm to the woman's autonomy than the possible gain from being given more attention or allowed to use one's sexuality to gain certain advantages. What counts as "job related" or "meritorious" has undergone a sometimes subtle shift, to the detriment of women workers.

III Female Exclusion from Full Participation

One of the things often ignored in discussions of sexual harassment is how it promotes male solidarity, especially a solidarity that keeps women in an inferior position and excludes them from full and equal participation in a practice. Think of a very minor form of sexual harassment, at least as compared to that suffered in the *Harris* or *Alexander* cases, namely, a *Playboy* centerfold placed on a locker door in an employee work area. Such an act is not likely to cause serious psychological distress to female employees, and it is not some kind of quid pro quo attempt to extort sexual favors. Nevertheless it resembles these more egregious acts in excluding women from full and equal participation in a work environment with their male colleagues, as we will see.

How is it that even such seemingly innocuous acts as posting the *Playboy* centerfold in a common area can contribute to a form of male bonding and solidarity that is aimed at, or at least has the known effect of, making females feel unwelcome?[16] My analysis is explicitly group oriented. The various forms of sexual harassment share, it seems to me, the effect of creating an environment in which women feel excluded. In this respect sexual harassment is best understood as a harm perpetrated by men against women. To see why this is a group-based problem as well as an interpersonal problem, one needs to recognize that putting the poster on the wall is a signal to any woman who enters the room that women are to be viewed as comparable to the woman in the centerfold picture—to be gawked at, drooled over, and reduced to the measurements of their breasts and buttocks—not welcome here as equals to men.

Even in the most egregious cases, sexual harassment often appears to be merely an interpersonal problem. One party, typically a male, is proposing sex to another party, typically a female, and the female does not welcome such a proposal. But again, one needs to realize that in many of these cases, including *Alexander v. Yale* and *Harris v. Forklift Systems, Inc.*, the woman who sues is normally not the only one being harassed. Other female students or employees often come forward to allege the same behavior toward them by the same male. The multiple victims of sexual harassers make it unlikely that theirs is only an interpersonal problem between an individual male and an individual female.

The type of behavior characteristic of sexual harassment rarely relates to the differences of individual women. The underlying attitudes of the men in question are contempt or at least condescension toward all or most women, not merely toward the one who is currently being harassed. In the next section we will see in more detail how this works when we examine the case of a heterosexual male who harasses a homosexual male. The thing that links the two cases is that exclusion is occurring because a person fails to occupy a certain category, not because of one's unique characteristics. A group-based harm has occurred whenever there is harm directed at a person because of features that that person shares with other members of a group.[17]

Indeed, it is common for sexual harassment to promote male solidarity in educational or employment contexts. Think again of the *Playboy* centerfold displayed in a prominent place in an auto mechanic's work area. If a woman should stray into the work area by mistake or in order to find the mechanic working on her car, she will be alerted right away that this is a male-only domain. Indeed, it may be the practice of the fellow mechanics to touch the breasts of the woman in the picture or to pat her buttocks as they enter or leave the work area, especially when women are present. Here is a good example of how pornographic images can be used to isolate women and separate them from men, but this image also solidifies bonds of men with men. Such a practice is obviously much less morally offensive than actually touching the breasts or patting the buttocks of real women in the workplace. But these practices serve as a reminder that the same thing could happen to women who stumble into the wrong place at the wrong time.

Here is another case.[18] A male graduate student displays a *Playboy* centerfold on a bulletin board in an office that houses half a dozen teaching assistants in philosophy, some of whom are women. The male students gather and comment on the physical dimensions of the centerfold woman's breasts and buttocks, laughing and joking and comparing the dimensions of the centerfold woman to those of their fellow female graduate students. The women find this behavior either annoying or humiliating or both. One woman finds it increasingly difficult to go into the office, knowing that her male colleagues may be discussing the dimensions of her breasts and buttocks. Another woman who complains finds herself the subject of ridicule for her lack of camaraderie.

In both of these cases male bonding and solidarity are furthered by excluding women from full and equal participation. Of course, it is not necessarily the intention of these men or of these practices to exclude women, although this is at least a reasonable thing to expect. The exclusion is by and large the unintended, but foreseen, consequence of the practices that build solidarity. But this is not a necessary result of building male solidarity, as we will see in the final section of this chapter. Indeed, men often find themselves today under siege because their practices of bonding have so publicly excluded women in ways that have deprived women of opportunities to advance, compete, and cooperate in the larger society. Men have been challenged in this domain, both in the courts and in various other public forums. It is not male solidarity that is the culprit, but the forms of harassment that have both supported the bonding between men, and also excluded women from full and equal participation with males.

One may wonder if it is always wrong for one group to adopt practices that have the effect of excluding another group. To answer this question one needs to think seriously about the moral principles that would be implicated in such exclusion. Exclusion is not always morally wrong or even suspect. But when exclusion affects a whole category of people and there is no reasonable basis for it, then it is morally suspect. The principle of moral equality is implicated whenever like cases are not treated alike. Excluding one group of people from a domain without good reason is a paradigmatic example of morally suspicious treatment. While it is obviously quite common for one group of people to exclude another group, moral criticism is appropriate when the exclusion is done for arbitrary reasons, especially if it perpetuates a pattern of exclusion in the larger society.

Is it necessary that there be a past pattern of exclusion for a current particular instance of sexual harassment to constitute group-based harm to women? This is a complex question that cannot be easily answered. Implicated here is the question whether harassment of a man by a female superior would constitute harm to men as a group. In part the answer could be obvious. If the man is sexually harassed merely for being a man, where other men have been similarly treated, then the man is clearly harmed in a discriminatory way and, in some sense, so are men as a group. But without the pattern of adverse treatment it is unclear that men as a group are *significantly* harmed by this seemingly isolated act by a woman. What makes sexual harassment a form of morally harmful sexual discrimination is that it contributes to a particular pattern of subordination.

If we are discussing these issues in a legal context, it is probably a mistake to say that a past pattern of exclusion is necessary for legally actionable harm, because on this construal a judge who does not see the pattern of past behavior will be entitled to disregard any current harm. But in the moral context, where we are not relying on judges who must decide whether to allow a suit to go forward, it is more reasonable to think that patterns of past discrimination are relevant to the assessment of harmfulness of what one man does to a female subordinate. While sexual harassment is often a form of group-based harm, it is not always so, and the harms involved in sexual harassment are not completely captured by focusing on the group. This point will become clearer, I hope, in light of some nonstandard examples of sexual harassment in the next section.

IV Discrimination and Harassment

I wish to investigate two cases of harassment that complicate the preceding analysis because of the sexual orientation of the people involved. I begin with a brief examination of a hypothetical case, then move on to a more developed treatment of an actual case and a variation on that case. The first case involves a bisexual man who harasses both men and women indifferently. The second case is that of a heterosexual man who harasses another man whom he believes to be a homosexual. A consideration of these cases will allow us to achieve a more adequate understanding of the moral harm involved in excluding someone on grounds of sexuality. A variation on the latter case, where the supervisee is actually a homosexual, is especially interesting for even though it does not involve harassment by a man of a woman, it nonetheless involves harassment of one person whose group, homosexual males, is subordinated on grounds of sexuality, by another person whose group, heterosexual males, is dominant. A consideration of this case also relates to the previous section's discussion of how sexual harassment contributes to male solidarity.

In the case of a bisexual man who sexually harasses both men and women indifferently, we can begin to see whether it matters morally that the harassment is based on men's historical dominance of women.[19] This harasser does not treat women differently from men, so there is no disparate treatment of women and therefore it appears that there is no sex discrimination occurring either. This case contrasts with the case of the male boss who simply harasses (in the sense of "gives a hard time to") every one of his employees equally; the harassment itself may be morally problematic, but not because of its connection with sexuality. The male bisexual harasser seemingly harasses men and women indiscriminately, but the harassment is on sexual grounds and takes a sexual form, either making sexual propositions or engaging in sexual jokes and ridicule that change the workplace environment.

It seems fair to say that the male bisexual harasser is engaging in sexual harassment since his behavior places both men and women in uncomfortable, and unwanted, positions, undeservedly restricting their autonomy. His propositions indicate that he views sexual favors as appropriate criteria in judging job performance. Insofar as the employees wish that this were not the case, the work environment has been rendered hostile. But the hostility is muted by the fact that this does not appear to be part of a larger pattern of hostile treatment by bisexuals in the larger society. What makes sexual harassment so problematic morally is that it contributes to a larger social problem, namely, the discriminatory treatment of women by men.

The male bisexual harasser does engage in sexual harassment, which creates a hostile work environment, but he does not engage in sex discrimination. Even though he sexually harasses women in the workplace, creating a hostile work environment for them, even sexually intimidating them in some cases, his behavior does not necessarily contribute to a society-wide pattern of sex discrimination. The main reason for this, of course, is that he does not treat the men in his employ any differently. This is not to deny that the women may respond quite differently from their male colleagues to his propositions, because of differential socialization. And this socialization may make things worse for the women, who find it harder to resist the propositions than the men. But the acts of the bisexual harasser are not themselves instances of sex discrimination and hence do not violate the moral principle of equal treatment and equal respect.[20]

Now consider a case of a heterosexual male who harasses a male supervisee. A recent case arose in Springfield, Illinois.

The suit alleges that the supervisor, John Trees, created "a sexually offensive and hostile work environment" at a Transportation Department facility in Springfield, repeatedly making comments in front of other workers indicating he believed that [Jim] Shermer was a homosexual. . . . Shermer isn't gay, the suit says. He alleges he "suffered emotional distress to his reputation, embarrassment, humiliation and other personal injuries," as a result of Tree's behavior. . . . A federal judge in Springfield dismissed the suit in August [1996], in part because of the state's novel argument: As a man on an all-male work crew, it was intrinsically impossible for Shermer to prove he was the victim of sexual discrimination, a necessary component of sexual harassment.[21]

I am inclined to agree with the judge in this case. There is no sex discrimination here because not all, or any other, men are being treated similarly
by the supervisor, and there is no indication that the supervisee is being
harassed because he is male.

In a variation of the above case, where the heterosexual male supervisor
was harassing a homosexual male, we can begin to see whether it matters
morally that harassment is directed at women for it to be pernicious. Here
the history of the discriminatory treatment of homosexual men by the larger
society makes the act of sexual harassment of a homosexual man more like
the standard cases of men harassing women than like the original case, one
heterosexual male harassing another, or like the hypothetical case of the
male bisexual harasser. But even in this case, sexual harassment is not a form
of sex discrimination, because it is not directed at someone by virtue of
being a member of a certain gender group. As long as heterosexual men
are not subjected to the same mistreatment, then it is not clear that the
mistreatment is based on belonging to a gender group. But it may be
discriminatory nonetheless if it turns out that the harasser only mistreats
homosexual men, and no others, and such mistreatment is arbitrary.

Illegal discrimination occurs whenever one group is arbitrarily and adversely treated differently from another. Harassment of homosexual men
is a clear example of discrimination even though it is not a form of sex
discrimination. Discrimination against homosexuals is still in the stage of
being quite blatant in most of Western society. The acts of gay bashing and
ridicule of gay lifestyles occur largely unabated and unchallenged. In this
sense discrimination against homosexuals is in a different stage, and perhaps
a worse stage, from that of discrimination against women. The main way to
see that it is, is to think about discrimination as a form of exclusion from
full and equal participation in social practices. Discrimination against homosexuals, especially men, is so virulent that it virtually excludes this group
from mainstream society in ways that are not now true for the way discrimination against women works.

Discrimination against women and discrimination against homosexual
men share this much: they are both instances of dominant males excluding
from full and equal participation those who are different from them and
thereby building solidarity within the dominant group. But such solidarity
is morally problematic, especially when it is purchased by virulent antiho-
mosexual behavior and attitudes. When solidarity is purchased by strong
exclusion, two sorts of moral wrong occur. First, of course, there is harm to
the excluded group, and its members. Second, the group that does the

excluding is also morally harmed and, in this sense, harms itself by its irrational aggression and anger, emotional responses that make it much harder for its members to know and do what is right and hence to attain certain moral virtues.

Aggression and anger often block one's ability to perceive a moral situation correctly. Indeed, the kind of exclusion-oriented aggression and anger characteristic of discrimination against homosexual men have made it very difficult for heterosexual men to recognize their behavior as discriminatory and their attitudes as displaying a lack of respect for fellow humans. Exclusion of one group by another is not always, but quite often, associated with characterizing the excluded group as one which is deserving of its exclusion. In the case of discrimination against homosexual men in Western society, and also in many areas of the non-Western world, the exclusion has been joined by strong emotional reactions directed against the "pernicious" lifestyles of gay men. These strong emotional reactions have created moral harms both for those harassed but also, interestingly, for those who do the harassing.

What would it take for a society to restructure itself so that women and homosexuals were not excluded and vilified for failing to conform to heterosexual male standards? It is beyond the scope of my project to attempt to give a full answer to this question. But one thing does seem clear to me. If heterosexual men could find alternative mechanisms for building solidarity which did not rely on exclusion, then a major part of the motivation for discrimination might be eliminated. I next turn my attention to such alternative bases for building solidarity among heterosexual men, some of which seem promising and some of which do not. I will be chiefly interested in examining a group which calls itself the Promise Keepers, and also groups of men which have chosen non-competitive athletic activities.

v Inclusion and Male Solidarity

Can solidarity be built around nonexclusionary practices and ideologies? Is it likely that men will be able to maintain solidarity by stressing inclusiveness rather than exclusiveness? Male athletes and soldiers have often formed strong bonds of inclusion. In some contexts they have managed to do so without also excluding women, but this has not often happened by chance. Instead, it takes planning and imagination for men to find methods of solidarity building that do not also exclude women. In Chapter 7, the next chapter, I discuss several military examples in some detail. After providing some conceptual background considerations, I will here focus on an athletic example and one drawn from a quasi-religious context.

As I have argued elsewhere, solidarity involves the following overlapping components:

conscious group identification,
bonds of sentiment,
interest in the group's well-being,
shared values and beliefs, and
a readiness to show moral support.[22]

The first component, conscious group identification, requires some sense that one's own group is different from other groups, and so there is some conceptual exclusivity built into the notion of solidarity from the start. But the kind of exclusivity here required for solidarity does not entail the kind of exclusivity that is involved in sexual harassment. One can distinguish oneself from others without needing to exclude from full and equal participation those others or needing to demean these others in order to boost oneself.

The second component, bonds of sentiment, and the fourth, shared values and beliefs, certainly put a premium on one's own group and what is shared therein. But this does not begin to rule out also having bonds of sentiment with non-group members or sharing values and beliefs with members of a larger unit, such as a society or nation, or even with other groups of which one is also a member or to which one feels some loose kinship. To feel bonds of sentiment with my family members does not mean that I cannot also feel bonds of sentiment with my neighbors, or with the members of another family half a world away. Bonds of sentiment do not necessarily compete with each other; one bond does not rule out another.

The third component, an interest in the group's well-being, may also be thought to require exclusivity, since having such an interest seems to preclude having an interest in the well-being of others, or at least it cannot countenance the kind of indiscriminate interestedness I have suggested. But this is also mistaken. Well-being is not always, or even often, a zero-sum game. This should be obvious but if it is not consider one's own health. In order to enjoy good health it is important that one eat in moderation and exercise regularly. One can garner these two essential ingredients of good health without denying them to anyone else. In some limited contexts, if food is in very short supply, then my continued good health is in competition with yours, and I suppose the same may be true if there is a limited amount of available space for us to exercise. But given the wide variety of acceptable foodstuffs available in most societies and the wide range of possible exercise regimens, it is not very often that one person's pursuit of his or her good health is at odds with anyone else's. Indeed, my good health requires that others remain relatively healthy as well so that they do not infect me.

The fifth component of solidarity, a readiness to show moral support, is perhaps the most problematic for my analysis, for surely a person's time is limited, so that if one shows moral support for a person in one's group, one will be less likely to have time to show moral support for someone not in one's group. But there is no reason to think that not having time to show moral support for members of another group than one's own means that one needs to show contempt for or to demean these folks. Indeed, showing contempt for someone is itself time-consuming, whereas not doing so is not time-consuming. Those who actively exclude others by deriding, defaming, or harassing them surely take time away from displaying moral support for their own group, unless showing contempt for another group just is showing support for one's own group. But this is simply not true except in limited contexts. Booing another team may be seen as showing support for one's own team. But acting hostiley toward a woman cannot be conceived as showing support for one's maleness without a very special, and extremely odd, set of circumstances, since men and women, as members of their respective gender groups, are generally not engaged in a zero-sum game in the workplace or educational setting.[23]

The movement called the Promise Keepers is an attempt to provide men with a sense of pride in being men and a sense of solidarity that is explicitly aimed at dissuading men from being intimidating, contemptuous, or hostile toward women. The idea behind the "promise" is explicitly that men have made commitments to those women with whom they are in relationships, and their main duty is to keep these commitments. But in addition, the men are looking for a group to join to provide them with support and motivation to help them become "men" in some positive sense of that term, especially good Christian men, men who follow the example of Jesus Christ in their daily lives. It is no accident that this group has held rallies that look like sports events, often actually held in large sports arenas.

The chief positive image of men which the Promise Keepers use to build solidarity is the image of men as providers and protectors of women and children. In this revitalized vision of the traditional male role, men are asked to put wife and children ahead of careers and to become the true spiritual leaders of their families. The men who have taken this route report that they have better relations with their children, that their marriages are revitalized, that they have surrendered themselves to God. Indeed, the whole point of the movement is best expressed as a call for each man to become less of "an independent person."[24] This call is successful evidently because while it criticizes certain aspects of traditional male roles, it also provides a positive model for change which draws on other aspects of traditional male roles.

The image of men as providers and protectors of women will not necessarily diminish the exclusivity of the male domain, especially if men still see themselves as the leaders or heads of the family unit. The Promise Keepers have left themselves open to the criticism that they are reinstilling in men the idea that they are superior to women as leaders, in both spiritual and nonspiritual ways, and this could function to restrict women from full and equal participation in the decision-making domain of family life. It is clear that what many men find attractive here is that they have found a new way that they can assert themselves, and draw on their traditional strengths, and not feel guilty about doing it. Much of this seems right to me. But we must be wary of this new movement merely reinforcing the prevalent cultural view that men should be in charge and women should be excluded from major decision-making roles. This already seems evident in the way the leaders of this group often talk about the role of women, and exclusionary practices are also evident in the sometimes hostile way this group has tried to exclude gay men from its ranks.[25]

To overcome some of these potential problems, I propose that we think about a different movement, perhaps called "Consensus Seekers," which would be more inclusive than the Promise Keepers, and not so closely tied to a particular religious creed. Here the idea would be that men can draw strength from their traditional roles as those who are good at practical tasks such as compromise and consensus building in the political and business arenas. Alongside the tradition of men acting independently and aggressively, there is also a tradition of men being good team players and facilitators. Men could use these consensus-building skills to find solutions to social, familial, and small-group problems, especially concerning mixed-sex situations, which allow both gender groups to feel as if their interests have been well respected. The model for such groups is the sports arena, where men have often excelled at finding a common basis for fellow members to draw strength from the team and to put their best efforts into the common goals of the group.

Men can find strength, support, and solidarity from interacting with other men to create new patterns of socialization for younger men which stress these traditional male virtues but downplay the aggressiveness and combativeness that also often accompany all-male groups in sports and other domains.[26] But unlike the Promise Keepers, the idea is not that men need to do something for women that women cannot do for themselves. Rather, the idea is that men can facilitate the greater participation of both sexes by exercising some traditional male virtues. And it should be apparent that these virtues can be exercised effectively only in a nonexclusionary way that does not express hostility toward any other group, be they women or homosexuals.

In some sports contexts we can find the rudimentary basis for a model of nonaggressive and nonexclusionary masculinity which I wish to defend. Pre-high school, and some informal adult, sports such as soccer, volleyball, and softball are often conducted with mixed teams of men and women. And in some of these cases, the boys or men manage to become true team players, adapting themselves to the variable range of skills of the players, rather than becoming disdainful of the girls or women on the team. Here is an example of the kind of non-zero-sum game I mentioned earlier. Males can feel good about what they accomplish as males in a way that enhances rather than diminishes the status of females. If these same men try to exclude women or demean them, they make it far less likely that they themselves can excel and display virtue, whether on the sports field or as moral agents.

Sexual harassment in employment and educational contexts is similarly situated with rancor or exclusion in the gender-mixed team. The man who expresses rancor toward female teammates lowers team morale and makes it generally less likely that these women will want to cooperate with him down the road. This reaction will adversely affect his own ability to display excellence and virtue, both on and off the field. In a very real sense the sexist diminishes himself. The solidarity built upon sexual harassment will often alienate those who are excluded, even though men may have to depend on the cooperation of those they have just alienated. Sexual harassment is morally suspicious and also practically problematic. Men should come to see sexual harassment as wrong on both of these counts, just as many men currently see rape as wrong.

7

Socialization and Separatism

For an awkward teenager with a serious acne condition, going
to an all boys high school had certain advantages, although I certainly didn't
see them at the time. I gravitated toward other socially outcast kids, and
found areas where I could excel without having to worry about whether I
was attractive to girls or not. The sports ethos pervaded our school, but for
those of us who were "not good at sports," there were many other options,
including public speaking, debate, and model United Nations. Good looking, well-built, popular boys picked on those who were not, but it all seemed
relatively mild compared to what went on at the co-ed high schools some of
my acquaintances attended. It seems in retrospect that boys in this all-male
environment were given a certain amount of space to define themselves
away from the glare of the public spotlight where appearance seemed to
matter so much.

When the Citadel and the Virginia Military Institute came under fire for accepting public funds while excluding women, the leaders of these colleges argued that it was important for men to have an environment in which traditional male values could be instilled without criticism or pressure from the larger society, especially from women. The arguments advanced by the leaders of these colleges were strikingly similar to those offered by women defending all-female schools and women's collectives.[1] The similarity derives from the common support for the value of separatism, that is, for providing an exclusive space for a group to occupy that would help sustain the group in its uniqueness and diversity from the larger community. But something different was at stake here too, in that a well-established pillar of male culture was claiming that it could sustain itself only when hidden from the scrutiny of women.

In this chapter, I argue that there are indeed good reasons to support male separatism, but not those reasons advanced by the Citadel and VMI. These military academies seek to perpetuate a form of masculinity that does not need special protection and nurturance. That form of masculinity is already supported by all-male sports settings, all-male clubs, and other social contexts that perpetuate the model of patriarchal man. What is needed instead is a realm where alternative models of masculinity can be allowed to flourish unhampered by the normalizing devices of the wider community. One commentator has suggested that the Citadel does offer some men such an alternative lifestyle different from the dominant one in our culture.[2] If this were true, which I doubt, then a case could be made for allowing it to remain sex segregated. But this would not resolve rather complex questions about public funding for such a school.

▎ Adversative Socialization

Military boot camps, fraternity initiations, football drills, and tribal puberty rituals all have in common the creation of an artificially stressful environment in which a boy is placed in order for him to become, or prove that he is becoming a man. That there are few if any parallel forms of socialization for girls indicates just how strongly gender-linked is this form of socialization.[3] Indeed, these forms of socialization are often claimed to be impossible to maintain unless females are excluded (even from view). The presence of females in these environments is not merely said to be a distraction to the boys/men.[4] Also, as was argued in both the Citadel and VMI cases, it is claimed that the presence of females will completely disrupt these forms of socialization. The stressful environment created by these forms of socialization will be dissipated when boys and men are forced to interact with girls and women, at least when they are forced to interact as equals.[5]

Why does the mere presence of women have such a disruptive effect on what is often called "adversative socialization"?[6] To answer this question, let us first look at some of what is typically involved in adversative socialization. Here are a few brief quotations from the Findings of Fact in the first VMI case to be decided by an appellate court, "The VMI method conforms generally to an adversative . . . model of education. Physical rigor, mental stress, absolute equality of treatment, absence of privacy, minute regulation of behavior, and indoctrination in desirable values are the salient attributes of the VMI educational experience."[7] Moreover, "the barracks are stark and unattractive. The windows and doors ensure that the cadets are never free from scrutiny. There is constant intermingling of cadets as a result of the close and intimate quarters and the number of cadets assigned to a room. Ventilation is poor. Furniture is unappealing. A principal object of these conditions is to induce stress."[8] In addition, upperclassmen are required to enforce the minute regulation of underclass behavior, administering frequent punishments and even beatings to these underclassmen.

The adversative socialization at VMI or the Citadel is meant to break down certain ego characteristics and values and to rebuild the cadets in the image of a "citizen soldier." The hardship of the first year in what is called "the rat line" is "sufficiently rigorous and stressful that those who complete it feel both a sense of accomplishment and a bonding to their fellow sufferers and former tormentors."[9] Such training instills a certain form of self-discipline and esprit de corps that is thought to be essential in developing leadership skills and character. The goal is to transform these boys into men who take their duties of service to community and nation to be of paramount importance. Many of these citizen soldiers go on to distinguished careers in the military,[10] politics, and business.

The attorneys for the Citadel and VMI argued that the presence of women in the adversative environment would create discomfort for the boys/men involved, and it would also destroy the artificially created stress. At least in part this is because the presence of women would introduce a normalizing element into an otherwise abnormal situation. Indeed, the presence of women would destroy a situation which is completely dependent on an abnormal scrutiny to create the desired effects. "The introduction of privacy required by admission of women to VMI would contradict the principle that everyone is constantly subjected to scrutiny by everyone else. The honor code would cease to be the absolute boundary between VMI and the outside world because it would become possible for cadets to take action at VMI without being observed."[11] Because of these effects, the mere presence of women was seen as disruptive of the adversative socialization coveted by the military-style academies at VMI and the Citadel.

Adversative socialization is deeply inculcated in modern Western, as well as many non-Western and premodern, conceptions of masculinity. In Greek mythology, various tales relate the trials young men undergo to prove their manhood. Ancient Sparta was known for its harsh conditioning of adolescent boys. David Gilmore has documented many Western and non-Western societies that have initiation rites for boys passing into manhood. Many of these rituals involve extremely risky undertakings or violence.[12] All the rituals are meant to create an environment very different from the actual one these males will encounter in their normal lives. And many of these rituals, especially the puberty rituals, are male-only affairs.

The adversative socialization employed at VMI and the Citadel is aimed at instilling certain masculine ideals into the consciousnesses of the boys/men they train so as to socialize within them leadership and strong character. The army, air force, and naval military academies at West Point, Colorado Springs, and Annapolis ceased to employ adversative socialization when women were admitted into these academies more than a decade ago. Since the service academies have continued to turn out military leaders with strong characters, both men and women, VMI and the Citadel could not argue that retention of adversative socialization was necessary to accomplish those goals. Instead, VMI and the Citadel chose to argue that they should retain their distinctive educational environments because they sustain diversity by providing an environment that fosters a certain kind of male socialization not found elsewhere.

▋▋ Separatism and Diversity

For a number of years, many French Canadians have been demanding their own state in order to maintain their distinctive culture against the onslaughts of the dominant English-speaking community. American Indian tribal councils and the Association of Black Social Workers have argued that only members of their respective groups should be allowed to adopt babies from their communities lest the children and the community lose their distinctive cultural identity. When these minority groups request different treatment or separate space from the majority, they often support their requests with arguments based on the value of diversity. If the society at large becomes homogeneous, something important is lost. The range of options and sources of traditional wisdom are diminished when a minority group is stifled or assimilated.[13]

Separatism comes in various degrees, but at the extreme end of the spectrum it involves a way of thinking that places ultimate value in an exclusive social order, a space in which people who do not have certain characteristics are not permitted to enter. Lesbian separatists, for instance, sometimes form their own communes in the wilderness so that outside contact with non-lesbians is cut off completely; or they sometimes remain within a larger society but choose to associate only with other lesbians, unless contact with nonlesbians is absolutely necessary.[14] The value of diversity is more easily recognized in the second of these two examples, since the larger community can gain by the contributions of this group to the larger society. But even in the lesbian separatist example, diversity may be advanced in that a range of options are afforded to homosexual women that would not normally be available if the separatist collectives did not exist.

Perhaps the classic examples of separatism are the cloistered convent and monastery. In the Middle Ages the walls of the monasteries and convents were quite literally meant to keep out the infidels, those whose very beliefs and way of life would pollute the nuns and monks if they came into contact with them. The very presence of others from the larger society was thought to jeopardize these fragile communities. Their coherence could not be sustained in the presence of those who did not share their beliefs and behaviors. In the Dark Ages, especially the tenth and eleventh centuries, these communities were so divergent from, and even antithetical to, the dominant society in which they resided that their coherence could not be guaranteed without complete separation. The justification of the separateness of these monastic communities turned on the value of the truths upheld within these communities, truths which were under attack by the so-called infidels.[15]

The defenders of male separatism at the Citadel argued that their institutions are the last vestiges of "traditional male values" which are constantly under assault especially from women and feminists within the larger society. Rather than defending traditional male values as expressing certain truths worth preserving, the defenders of the Citadel chose a more modern defense, namely, that the maintenance of these values is important for the goal of diversity within a pluralistic society. But as the appellate courts have noted, this defense is difficult to sustain, since the larger society continues to offer many venues where traditional male values are preserved. Indeed, while it is true that there is a lively debate about the worth of traditional male values, these values are still dominant in most of American society, as I will argue later.

In the past, arguments for exclusive communities have been put forth in support of groups that are fragile minorities within the larger society. What is odd about the Citadel and VMI defenses is that they are based on providing protection for a group which seems not at all to be a fragile minority. The defenders of the Citadel and VMI could counter that it is not males generally that they are trying to protect but a vulnerable minority who try to lead their lives according to "traditional male values." It is widely reported that white middle-class men are angry and at sea because they do not know how the larger society expects them to act, given that they are ashamed to be traditional men and given that they are not members of currently "privileged" minorities.

It is fair to say that many men today do not know what is expected of them and yearn for the return of an old order in which men were simply "men." One bumper sticker announces, "Real men are back." And one movement called the Promise Keepers, as we saw in the previous chapter, has as its main goal to give men a sense that they are in charge again, that a man is "the spiritual leader of his household." [16] A book by the humorist Dave Barry was advertised with posters proclaiming "Guy Pride." All of this is aimed at providing some kind of mooring for men who seem to be drifting. The Citadel and VMI are attempting to situate themselves in the midst of this masculine aporia. But the case they make is for a set of male values that have historically produced hatred and abuse toward women, and in any event these values have not proven to be fragile.

Diversity is not valuable in and of itself. What is valuable is to have a diverse collection of worthy sets of values and behaviors. Diversity derives its value from what already has value or worth. If a person obtained a greater diversity of disvalued things than before, the set of new, more diverse disvalued things would not be more valuable than the set of old, less diverse things. Similarly, having more rather than fewer options for men is not itself valuable; it is only so if the options themselves are worthy of pursuit. It is no advantage to have a society with active neo-Nazi or Ku Klux Klan organizations given that these groups are so self-confessedly racist and are engaged in violent intimidation of those who disagree with them. Diversity as a value is limited in that it posits that "the more options *worthy* of pursuit, the better," rather than "the more the merrier."

Greater diversity is valuable, especially in an already pluralistic setting, for two main reasons:

(a) greater diversity provides an increased pool of knowledge, especially practical knowledge, for a society to draw upon; and
(b) greater diversity provides an increased pool of behavioral and value options for individuals.

In each case, the sheer increase may have some minimal value, but the main value is had when each new instance of diverse behavior and values is itself worthy of pursuit. Some have argued that, given a free marketplace of ideas, sheer diversity has greater value than I have indicated.[17] But regardless of one's stance in this debate, weighty arguments would have to be marshaled to support protecting a set of behaviors and values that are not in short supply but are widespread today.

The value of diversity may be defended on the following grounds. It could be said that diversity of cultural forms, like diversity in the gene pool, is a good because it provides us with resources to meet whatever unforeseen situations could arise in the future. Indeed, in the case I am considering, it could be argued that traditional male values are in need of protection from extinction in case we return to a time when war is more common and defense of nation, city, and family is given high priority again. If there are not men who are still tough enough to do battle for just causes, dire consequences could result. Such an argument is not without merit, but as we will see, it fails to establish sufficiently weighty considerations to outweigh the harms that occur, especially to women, by the public support of traditional male values.

III Protecting Patriarchy

On Wednesday, June 26, 1996, the United States Supreme Court ruled against the male-only policy at Virginia Military Institute and the Citadel. In the case of *United States v. Virginia*, the court voted seven to one that the state of Virginia could not justify keeping women out of its state-supported military college. Justice Ruth Bader Ginsburg wrote the majority opinion, contending that "the constitution's equal protection guarantee precludes Virginia from reserving exclusively to men the unique educational opportunities V.M.I. affords." She argued that

neither the goal of producing citizen soldiers nor V.M.I.'s implementing methodology is inherently unsuitable to women. And the school's impressive record in producing leaders has made admission desirable to some women. Nevertheless, Virginia has elected to preserve exclusively for men the advantages and opportunities a V.M.I. education affords. . . . The burden of justification is demanding and rests entirely with the state. The state must show "at least that the (challenged) classification serves 'important governmental objectives and that the discriminatory means employed' are 'substantially related to the acheivements of those objectives.' " Such classifications cannot be used, as they once were, to create or perpetuate the legal, social and economic inferiority of women. Measuring the record in this case against the review standard just described, we conclude that Virginia has shown no "exceedingly persuasive justification" for excluding all women from the citizen soldier training program afforded by V.M.I.[18]

Legally, VMI and the Citadel failed to establish that allowing women to enter their programs would destroy the form of education, adversative socialization, they had championed.

In what follows I will provide a somewhat different set of arguments from those employed by the United States Supreme Court against public funding of the Citadel and VMI. I will argue that the stated mission of protecting traditional male values does not justify allowing these schools to remain all male and this goal is not worthy of public support. First, I will say quite a bit more about the nature of these traditional male roles, arguing that they contribute to the oppression of women, and thus that they (perhaps unwittingly) protect patriarchy. Second, I will challenge the idea that adversative training programs should be restricted to men only. And finally, I will argue that the main argument in favor of public support for such programs, the market-based argument that many men want such an educational option, is not morally significant enough to outweigh the harms caused by such programs.

From a moral perspective, the defenders of the Citadel and VMI needed to demonstrate two things: that they are pursuing morally permissible purposes and that male-only education is necessary to achieve these moral purposes. In this context these defenders need to confront the strong misogyny which is reported to exist at these schools. To cite just two examples, in the trial briefs it was contended (and not challenged) that the worst thing a cadet could call another was "woman" or "girl" and that there was a worrisome amount of violence toward women by the cadets.[19] It is of course also true that these schools have produced strong military, political, and civic leaders over the years. But they needed to establish that the adversative socialization they provide bears some relation to the leadership roles its cadets come to assume in the society at large.[20]

To make the moral case against protecting patriarchal values by public funding of the Citadel and VMI, I need to say more about the nature of patriarchy and its presence in society today. Patriarchy is a system of oppressive practices by men against women, which is coordinated by the common interests of men but which is not necessarily intentional.[21] Since it is not necessarily the intention of any man to oppress women, patriarchy can flourish at a prereflective or unconscious psychological level. It is for this reason that many men now, as well as in earlier eras, are not aware of having attitudes, beliefs, and dispositions that contribute to the oppression of women. And it is for this reason that many men may feel that their attitudes and behaviors are not oppressive when in fact they are.

Patriarchal behaviors and values are well entrenched in contemporary American society, although they are perhaps not as blatantly displayed as they once were. Many men claim to be committed to egalitarian marriages. Yet, most men do not do anything like their fair share of housework or child care.[22] Indeed, it is common to hear men talk about "helping out" with the dishes or with the children. The terminology is telling. If they regarded housework and child care as a significant responsibility, they would not say that they were "helping out" but rather that they were "doing some work around the house." By being reluctant to take responsibility for housework or child care, men are not necessarily intentionally oppressing women, but men's behaviors are nonetheless patriarchal in this respect, and there is no sign that they are changing.

Another domain, in addition to marital relationships, of traditional male values and behaviors concerns strenuous physical activity in work, sports, and military life. It is now rare to have women excluded from these domains, but it is not rare for men to belittle the attempt by women to compete in these domains. The possibility of women in combat or women in professional baseball, basketball, hockey, or football elicits contempt from many men. Indeed, schools are still discouraging girls from competing in the most physically strenuous sports, which are often those given very high prestige as well.[23] At present there are still no women in any of the highest levels of the four most prestigious professional sports (basketball, baseball, football, and hockey) in the United States.[24]

The restriction that keeps women out of combat positions could be defended on the grounds, advanced earlier, that the protection of nation, city, and family is of paramount importance. Assuming it is true that women will never be able to be trained to be, on average, as strong as men, doesn't it make sense to train men for combat and restrict women to noncombat roles in the military? Similar kinds of arguments could be advanced for keeping women out of strongly combative professional sports and for restricting attendance to men only in sports camps and military academies. These practices could be justified, at least potentially, by reference to the need to keep males strong enough to protect the society, should such protection be needed in the near future.

But is it true that women could not be as successful as men in defending nation, city, and family from aggression? When wars are fought, hand-to-hand combat is no longer the dominant mode of battle. Instead, wars are increasingly high-tech affairs, and there is no evidence to suggest that women cannot be trained to push buttons and steer aircraft or ships as well as men. Perhaps there is still the old argument that women are more vulnerable because they can be raped if they are captured by the enemy, whereas men can only be tortured. Such an argument, if it makes any sense at all in modern warfare, needs to be made against a backdrop of women who have entered a wide range of previously all-male domains, where their gender has not been a hindrance. Women police officers were once also thought not to be capable of defending the city streets because of the potential that they could be raped. But this myth has been exploded by the contrary evidence of large numbers of successful women police officers.

Even if it were true that there was a positive value to protecting these particular traditional male values within the society at large, the defenders of the Citadel and VMI would still not be out of the woods. For in addition they would have to show that this value was great enough to be considered a value deserving of receiving public funding. It is ironic that the Citadel and VMI used market arguments to justify the absence of a parallel publicly supported military academy for women in their states. But market arguments can be like two-edged swords. The question that needs to be asked is why the Citadel and VMI could not support themselves without public funds. If the market for education in traditional male values is not strong enough to support private military academies, why should the state consider the need important enough to warrant spending tax dollars on it.

At least one possible answer to this objection is that the Citadel and VMI need to offer such a valuably diverse training because there is so little demand for it. The low demand indicates that traditional male values are about to become extinct. As with other groups faced with extinction, the spotted owls for example, perhaps traditional males should be considered an endangered species in need of special protection. Low demand should not be seen as an indicator that the values are unworthy of state support. Indeed, low demand seems to indicate that the values are even more in need of public support than if they were rampant in the population. Even if such an argument is succesful, it has the unfortunate side effect of undercutting the claim that women should not have access to these military academies because of lack of demand, an argument made in both the Citadel and VMI cases.

With affirmative action programs under attack and a generally smaller role sought for government, it was curious to hear the Citadel and VMI argue in favor of large-scale governmental funding of their institutions in order to secure diversity. Nonetheless, these same arguments could be used to preserve the Citadel and VMI as fully private institutions as well. I have sought to show what is wrong with their arguments, regardless of the issue of public funding. But in the end the practical side of this dispute will surely make it harder and harder to keep publicly supported all-male military academies from budget axes, especially given that the federally funded academies at West Point, Annapolis, and Colorado Springs have opened their doors to women.

What is in need of protection from change? Perhaps it is the actual traditional values and behaviors of men that need protection. Yet, such values are not significantly less traditional now than they were in previous generations. Perhaps it is the exclusivity of the aggressive military sphere which needs to be protected. But that battle is effectively over since the major military academies, which began accepting women cadets over a decade ago, have found that these women respond surprisingly well to dangerous and aggressive situations. Perhaps it is the corresponding loss of confidence that men now feel needs to be corrected. The previous pervasiveness of patriarchy has been somewhat lessened in recent years, and with this has come a lessening of the celebration of the inferiority of women. With these changes has come a period of uncertainty for men, for the overt justification of male privilege is indeed taboo, and this has made some men uncertain about which roles they should pursue. Perhaps some would argue that this is why a publicly funded Citadel or VMI is needed: to give men a positive sense of roles that are deserving of celebration. As I will argue in the next sections of this chapter, such a goal can be achieved with far fewer disadvantages in other ways than those practiced at these military academies.

IV "Conversative" Socialization

My contention is not that all forms of male separatism are pernicious. Rather, I agree with the claims of the defenders of the Citadel and VMI that there is a need in our society for a place where men can withdraw from the demands of the larger society and come to terms with what it means to be a man. Traditionally, colleges and universities have provided the best environments for the kind of reflective disengagement with the world which the project of understanding and perhaps reshaping masculinity would require. In this section I discuss the kind of male separatist society that in my view would be worthy of public support.

Many men are indeed at sea today about the roles they should be pursuing, roles deserving of celebration by the society at large. One of the lawyers who defended both the Citadel and VMI has said: "VMI studied what the effects of co-education had been. It observed that the extreme adversative methodology did not survive co-education. VMI asked itself whether there is value in that system, and the conclusion was that there is, especially for late adolescent males trying to work out inherent senses of aggression. For these young men it is important to have the opportunity to experience the discipline of the VMI system."[25] These boys are looking for roles that will allow them to channel their teenage aggressiveness into socially acceptable behavior. Any alternative proposal about male separatist education would have to respond to the felt need of many boys to express themselves aggressively.

What is worrisome about the Citadel and VMI is that they have disciplined male teenage aggressiveness in a way that is not opposed to its display in the form of violence against women (and other men). Indeed, the extreme reactions against Shannon Faulkner, the first woman to enroll at the Citadel, points to serious problems in the way the adversative method channels aggressiveness.[26] My proposal is that we need an alternative that does not have this unacceptable result. Specifically we need an alternative form of socialization to "adversative" socialization that will channel aggressiveness into less hostile and more cooperative avenues. I propose to call this form of socialization "conversative." Rather than stressing the confrontation and opposition characteristic of adversative socialization, conversative socialization will stress communication, cooperation, and role reversal.

The term "conversative" is not now in common usage. As I use the term it has roots in both "conversation," the kind of communication with which men have traditionally had trouble in personal relationships, and "converse," a reversal of something which is not necessarily truth preserving, perhaps the kind of role reversal that men have also traditionally had trouble with.[27] Just as debate is different from combat, so conversative socialization will be different from adversative socialization. And just as the goals of role reversal are different from the goals of some traditional male roles, so the goals of conversative socialization will be different from those of adversative socialization. But there are nonetheless good reasons for conversative socialization to be done in male-only settings, just as was said to be true of adversative socialization.

The main reason for urging that conversative socialization occur in male-only settings is that if men are going to find alternatives to traditional patriarchal roles, they need the space to do it where they will be shielded from possible embarrassment or ridicule. The best way to allow male teenagers to open up to possibilities that they have previously not seen as viable options is to provide room to experiment with shedding the role trappings that they believe the rest of society expects of them. As in the case of role-reversal games such as charades, males often feel embarrassed when they try out new modes of behavior. If they have a supportive environment, boys/men will be more likely to discover options beyond the traditional roles that the society at large still foists upon them. Such an environment is indeed likely to be all-male.

In a "conversative" environment there will have to be outlets for teenage male aggressiveness. In this respect sports should continue to play a prominent role in teaching boys how to become "new men." But unlike sports at the Citadel and VMI, noncompetitive sports should be stressed for conversative socialization. Teamwork should be more important than individual achievement, and even in individualized sports, such as squash, handball, and racketball, the emphasis should be on providing your partner with the best workout possible, rather than beating the opponent into the ground.[28] And the best way to achieve this result is to see yourself as competing against yourself rather than against your partner.[29]

The stress on sports in conversative socialization is important for channeling teenage male aggressiveness into socially productive avenues. In non-competitive sports contexts, there can still be hard physical exertion, as well as aggressive play, but the aggression is not directed at one's partner or fellow players. When one does not see one's fellow player as an opponent, then the aggressive play one displays will not lead to an attitude of me or my team against the other player or team. And the lack of oppositional thinking will open the door for a form of aggressiveness that is compatible with attitudes of cooperation.

Another important dimension of conversative socialization (which clearly separates it from adversative socialization) is the idea that each person is deserving of respect and each person's beliefs and feelings need to be taken seriously. Just as adversative socialization seeks to promote ego development through a complete denial of the uniqueness of each person, so conversative socialization seeks to promote ego development through support for each person as a unique fellow member of one's community. And here we can see how conversative socialization is not as likely to risk the negative consequences for women which have haunted adversative socialization. For it is only a slight step from thinking that you are "a rat" to thinking that women, generally portrayed as even less deserving than you, are less than a rat and beneath contempt.[30]

As the name of the model indicates, conversative socialization will also stress dispute resolution through dialogue rather than through physical intimidation, or through verbally adversarial methods. Men have not been traditionally good at dialogue and this has contributed to their difficulties in finding roles worthy of celebration today. For pluralistic, multicultural societies are increasingly moving toward dialogic models of dispute resolution, rather than adversarial ones, and many men have found themselves badly served by their socialization for such a change. For example, lawyers now spend much more time in plea bargaining and alternative forms of dispute resolution than in the adversarial courtroom, and yet male lawyers are often not well suited to this change in a lawyer's role.[31] And today's American army officers are increasingly likely to find themselves negotiating a peaceful settlement of a border controversy or brush-fire war and less likely to be leading troops in violent clashes with "the enemy."

A further dimension of "conversative socialization" involves training in role reversal, acting out what it would be like to be another person. A key component in combating prejudice is to get the various parties to come to an understanding of what it is like to be the other.[32] Sensitivity training sessions have long employed the method of role reversal to offset the prejudices that have fueled racial violence or sexual harassment. But adolescent boys, in my experience, are reluctant even to play charades in mixed audiences. I propose that these same adolescents will find it easier to enage in dramatic productions or sensitivity-training sessions that employ role reversal if they are conducted in the presence of all-male audiences.

Role reversal and training in conversation skills will make it possible for males to become more sensitive and empathetic in their dealings with others. I talk in the final chapter about the importance of developing empathy with women. Here I wish to discuss briefly the importance of increasing sensitivity and empathy with regard to other males. Elsewhere Robert Strikwerda and I argue that men have a very difficult time relating to other men and forming male friendships because they lack skills and abilities for listening and talking to other men about what is important in their lives.[33] Male friendships with other men, at least in Western societies, tend to be based on shared activities, such as sports events, rather than shared stories of life experiences. As a result, it is quite common for men to say that they really don't know the other men in their lives, even their best friends. Role reversal will enable men to become more intimate with each other and hence will strengthen male solidarity, but it will do so without a corresponding exclusion of women.

An opponent of my proposal could claim that conversative socialization will not provide a basis for men to feel good about themselves *as men*, since women can be just as good, if not better, at the skills stressed in this form of socialization. But, as I argued in the previous chapter, there is a difference between the roles of men and women here.[34] Men have traditionally been very good at forging cooperative settlements of disputes in such areas as business and law, for instance; there is an opportunity with conversative socialization to extend this skill to personal relationships that will build solidarity between men and other men, and between men and women. Such a traditionally male skill would be of crucial importance in conversative socialization; indeed, it is this traditional skill which is most to be protected in this form of socialization. Men will gain a renewed sense of their self worth that is truly worthy of such sentiments.

Conversative socialization is better suited to training young men for careers in civic and professional life than is adversative socialization, given the changes occuring in the military and other professional contexts such as law. And conversative socialization is far less likely to have the detrimental side effects found in adversative socialization. If I am right to think that teenage male aggressiveness can be channeled at least as effectively through conversative as through adversative socialization, then there is little argument remaining in favor of special consideration for the types of male socialization that occurred at the Citadel and VMI. I next turn to this issue of channeling aggressiveness in teenage males.

∨ Young Male Aggression and Socialization

Young males, especially teenagers, display a disproportionate amount of aggression as compared to women at all ages and men of younger and older age groups. The popular conception of this pheonomenon, that teenage boys have runaway hormones, is not far from the truth, although, as I have discussed in Chapter 1, sexual aggressiveness is not truly out of control.[35] There are of course two ways for humans to bring a strong impulse under control: through the will and through various forms of socialization. Many boys and men are able to control their aggressiveness by will, but many find it extremely difficult. It is for this reason that socialization of male aggressiveness into acceptable pathways is so important for the maintenance of a nonabusive community.

Socialization is part of a whole panoply of influences that provide the environmental side of a human's character formation. Because of its grand scale, it is often hard to predict what changes in individual upbringing will produce what character changes.[36] Socialization is a form of learning which affects the development of attitudes, beliefs, habits, and behavior. Socialization is merely one form of learning among many others, where the learning is facilitated through various social institutions, primarily family and school. This connection with social institutions is what marks socialization off as different from many other forms of learning. As we saw in the discussion of sexuality,[37] the way that socialization occurs can sometimes be at odds with the publicly perceived messages of various institutions.

One of the most important ways that socialization occurs is through channeling existing capacities and tendencies in new directions, often by restricting the acceptable display of an emotion or behavior to a certain realm or by creating alternative ways of exercising this tendency. It is in this way that tendencies and capacities that are hardwired, that is, not a product of environmental influences, may be nonetheless contained by environmental factors. This is possible because while certain behavioral or attitudinal features may be hardwired in the sense that they will manifest themselves, the way that they manifest themselves is not pre-set. While all people have natural desires for food and sex, there is no pre-set time or place for satisfying those desires. Social institutions and customs can influence when and where these desires can be expressed in behavior and, to a certain extent, where they can not.

Young male aggressiveness may be hardwired in the sense that it is a function of hormones which create certain character traits and tendencies. The socialization process that many males experience partially channels this aggressiveness by restricting its expression to the organized violence of football scrimmages and soccer games. What many of us have come to realize though is that there are spillover effects — socialization cannot completely restrict the behavioral and attitudinal expression of deep-seated tendencies and capacities. As I have noted, sports figures find the controlled aggressive settings sometimes not sufficient for the expression of their aggressive tendencies.[38]

The Citadel and VMI have tried to channel young male aggressiveness into socially acceptable avenues to create citizen soldiers. Adversative socialization is designed to give maximum expression to young male aggressiveness while still steering it into acceptable domains of behavior, such as military life and business leadership roles. But as we have seen, this type of socialization can also result in a learned hatred and contempt for women. And while adversative socialization may not have this result, this correlation is a significant drawback to its continued use in our society. Just as athletes have trouble containing their aggressiveness on the playing fields, so the citizen soldiers have trouble containing their aggressiveness in simulated combat situations. At least in part this is because when aggression is rendered acceptable, this sometimes makes it more likely that a man will display more and stronger aggressiveness than would otherwise be true.

Adversative socialization creates even more stress than the typical teenage boy would be exposed to, as for instance when upperclassmen stand in front of the "rats" and scream into their faces or smack them in the face for no apparent reason. These boys are forbidden to show any aggressiveness toward those who have verbally or physically assaulted them. But sometimes the strategy of training boys to restrain their normal aggressive impulses backfires, and the boys only temporarily restrain themselves, later displaying their heightened aggressiveness to other rats or to women they encounter outside the confines of the academy.[39] Creating greater stress for normally aggressive boys can create a situation where even more aggression needs to be expressed than would have been otherwise true.

My proposed "conversative" socialization will also have to have a way of channeling young male aggressiveness if it is going to be effective in socializing boys into acceptable attitudes and behavior. One way this might be accomplished, as I suggested, is in cooperative rather than competitive sports events. Another way might involve intense dialogic practices such as are found in various debating contexts. Negotiators, facilitators, mediators, and advocates of various sorts all use a heightened form of intense energy to keep themselves focused on achieving compromise or consensus with a group of individuals whose interests otherwise conflict. The intense exertion of energy necessary for success in these projects will require men to channel their aggressions into socially acceptable avenues. But the intensity here is not of the same sort as that in adversative socialization; indeed, it is not adversative.

Aggression can be channeled in many ways which lead to socially useful results. On a traditional model of masculinity, male aggression is channeled into such practices as the intense pursuit of protection and support for family.[40] The "breadwinner" role for men in families can be seen as a way to channel male aggression in a socially productive direction. Unlike adversative socialization, such channeling also dissipates the aggression rather than intensifying it. But the "breadwinner" role is not without its problems, since it is often linked with a view of men as dominant over women in family life. In this respect, the channeling of male aggression here through this form of nonadversative socialization is not necessarily supportive of respect for women.

If the "breadwinner" role is not linked to male domination and female subordination, then there are fewer problems, but one may still wonder what it is about being a man that makes one so much better suited to be "the breadwinner" than a woman. Blankenhorn claims that it is the differential socialization that makes men better suited here. While I will later somewhat embrace this type of argument, at the end of the next chapter when I argue against androgynous gender roles, I am troubled by this particular version of the differential socialization argument. When the "breadwinning" role is linked to being a man, it will almost always lead to wide inequalities of income between men and women in the larger society, even if it does not lead to this result in a particular relationship. In my experience, when men are seen as the "breadwinners," women will be less likely than men to push for raises or to promote their own careers. Consider the case in which both male and female partners have advanced college degrees. When someone in the relationship needs to sacrifice for the larger family unit, it will more likely be the woman in those relationships who sacrifices when the man is thought of as the "breadwinner."

Will "conversative" socialization be better than "adversative" socialization at minimizing the harmful, exclusionary residues of contained aggression? One reason to have hope here is that "conversative" socialization does not proceed by creating more stress than these young men would already feel. What "conversative" socialization does, that "adversative" socialization does not, is to create a sense of one's ability to interact with others, and to make a difference in the lives of these others, by treating one another as deserving of respect and dignity. One of the scarier sides of adversative socialization is that, at least in the short run, it promotes the view that some people, including oneself, are not deserving of respect.

If there is a future for all-male educational environments, it will be to provide males with a safe haven where they can try out various alternative forms of masculinity. In this respect the defenders of the Citadel and VMI are correct; the harsh light of the public forum does make it harder, especially for teenage males, to push aside the world of expectations created by others. My own experiences in an all-male high school bear out this observation. But as in any, even temporarily, exclusionary environment, there are many subsidiary difficulties to be overcome or minimized. In my high school, some boys became contemptuous of all of those, especially girls, who were not members of our community. Such reactions are likely in any all-male setting. In some cases, perhaps the risks are worth it. Male separatism can be defended, but not on the grounds advanced by the defenders of the Citadel and VMI. If there is a future for all-male colleges or universities, I believe that it is better to look to the model of conversative rather than adversative socialization, better for the future prospects of the schools and better for the futures of boys and men in contemporary Western culture.

8

A Progressive Male Standpoint

Throughout this book I have adopted a progressive male standpoint, that is, an egalitarian and practical position from which men can critically assess male experience and traditional male roles.[1] This standpoint is similar to feminist standpoint epistemologies which have been developed in the last decade.[2] As I use the term, "progressive standpoints" are perspectives that intermix considerations of knowledge and politics in such a way that practical knowledge (or praxis) is created.[3] People who attain a progressive standpoint come to understand how their participation in certain social arrangements may contribute to inequality and oppression. In the context of gender, progressive standpoints allow men and women to understand their roles in gender inequality. While progressive female standpoints on gender have proliferated, progressive male standpoints have not. The chief question asked is this: Can men get enough distance on their privileged position in society to assess it critically and attempt to create an egalitarian model of masculinity?

In this chapter I describe a progressive male standpoint that was implicit in the previous chapters. This model has four dimensions which overlap and collectively provide sufficient conditions for a progressive male standpoint. First, there is a striving for knowledge or understanding based on experience, especially personal experience of traditional male roles and activities. Second, there is critical reflection on that experience in light of the possible harms to women, as well as men, of assuming traditional male roles and engaging in traditional male activities. Third, there is moral motivation to change at least some aspects of traditional male roles and activities. And finally, there are practical proposals for changes in traditional male roles that are regarded as believable by other men. In what follows I devote a section to each of these four aspects (personal experience, critique, moral motivation to change, and believable practical proposals) of one version of a progressive male standpoint.

▌ Personal Experience

For most of recorded history, the voice of knowledge has been a male voice. When women theorists began to challenge that voice they seized upon the idea that there were certain subjects, such as pregnancy and childbearing, that men could not understand as well as women could.[4] If experience is intimately connected to understanding, then those who have not had a relevant experience will have to work harder to attain the understanding, in most cases, than those who have had the relevant experience. Any person should be able to gain understanding as long as he or she can at least imagine experiencing the relevant phenomena. But in most cases, the task of imagination needs to be guided by someone who has had the relevant experience. I will begin my inquiry into the components of a progressive male standpoint with a discussion of the importance of personal experience.

A progressive male standpoint is an epistemic standpoint that places personal experience at center stage.[5] By experience I simply mean a state of affairs, or a process, in which one comes into contact with the world through the use of one's senses. Personal experience is experience based on having lived through a particular event (such as giving birth or having a vasectomy), having assumed a certain role (such as becoming a mother or a father), or having perceived a certain state of affairs (such as that one is an object of sex discrimination or that one has contributed to the rape culture). Personal experience can also involve observing someone else who is experiencing something (such as being present when someone else is giving birth to a child) or being told about someone's experience by a person one has reason to trust (such as being told about a friend's experience of being the victim of sexual harassment).

It is a commonplace for people to say that they can only really understand a thing if they have lived through it.[6] Those who have directly experienced something seem to be better placed to understand that thing than someone who has not had this experience.[7] If one has not experienced something personally, one must rely on the accounts of others. Yet, there may be a gap between what others experience and what they report they have experienced. Such a gap may exist because of intentional distortion or because of unintended distortions. Even when undistorted we may not be able to comprehend what another person reports because of problems of communication or lack of a common basis of shared experience. It seems that these problems of distortion and communication do not exist (at least to the same extent) when one learns something from one's own experience as opposed to learning from the reports of other persons whom one does not know.

In some cases, "perceiving" is not a simple matter of sense perception; a moral "perceiver" relies on his or her value orderings and conceptions of moral saliency.[8] Value orderings and rules of saliency are not themselves infallible. Accounts of one's moral experience are difficult to justify as well as difficult to transmit to others so that others can judge the cogency of what one claims to have experienced. A person may morally misperceive a situation he or she is personally experiencing. Of course, when one is forced to rely solely on what others experience, this problem may be compounded since the possibility of misperceiving a situation may increase the farther removed one is from the initial experience.

Consider two examples of assessing the degree of pain that a man experiences. In the first case the man suffers while undergoing a vasectomy. In the second case a man suffers when he is denied his paternal right to decide whether his biological child should be given up for adoption. Men who have had such experiences have a fairly straightforward way of assessing these types of suffering; they merely remember what they felt when they went through it. But here distortion is possible on two levels. First, one's memory may be faulty or clouded by other experiences. Second, one's initial experience may have been influenced by painkillers or depression and not easily generalizable. In order to generalize on the basis of one's personal experience, these men will also have to imagine what other men would experience. Because of this, one's ability to understand some general state, such as the degree of pain one is likely to suffer from having a vasectomy, is never based only on one's personal experience.

We cannot literally feel the pain or suffering of another person. We must reconstruct that pain or suffering on the basis of information that is problematical in several respects. Those who have not had the experience in question will often need to rely on people who have had the experience to help them test or check what they have imaginatively come up with. If one is having a direct experience of pain, one has what seems to be nearly immediate access to data that can confirm or deny that the pain is intense.[9] But of course, one can be deluded here, as in the case of people who have lost a limb, yet still feel pain in that limb.

Many men who have not had a vasectomy, or been denied paternal rights, have had other operations, or denials of rights, on the basis of which they can extrapolate. And this is also true of many women, who, after all, are more likely to experience pain and discomfort in the groin area than are men, and also more likely to have been denied their rights. If one is going to have to extrapolate to understand what others are experiencing, why should it matter whether one has had the relevant experience oneself or not? And if one has not had the experience, why would it matter whether one was male or female in being able to imagine the psychological pain of the man who does experience these things directly?

Can a woman imagine what it feels like to be repeatedly "kicked in the balls" (the account many men give of what it feels like to have a vasectomy)? Obviously she can at least partially imagine this sensation by extrapolation from other intensely painful experiences she has had. But at least part of the psychological distress men feel in such events is wrapped up with the fear of castration or impotence. And the suffering involved in the loss of paternal rights is bound up with the idea of losing one's sense of manhood. In this respect men who are trying to imagine what it is like to have a vasectomy, or to lose paternal rights, will be initially better placed than women. For there is no comparable experience for women to the fear of castration and impotence or of losing one's manhood. It is true that some women have a fear of being rendered infertile, but this fear is not ordinarily associated with an intensely painful experience. Of course, this experiential difference does not completely block the ability of women to imagine what men experience in vasectomy operations, but it does mean that they will find it more difficult than most men to engage in reconstructive imagination. For as one gets further and further removed from the actual experience, and as the pool of experiences upon which one draws is less and less analogous to the actual experience, the powers of imagination are more and more strained.

Why isn't imaginatively reconstructed or simulated experience close enough to direct experience to be as initially useful as direct experience? At least one reason is that people have limitations to their powers of imagination. A person who is able to use his legs to walk could imagine having to use a wheelchair for mobility. But he would find it difficult to imagine what it would be like to have to use a wheelchair to get anywhere at all, that *every* time he needs to go somewhere he would have to get there in his wheelchair. Our imagination can replicate certain kinds of temporally limited experiences, but it has trouble being sustained so as to replicate temporally extended experiences.[10]

The general point is that it is harder to achieve and to sustain an understanding of something if one has not experienced the thing oneself. The image fades more quickly if it was not implanted through some kind of lively experience. And as we will see, some faint images don't motivate as well as more lively ones do. But it is not impossible to replicate a set of experiences through imagination. For this reason, all that can be concluded is that personal experience of something initially makes it easier for a person to gain a certain kind of knowledge or understanding of that thing than if one has not had personal experience. But it cannot be said that such knowledge or understanding is blocked by lack of personal experience. Thus we have a reason for thinking that personal experience is initially valuable in attaining a progressive male standpoint but not a reason for thinking that this standpoint is unattainable by those who lack certain personal experiences.

❚❚ A Critical Point of View

There is more to the formation of a progressive standpoint than merely having a certain type of experience. We need to distinguish between merely having a viewpoint and attaining a progressive standpoint. As Nancy Hartsock has said, a standpoint is not merely something one assumes; rather it is an achievement.[11] To achieve a progressive standpoint one has to see certain experiences as part of a larger whole, not merely as isolated events. One must critically reflect on these experiences in light of a certain kind of enlarged consciousness, namely, one which filters out certain individual biases that one might impose on the interpretation of these experiences.[12] More important, a person must somehow come to an understanding of what it means to be oppressed, to be powerless rather than to be wielding power.

Consider the claim that women can understand the morality of abortion because of their personal experiences better than men can. A progressive female (or feminist) standpoint normally takes account of women's experiences in two respects. First, there is the experience of having had an abortion or having gone through pregnancy. Second, there is the experience of reflecting critically on the dominant institutions and roles that influence women's lives. It is the critical reflecton that turns the viewpoint of some women on their own personal experiences into a progressive standpoint. Not all women can achieve the progressive standpoint because not all women can attain a critical view of their own position in the world. But by virtue of being a member of an oppressed group, women are initially better placed to achieve a progressive standpoint than is generally true for men.

Members of oppressed groups, on this view, have fewer biases toward the maintenance of a certain status quo since their powerlessness allows fewer clear-cut interests in the continuation of the status quo than for members of oppressor groups. In this sense the members of oppressed groups can potentially attain an account of social reality that is more accurate than that attainable by members of oppressor groups. But members of oppressed groups also have interests, and those interests can block them from discovering certain kinds of social understanding. Just as the oppressors often have an interest in maintaining the social status quo, so the oppressed often have an interest in overturning that social status quo. So, there is also a sense in which oppressed group members will have trouble attaining a more accurate account of social reality than that attainable by members of an oppressor group, although it remains true that members of oppressed groups have fewer hurdles to overcome than do members of oppressor groups in attaining a progressive standpoint.

Many men have traditionally had "a male viewpoint" based largely on the experience of being in positions of privilege and power. The traditional male perspective has also virtually excluded the perspective of women, at least in certain domains. Can there be an alternative male viewpoint that does not merely replicate the existing position of privilege and power men have traditionally occupied? Does the fact that men are not systematically oppressed diminish the value of, or perhaps even make it impossible for them to attain, a standpoint from which critically to assess their lives? What unique practical problems are faced by men who try to achieve a progressive male standpoint? Is it necessary that a person be a member of an oppressed group in order to attain the enlarged consciousness that is central to the formation of a standpoint?

In order to answer these questions, I want to construct, and critically assess, an argument in support of the view that being oppressed is necessary for the achievement of a progressive standpoint. Perhaps the most obvious and commonsensical position would be that those who are not oppressed lack the motivation to challenge their own privileges and powers, since these contribute to the self-interest of the unoppressed. Hartsock argues that the viewpoint of those who are in an oppressor class is both partial and perverse.[13] It is partial because it cannot get beyond the self-interest of the oppressor group, and it is perverse because it seeks to nullify the interests of the oppressed group, thereby failing to afford women equal treatment and respect.

Can some men attain enough critical distance from the dominant position of their gender group to be able to approximate the standpoint of the oppressed gender group, namely, women? I am not suggesting that men must become women in order to achieve a progressive male standpoint on gender. Rather, I want to investigate whether men can attain a critical distance from their own positions of power and dominance over women which would be like the critical position that some women occupy? The answer I wish to offer is a qualified "yes." The qualification is that not many men will be likely to achieve this, and that they will no doubt be able only to approximate the progressive standpoint that some women can occupy.

As a first step, men need to be able to become critical of their roles in society, to see how the roles of husband and father, for instance, contain elements that contribute to the inequality of women and to sex discrimination. This is a necessary first step because otherwise men will be too likely to mistake what appears to be the normal functioning of a social role for the way that role should function morally. Men who are fathers and husbands will be inclined to see their roles in the narrow terms of whether they are successful at occupying certain roles, without recognizing that the successful fulfillment of these roles can, and often does, curtail the ability of women as wives and daughters to be afforded equal treatment and respect. Not only will men be inclined not to be self-critical because they are focused on conforming to the expectations of the role, but they will also be inclined to misunderstand the harmful effects of the role because it will be in their interests to have a positive public view of these defining roles for men. For these reasons it is important that men engage in critical thought and discussion about their roles, even though this will be quite difficult for most men.

Such critical thought and reflection, however, is probably not sufficient to afford some men the chance to achieve a progressive standpoint on their male roles and experiences. In addition, they will need to spend time interacting with women in nondominating ways to learn from them what it is like to be oppressed. Here is a legitimate role for imaginative reconstruction, especially in the context of role reversal. The critical perspective men need to achieve on their masculine roles is dependent on imagining the position of those who lack privilege and power, a feat of imagination which can be attained more easily by women since women normally in fact lack power and privilege. Men need to think about their own masculinity from a position where their interests are not so bound up with the maintenance of male privilege. In this sense, men cannot normally attain a progressive male standpoint unless they imagine and then come to understand the position of the oppressed, in this case the position of women.

Let us return to the discussion of role reversal begun in the previous chapter. Role reversal involves attempting to act in ways characteristic of another person. At its best, role reversal involves two people who take on each other's persona. In this sense, role reversal can be an aid for the imagination in helping men imagine what it is like to be a member of an oppressed group, especially what it is like to be a woman who is confronted by various men occupying traditional male roles. Role reversal acts as an aid to imagination here by confronting men with a dramatic enactment in which it is the woman who has the privilege and power and the man who lacks these things, and is hence relatively powerless and oppressed. Men can learn from such dramatic enactments, and their imaginative abilities will be enhanced.

Why not think that women are better able to reflect critically on masculinity and male experience than men since they do not need to imagine the perspective of the oppressed? I think there is a lot to be said for this view. Just as men are in a better position for data gathering about male experience and roles because of being directly acquainted with them, so women are better able to critically assess male experience since they are not as likely to be biased in favor of that experience.[14] Men will be better at certain aspects of the study of male experience and roles and women will be better at other aspects.[15] But in both cases, these are only initial advantages for some members of these groups. Other members of the group will still have difficulty attaining a progressive standpoint, and no one is completely blocked from attaining this standpoint just because he or she lacks certain experience.

Since men are generally not discriminated against on grounds of sex and are not treated unequally merely because they are male, it is not easy for them to take on the critical standpoint of one who has been adversely affected by a set of discriminatory roles and practices. Nonetheless, some men can potentially approximate such a stance either by engaging in role reversal or by extrapolating from other experiences they have, for instance as members of a marginalized subgroup of the larger group of men (as is true of men who are homosexual or bisexual, or of men who are nonwhite). In general men need to be able to become critical of the privileged position of men, while at the same time realizing that they will never be able to distance themselves completely from such privilege because they will continue to benefit from being male in ways of which they are often not conscious, such as the way all men benefit from the rape culture.[16]

III Moral Understanding

In addition to experiential and critical components, there is also a normative and motivational component in a progressive male standpoint. This third part of the progressive male standpoint involves that curious mixture of understanding and motivation to change which is characteristic of moral standpoints generally. What is the source of the motivation to change? Is the increased understanding of the harmfulness of rape and of a man's contribution to the environment that makes rape prevalent enough to spark a man to act in ways that would change that environment? Is the motivation to change merely internal to the understanding, or is there something added that brings about the motivational impetus?[17]

When a man gains a critical understanding of why it is wrong to contribute to the rape culture, what motivates him to respond by changing his behavior? In answering this question it is interesting to note that there are humans, most commonly referred to as psychopaths or sociopaths, who are unmoved even when they seemingly understand their role in producing harm. If one thinks that there is a necessary (internal) relationship between knowing what is right and doing it, there are at least two strategies that one can adopt to explain the psychopath or sociopath. First, one can attempt to deny that these people actually understand that others are harmed or that they have caused this harm. Second, one can admit that there are psychopaths or sociopaths but deny that there are very many of them, thereby downplaying the significance of their existence. Normal people are not psychopaths or sociopaths; normal people are moved by their moral understandings. There is a third strategy for taking account of these people which would call into question the necessary (internal) relationship between knowing what is right and doing it. This third strategy admits that there are psychopaths or sociopaths, and argues that moral understanding does not motivate without an additional element being present, for instance the threat of sanction or the hope of reward. Or even more basically, it might be claimed that understanding alone is not suffficient to motivate without some kind of caring disposition already in place, and that this is precisely what the psychopath or sociopath lacks.[18]

Let us first consider the strategy of denying the relevance of psychopaths or sociopaths because normal people are not sufficiently like them. This strategy runs into trouble whenever otherwise normal men, who have come to see that they are causing harm, display the same complete lack of motivation as is shown by psychopaths or sociopaths. Normal men often seem not to react to stimulations in their environment because they lack sensitivity or empathy. As a result of traditional socialization patterns, men have been less prone to display empathy and sympathy than have women.[19] Many heterosexual men in Western cultures are emotionally stunted and as a result have a harder time than women in changing their behavior even when they realize that they are causing or contributing to harm.

The second strategy, which claims that there are simply very few people like the psychopath or sociopath, runs into similar difficulties. Whether because of weakness of will or indifference or self-interest, many people in my experience do not do what they themselves think they morally should do. Of course many of these people are not psychopaths or sociopaths: they care about the harm they cause. The problem is that they also care about many other things, and so their caring about the harm they cause is not sufficient to motivate them to change their behavior. It is thus the third strategy that I am inclined to accept, since I find it implausible to deny the existence, indeed the prevalence, of psychopaths or sociopaths and others like them.

Would achieving a progressive male standpoint make it more likely that men would work to reduce sexual violence in their own lives and communities? This is a hard question to assess. While the example of the psychopath or sociopath shows that people do not always act on their normative understandings, this example tells us nothing about whether a motivational pull is necessarily associated with normative understanding. I believe that normative understanding of such things as men's complicity in the prevalence of rape will, under certain conditions, make it more likely, but not necessary, that men will be motivated to act to change the environment that contributes to the prevalence of rape.

Moral understanding, unlike other forms of understanding, is infused with understanding of how we should live our lives. Those who achieve a progressive male standpoint attain heightened moral understanding of male behavior and roles that will correspondingly heighten their motivation to change their own behavior and to influence the behavior of other men and the social institutions in their societies. But having heightened motivation to change does not guarantee that change will occur. Motivations can be offset by other motivations and hence fail to result in action. For moral motivation to result in action without additional sanctions or rewards, men must come to feel that changing themselves is a desirable thing.

Motivational change occurs because of some felt compulsion to act on what one already understands. The threat of external sanctions can induce a person to *feel* motivated to change behavior in a deeper sense than when one merely *believes* that one should change. Externally imposed sanctions add an extra impetus to change which often tips the scales, so that other motivations pulling us away from change can be overrridden. Socialization can also act as a kind of added sanction, although its force is felt as if it were internal rather than external. Emotions can perform the function of inner sanctions, motivating in a way that mere belief does not.[20] Socialized feelings of guilt and shame for instance can motivate as powerfully as fear of punishment.

For a progressive male standpoint to motivate men to change their behavior it must generate emotions, such as shame and guilt as well as compassion and caring, in addition to changing beliefs. One way this can occur is when men socialize boys to feel shame for sexual aggression. Then, later in life, when men criticize other men the earlier socialization is reinforced in a way that motivates men to change. In the case of complicity for rape, a profound sense of shame motivates some men to try to distance themselves from the rest of the group "men" by speaking out or attempting to raise their sons in a way that will break the pattern of male socialization which results in the increasingly violent rape culture. Men need to help motivate one another to change socialization patterns.

Women also can help emotionally motivate men to act on their normative understandings. It is important that women, especially mothers, aunts, grandmothers, and neighbors work to change male socialization and motivation. Because of the central role played by many women in early childhood socialization, women can contribute quite a bit to the progressive socialization of boys. So there is nothing in my view to support the contention that women should be marginalized in motivating men to change. But men may be better placed to effect these changes in adult men than are women because these are largely male problems and because, regrettably, men are more likely to listen to other men than to women.

Men are the perpetrators of rape and sexual harassment; they are the impregnators and the predominant buyers of pornography; they are the sexual aggressors and those most likely to exclude and diminish the status of women. But many men are also enraged, saddened, guilt-ridden, and ashamed of their position in society. Mostly, though, many men are confused about the alternatives that are available to them that would be more socially acceptable and yet not merely a pale reflection of the other gender group. And it is for this reason that men need to assume a progressive male standpoint and speak to their fellow men about ways to change patterns of male socialization in ways that are believable and plausible.[21]

IV Convincing Ourselves

In this final section I turn from discussions of how one acquires understanding to questions of how that understanding is best conveyed. A progressive male standpoint that seeks change in traditional male behavior will need to provide analyses and proposals for change that men will find believable in order for them to be motivated by these proposals. Whether someone is regarded as believable is often as important as whether his or her ideas are theoretically justifiable. Believability is affected by many factors that are not properly germane to justifiability, although the two are not completely separate. In this section I will briefly address this aspect of a progressive male standpoint, recognizing that it is fraught with problems.

The distinction between justifiability and believability is important in many contexts. A person who has just looked through a telescope may be quite justified epistemically in saying that what appears to be a shooting star is really a fast moving airplane. Yet, others may not consider this information believable unless it is known that the person is an astronomer, or it is known that she has just looked through a telescope, or until someone else looks through the telescope and publicly confirms the observation. Similarly, men often are more likely to believe other men than to believe women, even when the two are saying the same things. Believability is often a function of appearances, especially public appearances, rather than a matter of theoretical justification.

There is an obvious difficulty with this type of believability. When men give greater uptake to fellow men than to women concerning the critique of male roles, this sounds suspiciously like men's historical distrust of women as thinkers and scholars. We should not give credibility to men's discriminatory attitudes. If men were more likely to believe other men because of contemptuous attitudes toward women scholars, then this type of believability should not count for much. But if men tend to trust other men more than women because they believe that men will be better positioned to understand both the positive and negative aspects of male experience, then this is a type of believability that may be legitimately given some weight.

Here is an example. I have attended conferences where male speakers have made jokes or statements that are blatantly sexist. If this is pointed out by a woman in the audience, many men will roll their eyes or chuckle, often saying to one another, "she has too thin a skin," or "she can't take a joke." But when I or another man points out the sexist nature of the joke or statement, men in the audience, as well as the speaker, often look sheepish or guilty. There is no room for a conspiratorial nod or chuckle toward other men since it is not clear whether these other men will side with the speaker or with the man who has challenged the speaker. In addition, men cannot easily dismiss the criticism since it emanates from a position where it is assumed that male experience is taken seriously. For these reasons, criticism of male behavior will sometimes be more believable if it is issued by men rather than by women.

It is a regrettable fact that men generally take other men more seriously than they take women. But the regrettable aspects of this state of affairs can be overcome in some cases if the male voice of authority is used as an effective critical tool. Believability is not a substitute for justifiability. If a person lacks justifiability for a claim he has made, merely being believed counts for very little. But if a person has a reasonable degree of justifiability, then being believable can enhance his claim enough to make it preferable to other justifiable claims that lack this believability. The preference for the male critical voice, of course, is practical rather than theoretical: the truth of the claims themselves is not affected by believability.

At least part of the explanation for the greater believability men give other men is that many men see women's criticism of their experiences and roles as an affront to their manliness. It is harder to dismiss the call for change as an affront to one's manliness if it is made by another man. I must confess that I don't think much of the affront-to-manliness charge since the conception of masculinity that it rests on is in my view faulty; but if it is taken seriously by many other men, then I am inclined to take it seriously. It is for this reason that I have made positive suggestions about what men can do to build on the strengths they already have, rather than mere negative criticisms of male experience and traditional conceptions of masculinity.[22]

Another part of the puzzle of believability is now becoming clear. Men have more trust in men than in women not to discount the positive aspects of male experience and roles. Of course men can demonstrate that this trust was misplaced, as can be seen in the negative reaction by many men to certain writers in the men's movement. Such criticisms are not nearly as common as those directed at women who write about men. Indeed, the backlash against feminism is fueled by this general charge of male bashing, whereas there are few similar criticisms of male writers.[23] One does not expect a person to "bash" himself or his own group since such bashing seems so clearly self-hurtful. So men are afforded more trust than women not to be overly critical of male experience and of masculinity more generally.

There is a serious political problem here, though, that has epistemic ramifications. If men need to be perceived as not overly critical of male experience and roles in order to be believable, then this may put a constraint on their critical writings and this would jeopardize the justifiability of those writings. Purists who insist on providing a thoroughgoing critique of male experience and traditional roles will find that their message will not be taken as seriously as they would like by the very people they want most to affect, namely, other men. There is a fine line between doing respectable philosophical work, which calls for a healthy dose of critique, and not losing the trust of those to whom the critique is addressed.

A similar problem occurs in the fields of medical and business ethics. In order to be taken seriously by the practitioners in business and medicine, philosophers have found that they cannot be perceived as critical of the whole enterprise of business or medicine. But this recognition has sometimes meant that philosophers have shied away from systemic critiques of these disciplines so as to make sure that they do not lose the trust of the members of these fields. The integrity of the philosophical investigations is difficult, although not impossible, to maintain under these circumstances. Just the right balance needs to be struck between searchingly critical inquiry and sympathetic attempts to understand a person's or group's point of view.[24]

I have argued that it is possible for some men to attain a progressive male standpoint. Such a position involves observing male experience and traditional roles with a critical eye; being motivated to try to change certain traditional ways of behaving and thinking; and constructing believable proposals for change for other men. I have not argued that such a standpoint is blocked for women, but I have argued that men are generally better placed than women in two ways: they have better access to certain data because of their direct acquaintance with certain male experiences, and their criticisms are more believable by other men because it is presumed that they will not be excessively critical of those experiences. I have also argued that women are more likely to have a distanced, critical perspective on male experience and roles, and that women are often better placed to contribute to changing early socialization patterns so as to motivate change. Thus, men and women can each bring different resources and expertise to a progressive standpoint on masculinity.

A male standpoint that is progressive and morally responsive can be achieved. One of the obstacles to such an achievement is that men currently feel under siege. They are being asked to give up a lot — for instance, roles that they previously felt quite comfortable filling — and it is not yet clear to many of them what they will gain in return. Male philosophical writing about male experience and traditional roles needs to provide not only critical arguments but a new vision of what men can become.[25] There is no reason to think that men and women must become alike. Men can be distinctively men, but different from how they now are. A progressive male standpoint on male experience and traditional roles needs both to make that point clear and also to make a concerted effort to go beyond merely sketching out what the alternative conception of masculinity would be like.[26]

In the previous chapters I have made a start in this direction. My discussions of male anger, paternity, sexuality, pornography, rape, sexual harassment, and the exclusion of women from full and equal participation in society have all had a strong morally critical dimension.[27] But these discussions have also tried to indicate avenues for positive reconceptualization of male roles, building on some of the traditional strengths of those roles. In this way, I have tried to illustrate how a progressive male standpoint can produce reasonable critiques of male roles and yet still be believable enough to motivate men to change their lives. I have tried to lend some support to the growing, but still relatively small, number of men trying to provide a moral reconceptualization of masculinity.

Masculinity is merely the view that men have of their proper roles, as men, within a society. Masculinity is not something fixed for all time. Men can see themselves as out of control, at the mercy of their anger or sexuality, or they can see themselves as able to take control of their lives. Men can see themselves as mere procreators or as nurturing fathers. Men can see rape, sexual coercion, and harassment as badges of solidarity, or they can see these as matters for collective shame. Men can urge their sons to be aggressive and competitive on the playing fields, or they can urge them to be cooperative leaders. For any given type, or stereotype, of masculinity, there is an alternative type of masculinity. I have tried to sketch a number of these alternative male roles and experiences that still are definitive of a masculinity that is not reduced to femininity, or androgyny for that matter.

There are two main reasons for thinking that androgyny is not a desirable goal for our society. The first has to do with the value of diversity, and the second has to do with issues of socialization. Because both of these reasons also have their difficulties, I am reluctant to say that androgyny is unacceptable for all societies. I do think that the disadvantages of androgyny outweigh the advantages for our contemporary society. In any event, it would be enormously difficult to get men, and women, to abandon the gendered roles they now occupy. Here practical considerations tip the balance, even if other considerations do not.

The first reason why I do not endorse androgynous gender roles has to do with the loss of diversity that would occur from androgyny. Androgyny is premised on a radical equality, but like most radical egalitarian proposals, it fails to take seriously actual diferences among individuals. There are undeniable biological differences between men and women, and there are also clear-cut social differences. It remains controversial whether the ability of women to breast-feed a newborn makes them more suited than men to assume a nurturant gender role. But if men and women come to assume the same roles, then bottle feeding rather than breast feeding will become the norm. Whether this change would ultimately be harmful to the child or not, it does seem clear that diversity of types or styles of child rearing would be adversely affected. In the social domain, men more than women tend to educate their children to be aggressive, independent beings. While many, including me, have been critical of the excesses of socialization in aggression, the world would be less rich if all parents stopped socializing their children to be aggressive.

There is no reason in principle why men and women couldn't educate both male and female children in the same skills and dispositions. At this point my second reason for being skeptical of androgyny becomes relevant. Men and women who become parents are themselves the products of highly gendered socialization patterns. As a result, men will find it harder than women to educate their children in some areas; and women will find it harder than men to educate their children in some other areas. In our family, I found it easier than did my partner to take our daughter on outings when she was an infant, whereas my partner found it easier than I did to entertain our infant daughter in our house. Of course, I could have done either of these tasks, as could my partner. But it was not inconsequential that I felt more comfortable doing some of the tasks than she did.

Considerations of past socialization and current comfort need to be treated with a certain amount of skepticism themselves. We should not become complacent in our comfortable gender roles, especially when those roles contribute to various harms. Reconceptualizing masculinity in terms of a progressive male standpoint requires such changes in traditional male roles. But eliminating certain gendered roles does not mean that other roles should also be eliminated. And as a result, in order to overcome harmful gender roles we need not necessarily turn toward androgyny. Indeed, some nonandrogynous gender-role socialization can be quite healthy and instrumental in overcoming certain forms of gender oppression, as I have tried to indicate in the last few chapters.

Masculinity is a social construction of a particular culture at a particular time. Our conceptions of masculinity are malleable; yet they are often hard to change. I have provided various moral arguments for thinking that men should change some of their traditional roles and experiences. I have also sketched some alternative roles and experiences that would be achievable and also morally less problematical than some of the traditional ones. But I do not want to underestimate how hard it is for men to change, for I am the first to admit that in many of these respects I have not changed myself when I should have. Yet I have also been luckier than many other men in benefitting from the constructive criticisms, as well as enormous support, of my actions and attitudes over the years by male and female friends alike. I hope this book will similarly support and challenge many males to accept responsibility for the men they are and to strive toward the men they can become.

Notes

Introduction

1. See Larry May, *The Morality of Groups* (Notre Dame: University of Notre Dame Press, 1987); May, *Sharing Responsibility* (Chicago: University of Chicago Press, 1992); and May, *The Socially Responsive Self* (Chicago: University of Chicago Press, 1996).

2. Robert Strikwerda and Larry May, "Male Friendship and Intimacy," *Hypatia* 7 (Summer 1992): 110–25.

3. May and Strikwerda, "Fatherhood and Nurturance," *Journal of Social Philosophy* 22 (Fall 1991): 28-39.

4. May and Strikwerda, "Men in Groups: Collective Responsibility for Rape," *Hypatia* 9 (Spring 1994): 134–51.

5. Larry May and James Bohman, "Masculinity, Sexuality, and Confession," *Hypatia* 12 (Winter 1997), 138–54.

6. Kenneth Clatterbaugh's book, *Contemporary Perspectives on Masculinity* (Boulder, Colo.: Westview Press, 1990), remains the most widely cited and most influential philosophical work even though it was meant to be introductory. Victor Seidler's books, including *Unreasonable Men: Masculinity and Social Theory* (London: Routledge, 1994), are in part theoretically rigorous, but they have not received much critical attention.

7. I would mention Liam Hudson and Bernardine Jacot's book, *The Way Men Think: Intellect, Intimacy, and the Erotic Imagination,* (New Haven: Yale University Press, 1991), as an example, although by no means the worst, of this literature.

8. I am not suggesting here that the moral study of masculinity is different from other moral studies. I would make the larger claim, if I had space to defend it, that using real events rather than hypothetical ones is the preferable strategy in most moral philosophy.

9. Throughout this book I will describe my own view as "progressive." I use the term "progressive" to mean roughly a standpoint which is sympathetic to the plight of those who are harmed or oppressed by various social practices and traditions. Implicit in the use of this term is that we need to be actively engaged in making "progress" on the agenda of eliminating bias and oppression in our society. I leave open the question of how much progress any one person can or should make on this agenda. But I do consider, in various chapters, why eliminating bias and oppression in sexual relations between men and women is a desirable goal.

10. See Susan Bordo, "Reading the Male Body," *Michigan Quarterly Review* (1994): 696–737.

Chapter 1. Anger, Desire, and Moral Responsibility

1. A public prosecutor I know has proposed, only somewhat facetiously, that the surest way to reduce violent crime in the United States is to incarcerate all males between the ages of fifteen and twenty-five.

2. On February 29, 1996 Belle was fined $50,000 for a profane tirade, and then following his assault on a photographer on April 6, 1996, he was ordered to undergo counseling and to perform community service.

3. For a good popular discussion of the issue of violent behavior among college football players, see Pat Jordan, "Belittled Big Men," *New York Times Magazine,* December 10, 1995, 68–75.

4. I am not trying to suggest that violence is more prevalent among athletes and soldiers than among the rest of the male population. My point is rather that even in those cases where men seem to have found a way to channel their angry responses into positive directions, anger-stimulated violence spills over into other aspects of life.

5. There is another commonly discussed excuse that does not stress the repeated pattern of past events so much as the intensity of stressfulness of the current situation, such as the now-classic example of a man who discovers his wife in bed with another man. Because of the limited range of such cases, I will not focus on such an excuse here. I am more interested in the kind of excuse that could explain, and possibly excuse, the prevalence of angry responses by men in contemporary society.

6. For a good discussion of this issue, see Kathleen Waits, "The Criminal Justice System's Response to Battering: Understanding the Problem, Forging the Solutions," *Washington Law Review,* 60 (1985), reprinted in *Feminist Jurisprudence,* ed., Patricia Smith (New York: Oxford University Press, 1993).

7. See the work of Elizabeth Schneider, especially "Describing and Changing: Women's Self-Defense Work and the Problem of Expert Testimony on Battering," *Women's Rights Law Reporter* 9 (1986).

8. It could be argued that in some cases men could adopt self-defense legal strategies since the conditions of their lives really were threatening to them. In cases where men are in mutually abusive relationships with their spouses or partners both the man and woman may have a legitimate basis for claiming self-defense to justify their violent behavior. But in most cases, the circumstances that "badger" the man are not so life-threatening.

9. See Robert Bly, *Iron John* (Reading, Mass.: Addison-Wesley, 1990). For a discussion of the views of the psychoanalytically oriented writers on masculinity see Chap. 3, section III.

10. There are no doubt other disanalogies that could be mentioned. In the case of the battered woman syndrome excuse, the series of past events all were perpetrated by the same person, the male spouse, whereas in many cases of the badgered male the past events were perpetrated by different people. So the target of the violence of the battered woman is more justifiably seen as connected to the past events than is true for the badgered male.

11. Certain forms of insult, directed at the ethnicity or race of a person, can certainly harm that person significantly. See the wonderful collection of papers on this topic by Mari J. Matsuda, Charles R. Lawrence III, Richard Delgado, and Kimberle Williams Crenshaw, *Words That Wound* (Boulder, Colo.: Westview, 1993).

12. For a discussion of thinkers who have held this view and for complications

in this standard way of thinking of responsibility, see the first chapter of my book *Sharing Responsibility*.

13. This doctrine has come down to us from Aristotle and is still largely accepted today. See *Nicomachean Ethics*, bk. 3, sec. 1, trans. Terence Irwin (Indianapolis: Hackett, 1985).

14. Results of various studies are summarized in Joseph H. Pleck, *The Myth of Masculinity* (Cambridge: MIT Press, 1981), app. A. See also the revised edition of Anne Fausto-Sterling, *Myths of Gender* (New York: Basic Books, 1992).

15. I discuss this issue at greater length in Chapter 4: Pornography and Pollution.

16. I will not here pursue the most obvious objection, namely, that excusing male aggression and violence makes it more likely that women will continue to be beaten by their mates.

17. See, for instance, Allan Gibbard, "Moral Judgment and the Acceptance of Norms," *Ethics* 95 (October 1985); and Gibbard, *Wise Choices, Apt Feelings* (Cambridge: Harvard University Press, 1990).

18. In this respect I find Patricia Greenspan's account of the morality of the emotions preferable to Gibbard's. See her *Practical Guilt* (New York: Oxford University Press, 1995).

19. Gibbard, "Moral Judgment," p. 8.

20. See Gibbard's assessment of this case in *Wise Choices*, pp. 58–61.

21. For more discussion of male parental roles see Chapter 2: Paternity and Commitment.

22. Gibbard does not make this mistake, but this mistake is indeed commonly made. See May, *The Socially Responsive Self*, chap. 5, for more discussion of this point.

23. There are nonstandard cases where sexual desire leads to rape, which obviously drives people apart, and where anger drives a person toward another in the sense that one is driven toward one's opponent so as more easily to strike out at the object of one's anger. But these are not the normal cases.

24. For much more detailed discussion of rape see Chapter 5: Rape and Collective Responsibility. For more discussion of sexuality see Chapter 3: Sexuality and Confession.

25. One of the most important works on the reactive nature of moral emotions is Peter Strawson, "Freedom and Resentment," originally published in 1962 and reprinted in many places including, *Perspectives on Moral Responsibility*, ed. John Martin Fischer and Mark Ravizza (Ithaca: Cornell University Press, 1993), pp. 45–66. As Strawson uses the term "reactive," sexual desire is not properly reactive, since it isn't necessarily reactive to what other people have done to us. I use the term "reactive" emotions in a somewhat broader way than Strawson.

26. See Chapter 4: Pornography and Pollution.

27. On some analyses of responsibility, it may make sense to blame someone even when he or she could not have changed his or her behavior, perhaps because he or she had not done things years ago which would have made it possible to change now. I do not think that this is a good way to analyze blame, but I do develop a similar analysis for shame in *Sharing Responsibility*, esp. pp. 152–55.

28. See Chapters 4, 5, and 6, respectively.

29. Lance Morrow, "Men: Are They Really That Bad?" *Time*, February 14, 1994, 56–57.

30. I suppose that Morrow could be making merely an evolutionary argument about what men are biologically destined to be like. If this is the way to read him, then what I have to say about such arguments in Chapter 5, section II would be relevant.

31. See my discussion of this point in May, *Sharing Responsibility*, chap. 2, where I draw the distinction in terms of being held responsible versus feeling responsible. See especially pp. 51–52.

32. This is not to say that there is no relation between being assigned responsiblity and taking responsibility. One early method of instilling a sense of responsibility which enables people later to take responsibility for their actions is to assign responsiblity to people, especially children.

33. For more discussion of male socialization patterns, see Chapter 7: Socialization and Separatism.

34. See one of my earlier essays on this topic, written with Marilyn Friedman, "Harming Women as a Group," *Social Theory and Practice* 11 (Summer 1985): 207–34.

35. Vonda Olson Long, "Relation of Masculinity to Self-Esteem and Self-Acceptance in Male Professionals, College Students, and Clients," *Journal of Counseling Psychology* 36 (1989): 84-87.

36. For more discussion of the reconfiguration of male roles in a positive way, see Chapter 8: A Progressive Male Standpoint.

37. This is the point of the discussion at the end of Chapter 7: Socialization and Separatism.

Chapter 2. Paternity and Commitment

1. Throughout I will use the terms "birth parents" and "biological parents" interchangeably. I am aware that many advocates in the adoption movement prefer the term "birth parents," but in the context of certain legal cases the term "biological parents" seems to be more suitable.

2. For a good account of these cases, see Mary Shanley, "Unwed Fathers' Rights, Adoption, and Sex Equality: Gender-Neutrality and the Perpetuation of Patriarchy," *Columbia Law Review* 95 (January 1995).

3. And in the similar case of Baby Richard, on June 19, 1995 the United States Supreme Court decided not to review, and hence to let stand, a lower court ruling that had overturned an adoption and awarded the child to the biological father, whose consent to the adoption had not been secured.

4. A very good collection of papers on the subject of substantive equality in parenthood is Joyce Trebilcot, *Mothering: Essays in Feminist Theory* (Totowa, N.J.: Rowman and Allanheld, 1983).

5. *Stanley v. Illinois*, 405 U.S. 645 (1972), at 651 (my italics).

6. See Janet L. Dolgin, "Just a Gene: Judicial Assumptions about Fatherhood," *UCLA Law Review* 40 (1993): 650–52, for a good summary of the dispute in the

Supreme Court opinions about this case. Contrary to my analysis, Dolgin claims that it is the relationship with the mother which grounds the father's rights in these cases. Many of the quotations from the case law are taken from Dolgin's comprehensive treatment of these cases.

7. The best piece on this topic is Deborah L. Forman, "Unwed Fathers and Adoption: A Theoretical Analysis in Context," *Texas Law Review* 72 (April 1994): 967–1045.

8. *Caban v. Mohammed*, 441 U.S. 380 (1979), at 397.

9. *Caban* at 397.

10. *Lehr v. Robertson*, 463 U.S. 248 (1983), at 260.

11. *Lehr* at 262.

12. Dolgin, "Just a Gene . . .", p. 661.

13. Recent developments in reproductive technology cloud the issue of whether it is nature alone that makes women mothers. I am grateful to Richard Hiskes for reminding me of this point.

14. For a discussion of the facts of the case, which was officially titled *DeBoer v. Schmidt (In re Baby Girl Clausen)*, see Shanley, "Unwed Fathers' Rights," pp. 96–97.

15. This case is officially known as *In re Doe (Baby Boy Janikova)*. See the news story "Man Who Battled to Regain Son after Adoption Leaves Wife, Boy," *St. Louis Post-Dispatch*, January 21, 1997, 6A.

16. Daniel Callahan, "Bioethics and Fatherhood," *Utah Law Review*, 3 (1992): 737.

17. Ibid.

18. Ibid., p. 738.

19. Ibid.

20. Ibid., p. 744.

21. See May and Strikwerda, "Fatherhood and Nurturance," pp. 28–39.

22. In certain institutional, and some noninstitutional, settings things may be different. If a person is literally given a role which has a range of obligations connected to it, then criticism for non-fulfillment of those obligations must be premised on the person having also had certain rights which would enable him or her to fulfill those obligations. This is not the kind of case that Callahan is discussing. I am grateful to Carl Wellman for this point.

23. *Webster's Third International Dictionary* (Springfield, Mass.: Merriam-Webster, 1986) mentions only one meaning of mothering, visiting one's parents on mid-Lent Sunday and giving gifts, which is not in common usage except perhaps in the south of England where this custom originated.

24. It might be useful to ponder the case of surrogacy in what follows, since in that case maternal rights may be contested between the biological and nurturing mothers.

25. Shanley, "Unwed Fathers' Rights," p. 82.

26. But in some cases, where the pregnancy is difficult and where the pregnant woman sacrifices a lot, for instance being forced to lie flat in bed for several months at the end of the pregnancy to avoid miscarriage, it will be difficult for the man to reach an equivalent level of care before birth. After birth, of course, there may be

greater opportunities for rough equivalences to be built up. I am grateful to Marilyn Friedman for pressing me to see that some pregnancies take such a toll on the woman that the man may not be able to catch up until after birth.

27. This line of argument could set the stage for men who have no biological link to a child, but who have engaged in significant nurturance of a pregnant woman, to have a claim on decision-making concerning that child's welfare. While I would be concerned about potential abuse of such an extension of my argument, I would also point out that some men have developed loving relationships with a woman and her children where it would not be implausible to grant them some say in decisions concerning that child's welfare.

28. I am indebted to Iris Young for crucial comments on this part of my argument.

29. See Hugh LaFollette's prescient piece "Licensing Parents," *Philosophy and Public Affairs* 9 (Winter 1980). LaFollette points out that the screening for adoptive parents works so well that they are five times less likely to be abusive toward their children than are "biological" parents.

30. On this point, see the excellent essay by Barbara Bennett Woodhouse, "Hatching the Egg: A Child-Centered Perspective on Parents' Rights," *Cardozo Law Review* 14 (1993).

31. See Hugh LaFollette's wonderful essay "Real Men," in *Rethinking Masculinity*, ed. Larry May, Robert Strikwerda, and Patrick Hopkins (Lanham, Md.: Rowman and Littlefield, 1992).

32. *Webster's Third International Dictionary*, p. 828.

33. *Jhordan C. v. Mary K.* (1986) 179 CA3d 386, 224 CR 530, as quoted in Thomas W. Lacqueur, "The Facts of Fatherhood," in *Conflicts in Feminism*, ed. Marianne Hirsch and Evelyn Fox Keller (New York: Routledge, 1990), p. 216.

34. I owe this point to Marilyn Friedman.

35. *In Re Raquel Marie X* 559 N.E.2d 418 (1989). Woodhouse, "Hatching the Egg," pp. 1799–1802, has a good summary and analysis of this case, upon which I draw.

36. This is Woodhouse's summary of the Court's observations, "Hatching the Egg," pp. 1800–1801.

37. Forman, "Unwed Fathers and Adoption," p. 1024.

38. While standards for adoption vary from state to state, social workers and judges engage in close scrutiny of prospective adoptive parents in every jurisdiction within the United States. In my experience, couples are routinely turned down by adoption agencies, or by judges, if either person has a history of violent behavior.

39. Forman, "Unwed Fathers and Adoption," p. 1037.

40. A Florida appeals court recently agreed with a lower court that a man convicted of murdering his first wife should have custody of a child he fathered instead of the child's mother, who is a lesbian. This seems to be a caricature of the position that Forman defends, and could be dismissed as that were it not now an established precedent in Florida. See Mireya Navarro, "Appeals Court Rebuffs Lesbian in Custody Bid," *New York Times*, August 31, 1996, A7.

41. In making this proposal I am influenced by LaFollette's similar claim in "Licensing Parents."

42. This is Shanley's summary of the major provision of the bill, A. 8319A, N.Y. Legislature, 1993–1994 Reg. Sess. (introduced by Member of the Assembly Lopez at the request of the governor). See "Unwed Fathers' Rights," p. 92.

43. Until the next section, I here leave largely unaddressed the question of what paternal obligations should be like.

44. See Shanley, "Unwed Fathers' Rights," p. 93.

45. I am here speaking only of genetic claims. As I said earlier, 9 months of pregnancy often changes things.

46. George W. Harris, "Fathers and Fetuses," *Ethics* 96 (April 1986): 596.

47. Virginia Held, "The Obligations of Mothers and Fathers," in *Mothering: Essays in Feminist Theory*, ed. Joyce Trebilcot (Totowa, N.J.: Rowman and Allanheld, 1983), p. 7.

48. I here draw on Virginia Held's lucid account of the first and second phases of the feminist movement in her book *Feminist Morality* (Chicago: University of Chicago Press, 1993), pp. 160–68. I also embrace her distinction between procedural and substantive equality.

49. James Sterba argues for a similar view in *Contemporary Social and Political Philosophy* (Belmont, Calif.: Wadsworth, 1996).

50. Held, "Obligations of Mothers and Fathers," p. 16.

51. Ibid. For more on this topic see my discussion of androgynous gender roles in the final section of Chapter 8.

52. See May and Strikwerda, "Fatherhood and Nurturance," for an extended discussion of this point.

53. Held, "Obligations of Mothers and Fathers," p. 19.

Chapter 3. Sexuality and Confession

1. See Alan Soble, *Pornography* (New Haven: Yale University Press, 1986).

2. Touching oneself as well as forcible sex is a form of "pollution" and is "intrinsically forbidden." This pre-Vatican II Catholic dogma is clear in canonical writings such as Thomas Tamburinus, S.J., *Explicationes in Decalogum* Lyons, 1651), 2: 72–73. Both masturbation and rape were considered sins in the same category, "mortal sins ex toto genere suo" (intrinsically bad in themselves). In this category sins did not admit of degrees of seriousness; they were all equally serious. Patrick Boyle, "Parvitas Materiae in Sexto," in *Contemporary Catholic Thought* (Lanham, Md.: University Press of America, 1987), pp. 2–3.

3. Quoted in Eli Zaretsky, "Female Sexuality and the Catholic Confessional," in *Women, Sex, and Sexuality*, ed. Catherine R. Stimpson and Ethel Spector Person (Chicago: University of Chicago Press, 1980), p. 327.

4. Ibid., p. 333.

5. For those who still do not accept our arguments, it may be of interest that in the summer of 1995 the Vatican issued a statement in which it accepted its complicity in certain historical practices that oppressed women.

6. See the discussion of the views of the Thornhills in Chapter 5: Rape and Collective Responsibility.

7. In the most recent version of the *Catechism of the Catholic Church* (Liguori, Mo.: Liguori Publications, 1994), para. 1455, p. 365, it is stressed that some sort of "reconciliation" with others is called for. It is not clear to us how the new version of the catechism has changed the practice of confession. In any event, when we were growing up this kind of "reconciliation" was never mentioned.

8. Erik Berggren, *The Psychology of Confession* (Leiden: E. J. Brill, 1975), p. 8.

9. Michel Foucault provides an analysis of Catholic confession that is in some respects similar to ours, but Foucault draws conclusions about the notion of truth and eschews explicitly moral and social critique. See the first section of *The History of Sexuality*, vol. 1 (New York: Vintage Books, 1978), pp. 17ff., as well as 59ff.

10. Ibid., p. 20.

11. Blu Greenberg, "Female Sexuality and Bodily Functions in the Jewish Tradition," in *Women, Religion, and Sexuality*, ed. Jeanne Becher (Philadelphia: Trinity Press International, 1990), pp. 30–32.

12. See Riffat Hassan, "An Islamic Perspective," ibid., esp. pp. 117-18.

13. See Michael Kimmel, "Masculinity as Homophobia," in *Theorizing Masculinities*, ed. Harry Brod and Michael Kaufman Sage (Thousand Oaks, Calif.: 1994). The latitude afforded dominant heterosexual identity is also expressed in the concern about transgression. The idea of male sexual aggressiveness establishes a certain latitude for action, but this aggressiveness must then be harnessed in conventional gender roles. Confession establishes permissions (of public actions) and prohibitions (of deviant heterosexual identity and sexual orientation).

14. In some respects, the phenomenon we are discussing is not unique to Catholicism. Any form of sexual socialization that relies on an operant moral code could function somewhat similarly. But the unique feature of Catholic sexual socialization is reliance on the legitimating act of confessing.

15. In this sense Foucault is correct in seeing the confessional as a social technology of power. See the section "Scientia Sexualis," in *The History of Sexuality*, 1:53–73.

16. Stephen Haliczer documents the large number of cases of sexual solicitation of penitents by priests in the confessional well into the nineteenth century. The practice was so common that Protestant anticlerics contended that the demand for sexual explicitness during confession was only a pretext for sexual solicitation. See Stephen Haliczer, *Sexuality in the Confessional: A Sacrament Profaned* (New York: Oxford University Press, 1996).

17. Charles Taylor, *Sources of the Self* (Cambridge: Harvard University Press, 1989), p. 28.

18. The conception of moral space is also useful for articulating the differences between our views of the confession and Foucault's. We accept Foucault's main insight that power is not merely restrictive and that confession stimulates discourse about sexuality. But it does so in order to articulate a moral space of evaluations, in which prohibitions also establish permissions and constraints also enable other actions as well as facilitate domination over others.

19. For more discussion of this point see Chapter 5: Rape and Collective Responsibility.

20. "Men are suffering right now—young men especially." Bly, *Iron John*, p. 27.

21. Mark Gerzon, *A Choice of Heroes* (New York: Houghton Mifflin, 1982), p. vii. It should be said that Gerzon at least broaches the subject of what it would mean for men to blame themselves instead of others.

22. R. William Betcher and William S. Pollack, *In a Time of Fallen Heroes* (New York: Atheneum, 1993), pp. 1 and 4.

23. Hudson and Jacot, *The Way Men Think*, p. viii. Also see p. xi where the authors say that men should not be apologetic about their sexual aggressiveness.

24. Ibid., p. 135.

25. See Robert Moore and Douglas Gillette, *The Warrior Within: Accessing the Knight in the Male Psyche* (New York: William Morrow, 1992). On p. x, they say: "There is no way to socialize aggression away. The Warrior archetype is hard-wired into our brain structure. . . . With a growing sense of what masculinity entails, men today are claiming their birthright Warrior energy."

26. We are by no means the first to notice the similarity between Catholic and psychoanalytic confession. Among many others we would especially note the treatment of this topic by Foucault in *The History of Sexuality*, vol. 1; and by Berggren in *The Psychology of the Confession*.

27. For an account of what this involves see Chapter 8: A Progressive Male Standpoint.

28. In the next section of this chapter we describe this alternative form of confession.

29. Taylor, *Sources of the Self*, p. 462 and also p. 463.

30. John Stoltenberg, *Refusing to be a Man* (New York: Meridian Books, 1990). It is interesting that Stoltenberg couches his confessional discourse in a way that makes it stand for all men. This representative group confessional mode is becoming more common. For a very good example of progressive confessional writing, in many different voices, we would recommend the books that have originated in the writings of the Achilles Heel Collective, a men's group that has published a journal in London since 1978. See Andy Metcalf and Martin Humphries, eds., *The Sexuality of Men* (London: Pluto Press, 1985); Victor J. Seidler, ed., *The Achilles Heel Reader* (London: Routledge, 1991); Victor J. Seidler, ed. *Men, Sex, and Relationships* (London: Routledge, 1992).

31. Stoltenberg, *Refusing to Be a Man*, p. 5.

32. Ibid., pp. 24 and 17.

33. Ibid., p. 39.

34. See Chapter 8: A Progressive Male Standpoint.

35. See May and Strikwerda, "Fatherhood and Nurturance," pp. 28–39; and Strikwerda and May, "Male Friendship and Intimacy," pp. 110–25. Both essays are reprinted in *Rethinking Masculinity*, ed. May et al.

36. We do not mean to imply that consciousness raising must take on the confessional mode of discourse. Indeed, in early feminist consciousness raising in the

middle of the twentieth century, people were not shamed but rather accepted for who they were. We find this form of consciousness raising less valuable for men than it was for women. Men have been told for too long that their sexually aggressive behavior was acceptable, whereas women had hardly ever been told that their sexual behavior was acceptable.

Chapter 4. Pornography and Pollution

1. Unless noted in the text, whenever I refer to pornography this is meant to include only heterosexual pornography. See the last section of the chapter, where I address some forms of homosexual pornography.

2. I take these definitions from Joel Feinberg's well-known discussion of obscenity and pornography in *Offense to Others* (Oxford: Oxford University Press, 1985), p. 127.

3. My focus on the negative effects that pornography has on male sexuality is not meant to diminish the negative effects that pornography obviously has had on women, as should become clear as I rehearse and at least partially endorse various feminist critiques of pornography.

4. Seymour Feshbach and Neal M. Malamuth, "Sex and Aggression: Proving the Link," *Psychology Today* 12 (November 1978), cited in Pauline B. Bart and Margaret Jozsa, "Dirty Books, Dirty Films, and Dirty Data," in *Take Back the Night*, ed. Laura Lederer (New York: William Morrow, 1980), p. 215.

5. Dolf Zillman and Jennings Bryant, "Pornography, Sexual Callousness, and the Trivialization of Rape," *Journal of Communication* (Autumn 1982), reprinted in *Men Confront Pornography*, ed. Michael S. Kimmel (New York: Meridian Books, 1990), p. 213.

6. Edward Donnerstein and Daniel Linz, "Mass Media, Sexual Violence, and Male Viewers: Current Theory and Research," *American Behavioral Scientist* 29 (May–June 1986), reprinted in *Men Confront Pornography*, ed. Kimmel, p. 221.

7. Berl Kutchinsky, "Legalized Pornography in Denmark," in *Men Confront Pornography*, ed. Kimmel, pp. 244–45.

8. A large number of studies were conducted in the wake of the Meese Commission. This 1985 Attorney General's Commission on Pornography had concluded that there is a causal relationship between exposure to many forms of pornography and increased violence toward women. The majority of studies disputed the findings of the Meese Commission, claiming that the attorney general's own data did not establish this conclusion and that studies show no such causal relationship. See B. L. Wilcox, "Pornography Social Science, and Politics: When Research and Ideology Collide," *American Psychologist*, 42 (1987): 941–43; M. K. Condron and D. E. Nutter, "A Preliminary Examination of the Pornographic Experience of Sex Offenders, Paraphiliacs, Sexual Dysfunctional Patients, and Controls Based on Meese Commission Recommendations," *Journal of Sex and Marital Therapy* 14 (1988): 285–98; and W. A. Fischer and G. J. Greneir, "Violent Pornography, Antiwoman Thoughts, and Antiwoman Acts: In Search of Reliable Effects," *Journal of Sex Research* 31 (1994): pp. 23–38. For evidence that supports the Meese Commission, see C. E. Koop, "Report of the Surgeon General's Workshop on Pornography and Public

Health," *American Psychologist* 42 (1987): 944–45; and E. K. Sommers and J. V. Check, "An Empirical Investigation of the Role of Pornography in the Verbal and Physical Abuse of Women," *Violence and Victims* 2 (1987): 189–209.

9. Joel Feinberg, *Harm to Others* (Oxford: Oxford University Press, 1984), pp. 105–6, 54.

10. Ibid., p. 54.

11. Feinberg does distinguish harms from evils, where an evil may be said to occur to a person regardless of whether he or she was harmed, that is, whether her or his interests were set back. He cites as his chief example "prolonged states of intolerably intense pain." These can be considered evils even if they do not set back an interest. Feinberg also talks about the "ulterior interest in not undergoing torture even when the experience is not harmful as measured by its effects on other interests." For these reasons Feinberg could embrace something like my notion of non-relativistic harm, as long as it was not called a harm proper. But he does not seem to admit ulterior interests that do not extend to all members of the human race. In this respect our views will still differ. See Feinberg's brief discussion of this point in *Harm to Others*, p. 49.

12. See the fascinating analysis of a similar case in Irving Thalberg and Deborah Pellow, "Imagining Alternatives," *Philosophical Forum* 11 (Fall 1979).

13. For a representative critique of the view I am defending, see Alan H. Goldman, *Justice and Reverse Discrimination* (Princeton: Princeton University Press, 1979), chap. 3.

14. See Larry May and Marilyn Friedman, "Harming Women as a Group," *Social Theory and Practice* 11 (Summer 1985): 207–34. Also see May, *The Morality of Groups*, chap. 6.

15. In some cases, one corporation may adversely affect the profitability and hence the assets of another corporation by falsely describing a competitor's product. See my discussion of one such case that eventually made it to the Supreme Court in 1982, in *The Morality of Groups*, Chap. 2.

16. The United States Supreme Court applies a standard of strict scrutiny to race and ethnicity and seems to be moving toward regarding gender this way as well. Viewing something with strict scrutiny means that the burden of proof shifts to the state to show that it has a compelling interest in a goal that can be achieved only by discriminating against people on the basis of one of these categories.

17. William Prosser and W. Page Keeton, *On Torts*, 5th ed. (St. Paul: West 1984), p. 784.

18. Catharine MacKinnon, "Pornography, Civil Rights, and Speech," *Harvard Civil Rights–Civil Liberties Law Review* 20 (1985); Rae Langton, "Speech Acts and Unspeakable Acts," *Philosophy and Public Affairs* 22 (Fall 1993). There is another, less plausible philosophical defense of MacKinnon's claim provided by Melinda Vadas, "A First Look at the Pornography/Civil Rights Ordinance: Could Pornography Be the Subordination of Women?" *Journal of Philosophy* 84 (September 1987). A sympathetic but critical response to Vadas is W. A. Parent, "A Second Look at Pornography and the Subordination of Women," *Journal of Philosophy* 87 (April 1990).

19. Langton, "Speech Acts," p. 305.

20. Ibid., p. 311.

21. Ibid., p. 307.

22. Ibid., p. 312.

23. Cass R. Sunstein, "Words, Conduct, Caste," *University of Chicago Law Review* 60 (Summer–Fall 1993).

24. Article IV of the Constitution guaranteed that fugitive slaves would be returned to their owner's state where the owner could pursue legal action to regain them. There is no comparable provision of the Constitution concerning gender relations.

25. See Chapter 5: Rape and Collective Responsibility.

26. See Chapter 6: Sexual Harassment and Solidarity.

27. I will henceforth use the term "nonegalitarian pornography" to refer to pornography that portrays men in dominant positions and women in subordinate positions in that it is men's pleasure that is the focus of the pornography, and if women's pleasure is a focus at all, it is only secondary to men's pleasure. By contrast egalitarian pornography is pornography that does not make a woman's pleasure secondary to a man's pleasure.

28. I also contend that men's status is harmed by nonegalitarian forms of pornography.

29. In a very interesting study, "Women's Attitudes and Fantasies about Rape as a Function of Early Exposure to Pornography," *Journal of Interpersonal Violence* 7 (1992): 454–61, S. Corne and colleagues contend that women's positive attitudes toward sexual violence against women are influenced by early exposure to pornography.

30. I discuss later in this chapter how women are consigned to see themselves as restricted to only certain roles.

31. See Lucy Candib and Richard Schmitt, "About Losing It: The Fear of Impotence," in *Rethinking Masculinity*, 2d ed., ed. May et al.

32. The harms to men from repeated exposure to nonegalitarian forms of pornography are not as severe as harms to women, since men are consigned to roles of dominance, whereas women are consigned to roles of submission. But insofar as egalitarian sexual options are restricted, both men and women are harmed.

33. A good discussion of the subliminal effects of a variety of factors in the processing of information is provided in Norman F. Dixon, *Preconscious Processing* (New York: John Wiley and Sons, 1981).

34. Daniel I. A. Cohen, "The Hate That Dare Not Speak Its Name," *Law and Philosophy* 13 (1994): 236–37.

35. In this analysis I have been influenced by Joel Feinberg's treatment of cumulative harms in *Harm to Others*, pp. 225–32.

36. See Berl Kutchinsky, "The Effects of Easy Availability of Pornography on the Incidence of Sex Crimes: The Danish Experience," *Journal of Social Issues* 29 (1973): 163–81.

37. This approach follows the line of Supreme Court cases that leave it up to individual communities to set standards of obscenity.

38. MacKinnon describes these efforts in "Pornography, Civil Rights, and Speech."

39. Arthur W. H. Adkins, *Merit and Responsibility* (Oxford: Clarendon Press, 1960), p. 86.

40. Ibid., pp. 86–88.

41. Devlin does not, to the best of my knowledge, use the term "pollution." But his many discussions of how an entire society is affected by the morally corrupt attitudes of some of its members is clearly consistent with a concept of moral pollution.

42. Patrick Devlin, *The Enforcement of Morals* (Oxford: Oxford University Press, 1965), p. 11.

43. Ibid., p. 115.

44. H. L. A. Hart, *Law, Liberty, and Morality* (Stanford: Stanford University Press, 1963), p. 72.

45. Ibid., p. 70.

46. This is not to suggest that certain nonegalitarian forms of homosexual pornography are not harmful to relations between the sexes and within each gender group.

Chapter 5. Rape and Collective Responsibility

1. This paragraph is based on my experience growing up in upper-middle-class suburban U.S. society. My experiences and Bob's differ somewhat in this respect, but these experiences are common among men that we know.

2. Tony Post et al., "A Pattern of Rape," *Newsweek*, January 4, 1993, 32–36.

3. Susan Brownmiller, "Making Female Bodies the Battlefield." *Newsweek*, 4 January 1993, 37.

4. Catharine A. MacKinnon, "Turning Rape into Pornography: Postmodern Genocide," *Ms.* (July–August, 1993), p. 30

5. There is a fifth response, namely, that women alone are somehow responsible for being raped. This response will be largely ignored in our essay since we regard it as merely another case of "blaming the victim." See Diana Scully, *Understanding Sexual Violence* (Boston: Unwin Hyman, 1990), for a critical discussion of this response. Undoubtedly there are yet other responses. We have tried to focus our attention on the most common responses we have seen in the literature on rape.

6. Joyce Carol Oates, "Rape and the Boxing Ring," *Newsweek* February 24, 1992, 60.

7. Ibid., p. 61.

8. *St. Louis Post Dispatch*, March 27, 1992, 20A.

9. See Chapter 3: Sexuality and Confession.

10. See Susan Griffin, "Rape: The All-American Crime," *Ramparts*, (September 1971): 26–35, reprinted in *Women and Values: Readings in Feminist Philosophy*, ed. Marilyn Pearsall (Belmont, Calif.: Wadsworth, 1986), pp. 176–88.

11. Oates, "Rape and the Boxing Ring," p. 61.

12. Later in this chapter, section III, we explain who is responsible for this socialization pattern. Socialization is one of the main foci of the next two chapters as well.

13. See the analysis of this concept in section III of Chapter 4: Pornography and Pollution.

14. Robert Lipsyte, "An Ethics Trial: Must Boys Always Be Boys," *New York Times*, March 12, 1993, B-11, reports that the defense attorney used just these words to defend the star high school football players who raped a retarded girl in Glen Ridge, New Jersey. Also see Myriam Miedzian, *Boys Will Be Boys: Breaking the Link between Masculinity and Violence* (New York: Doubleday, 1991).

15. For more discussion of the mixed messages boys are given, see Chapter 3: Sexuality and Confession.

16. Post et al., "Pattern of Rape," p. 32.

17. Robin Warshaw, *I Never Called It Rape*, (New York: Harper and Row, 1988), describes a study of college men and women which indicates that one in eight college women had been forced to have sex against her will, more than two-thirds by men the women knew. One in twelve college men admitted to having committed acts meeting the legal definition of rape.

18. Studies, cited in Griffin, "Rape," p. 178, show that the average rapist is not psychologically "abnormal."

19. Studies, cited in Scully, *Understanding Sexual Violence*, p. 75, indicate that rapists "seemed not to differ markedly from the majority of males in our culture."

20. Randy Thornhill and Nancy Wilmsen Thornhill, "The Evolutionary Psychology of Men's Coercive Sexuality," *Behavioral and Brain Sciences*, 15 (1992).

21. Ibid., p. 363.

22. Ibid., p. 366.

23. Ibid., p. 364.

24. Ibid., p. 416.

25. Ibid.

26. Ibid., p. 375.

27. Ibid., p. 407.

28. Lionel Tiger, *Men in Groups* (New York: Marion Boyars, 1984), pp. 158–59.

29. Ibid., p. 159.

30. Ibid.

31. Ibid., pp. 159–60.

32. Ibid., p. 81.

33. Preface, ibid., n.p.

34. Ibid., and p. 191.

35. Ibid. pp. 191–92 and elsewhere.

36. Peggy Reeves Sanday, "Rape and the Silencing of the Feminine," in *Rape: An Historical and Social Enquiry*, ed. Sylvana Tomaselli and Roy Porter (Oxford: Basil Blackwell, 1986), p. 85; also see Sanday, "Androcentric and Matrifocal Gender Representation in Minangkabau Ideology," and Maria Lepowsky, "Gender in an Egalitarian Society," in *Beyond the Second Sex*, ed. Sanday and Ruth Gallagher Goodenough (Philadelphia: University of Pennsylvania Press, 1990).

37. Sam Keen, *Fire in the Belly* (New York: Bantam Books, 1991), p. 47.

38. Ibid.

39. This is not to say that violence is the only source of socialization that produces the rape culture. We discuss other sources in later sections of the chapter.

40. Women contribute to adult male socialization as well, but studies such as Tiger's indicate that adult male influence on other males is far stronger with regard to attitudes toward rape.

41. To say that men benefit from the rape culture does not mean that this is part of an intentional plan on the part of men, as we will explain later in the chapter.

42. We are not necessarily putting Keen in this camp.

43. See May, *Sharing Responsibility*, esp. chap. 2.

44. Ibid.

45. See May, *Morality of Groups*, esp. chaps. 2 and 4.

46. Recall the study referred to in the previous chapter where 50 percent of college men said they would rape if they thought they wouldn't get caught.

47. Scully, *Understanding Sexual Violence*, pp. 162–63

48. The full argument in support of this admittedly controversial claim is supplied in the second chapter of May, *Sharing Responsibility*.

49. Timothy Beneke, *Men on Rape* (New York: St. Martin's Press, 1982), p. 170. In his fascinating study of the climate of rape in American culture, Beneke also reports as one of his conclusions that the fear of rape at night "inhibits the freedom of the eye, hurts women economically, undercuts women's independence, destroys solitude, and restricts expressiveness." Such curtailments of freedom, he argues, "must be acknowledged as part of the crime."

50. Jill Radford, "Policing Male Violence, Policing Women," in *Women, Violence, and Social Control*, ed. Jalna Hanmer and Mary Maynard (Atlantic Highlands, N.J.: Humanities Press, 1987), p. 33.

51. Of course, men accrue most of the benefit inadvertently, and for this reason, the responsibility they also accrue is relatively small. But here we do have a case of responsibility that is not necessarily connected to causation. On this general topic, see the lengthy discussions of responsibility without causation in May, *Sharing Responsibility*, chap. 2.

52. See Charlotte Bunch, "Women's Rights as Human Rights: Toward a Revisioning of Human Rights," *Human Rights Quarterly* 12 (November 1990), reprinted in *Applied Ethics: A Multicultural Approach*, ed. Larry May and Shari Sharrat (Englewood Cliffs, N.J.: Prentice-Hall, 1994), pp. 41–50. Also see MacKinnon, "Turning Rape into Pornography."

53. See Roy Porter, "Does Rape Have a Historical Meaning?" in *Rape*, ed. Tomaselli and Porter, pp. 222–223.

54. The European Community's preliminary investigation into the reports of widespread rapes of Muslim women by Serbian soldiers in Bosnia concluded that "rape is part of a pattern of abuse, usually perpetrated with the conscious intention of demoralizing and terrorizing communities, driving them from their homes and demonstrating the power of the invading forces. Viewed in this way, rape cannot be seen as incidental to the main purpose of the aggression but as serving a strategic purpose in itself." *St. Louis Post-Dispatch*, January 9, 1993, 8A.

55. See Susan Rae Peterson, "Coercion and Rape: The State as a Male Protection Racket," in *Feminism and Philosophy*, ed. Mary Vetterling Braggin, Frederick Elliston, and Jane English (Totowa, N.J.: Littlefield, Adams, 1977), pp. 360–71.

56. See Claudia Card, "Rape as a Terrorist Institution," in *Violence, Terrorism, and Justice*, ed. R. G. Frey and Christopher Morris (New York: Cambridge University Press, 1991).

57. Carolyn M. Shafer and Marilyn Frye, "Rape and Respect," in *Feminism and Philosophy*, ed. Vetterling-Braggin et al.

58. Here is a possible sixth basis for thinking that men are responsible for rape. It was not identified as a separate category earlier because, to a large extent, it depends on several of the other bases.

59. We would also recommend recent essays by philosophers who are trying to come to terms with their masculinity. See our essay on friendship, Strikwerda and May, "Male Friendship and Intimacy." Also see LaFollette, "Real Men."

Chapter 6. Sexual Harrassment and Solidarity

1. I do not mean to dismiss the difficulty of distinguishing innocent pranks from those that constitute harassment. But I will sidestep this question and employ examples that seem clearly to be more than innocent pranks.

2. Throughout this chapter I use the term "solidarity" to refer to the phenomenon first discussed theoretically by Emil Durkheim as "cohesiveness within a group." See chap. 2, "Solidarity and Moral Support," in May, *The Socially Responsive Self.*

3. *Alexander v. Yale University*, 459 F.Supp. 1 (D. Conn. 1977), 631 F.2d 178 (2d Cir. 1980). The courts ruled the case moot since the student had already graduated and other students were not clearly adversely affected by the harassment of one of their friends.

4. I am assuming that female students generally do not want to have their sexuality become a basis for academic success. Cynics might dispute this assumption, but I have never met a female student who took such a cynical view.

5. John C. Hughes and Larry May, "Sexual Harassment," *Social Theory and Practice* 6 (Fall 1980).

6. See Larry May and John C. Hughes, "Is Sexual Harassment Coercive?" in *Moral Rights in the Workplace*, ed. Gertrude Ezorsky (Albany: State University of New York Press, 1987). One of the main problems is that the woman no longer has at least one choice she had before, namely, to be regarded just as a student. Even if she doesn't mind being seen as a sex object, there is a problem in that her position in an academic community is being defined in a way over which she has no control.

7. Laurence Thomas, "On Sexual Offers and Threats," in *Moral Rights in the Workplace*, ed. Ezorsky, p. 125.

8. Ibid., p. 126.

9. Ibid.

10. For instance, Peter may be motivated to look more or less favorably on Deborah's job performance based on how well they are getting along sexually. There is another way to view this whole business that I also find helpful. It might be that the mutually trusting relationship that Peter and Deborah had is now shattered

because neither can now trust the other to be "objective" about work-related matters. I am grateful to Ed Soule for providing this complemetary way of seeing the damage that is done merely by Peter making the offer.

11. See my discussion of the harm that occurs when options are restricted in section II: Conceptualizing Harm, in Chapter 4.

12. This doctrine was first embraced, by a unanimous Supreme Court, in *Meritor Savings Bank v. Vinson*, 477 U.S. 57, 106 S.Ct. 2399, 91 L.Ed.2d 49 (1986).

13. *Harris v. Forklift Systems, Inc.* 114 S.Ct. 367 (1993).

14. Ibid.

15. This is a quotation from the Eleventh Circuit Court of Appeals ruling in *Henson v. Dundee*, quoted by Chief Justice William Rehnquist in *Meritor Savings Bank v. Vinson.*

16. Esther Nevarez, who counsels employers for the New Jersey Division of Civil Rights, put the point quite well when she said that such behavior "affects the esprit de corps in an office because it eliminates certain groups of people from participating." She was quoted in Trip Gabriel, "New Issue at Work: On-Line Sex Sites," *New York Times*, June 27, 1996, B4.

17. See my discussion of this point in May, *The Morality of Groups.*

18. Both the case of the mechanic and that of the graduate student are based on examples of which I have had personal experience.

19. This hypothetical case is loosely based on several actual cases I have heard about in the last ten years.

20. This is not to say that nothing morally suspicious has occurred here. The case I have described clearly involves an abuse of power by the bisexual harasser.

21. Kevin McDermott, "Same-Sex Suit Pits Man vs. Male Boss," *St. Louis Post-Dispatch*, October 13, 1996, D1, 11.

22. I explain why each of these components is an important element of solidarity in May, *The Socially Responsive Self*, chap. 2.

23. There may indeed be competition for various goods, such as rewards or raises, but the main goods at stake in workplace and educational contexts are like health in that they are best garnered through cooperative methods since the size and extent of the good is dependent on working together.

24. Carol McGraw and Mike Eisenbath, "God's Guys," *St. Louis Post-Dispatch*, June 28, 1995, E1, 5.

25. For a rich account of this movement, and a devastating critique of their practices, see Clatterbaugh, *Contemporary Perspectives on Masculinity*, chap. 9.

26. I take up this theme in greater detail in the next chapter, Chapter 7: "Socialization and Separatism."

Chaper 7. Socialization and Separatism

1. In the Citadel's promotional material, "An Overview of the Citadel: Everything You Need to Know About the Citadel, the Military College of South Carolina," an explicit comparison is made between the historical success of women who attended all-women colleges and the success of the men who have attended the Citadel.

2. Susan Faludi, "The Naked Citadel," *New Yorker*, September 5, 1994, 62–81.

3. This is not to say that there are no spheres inhabited only by women. But it is to say that there are few if any spheres which are designed to provide trials by which a girl proves that she is now, or is becoming, a woman.

4. Similar arguments were used to justify the exclusion of women from liberal arts colleges. I started college at Georgetown University in the very first class to admit women to the College of Arts and Sciences. Despite dire warnings, women did not disrupt classes or unduly distract the male students. As far as I can tell, the environment did change, but clearly for the better. This has also been the overwhelming view of faculty and students at the three U.S. military academies since they began admitting women over a decade ago.

5. As Susan Faludi points out in "The Naked Citadel," there were lots of women at the Citadel. All the cafeteria servers are women; there are female faculty members; female students attend the night division; and there are female administrative and clerical support staff in great numbers.

6. The term is meant to imply that learning is accomplished through confrontation with and opposition by one's fellow cadets. As we will see, the confrontations are often violent.

7. *United States v. Commonwealth of Virginia (VMI)*, 766 F.Supp. 1407 (W.D.Va. 1991) at 1421.

8. Ibid., at 1424.

9. Ibid., at 1422.

10. Only 30 percent of Citadel graduates enter military service, according to the Citadel's own promotional material, "An Overview of the Citadel."

11. *United States v. Commonwealth of Virginia*, at 1438. Notice that the term "honor" is being used in an odd way if one's honor would be destroyed when others could not see you. Typically the expression "being on your honor" means that you will be trusted regardless of whether you are in view or not.

12. David Gilmore, *Manhood in the Making: Cultural Concepts of Masculinity* (New Haven: Yale University Press, 1990), esp. pp. 12–20.

13. For a discussion of these issues from a variety of perspectives, see Amy Gutman, ed., *Multiculturalism: Examining the Politics of Recognition* (Princeton: Princeton University Press, 1994.)

14. For a good discussion of the value of lesbian separatist communities, see Sarah Lucia Hoagland, "Separating from Heterosexualism," in *Feminism and Community*, ed. Penny Weiss and Marilyn Friedman (Philadelphia: Temple University Press, 1995), pp. 273–91.

15. See Alisdair MacIntyre's treatment of this topic in the final pages of *After Virtue* (Notre Dame, Ind.: University of Notre Dame Press, 1981).

16. McGraw and Eisenbath, "God's Guys." See the previous chapter, "Sexual Harassment and Solidarity," for a more detailed discussion of this example.

17. The greatest work on this topic is John Stuart Mill, *On Liberty* (1859); Indianapolis: Hackett, 1978). I have partially followed Mill in my account of the value of diversity. Mill goes further than I do in insisting that diversity has a value

in almost every case, primarily because it allows for a confrontation with the power of uniformity. I remain skeptical that mere diversity has this effect. If the diverse perspective is ridiculous, for instance, it will not necessarily confront the power of uniformity.

18. Excerpts from *United States v. Virginia*, printed in the *New York Times*, June 27, 1996, C18. Since the Citadel case was so similar to the VMI case, the Citadel has announced that it will begin changing to an academy that admits both men and women.

19. See Susan Faludi's discussion of these themes in "The Naked Citadel."

20. For many years Ivy League schools produced civic, military, and business leaders in an all-male setting that did not involve adversative socialization. Several all-male schools, Wabash College being the best known, continue to produce strong community leaders without employing adversative socialization. Such facts call into question the necessity of adversative socialization for the production of strong male leaders.

21. See Chapter 5: Rape and Collective Responsibility.

22. See Susan Moller Okin, *Justice, Gender, and the Family* (New York: Basic Books, 1989), pp. 153–55, for a summary of the data on this topic.

23. See Myra Sadker and David Sadker, *Failing at Fairness: How America's Schools Cheat Girls* (New York: Charles Scribner's Sons, 1994), esp. pp. 208–13 and 85–86.

24. In 1996 a women-only professional basketball league was formed, and women-only professional softball teams have surfaced as well.

25. Anne Marie Wittemore, "Single Gender Education and the Constitution," *Loyola Law Review* 40 (1994): 261–62.

26. Overt threats and vicious verbal abuse greeted Faulkner. Her home was spray painted with graffiti, and firecrackers were thrown onto her front lawn. Bumper stickers and posters referring to Faulkner as a "bitch" or a "bovine" were disseminated throughout the state by alumni groups. Female faculty members have been subjected to similar forms of harassment for years. See Faludi, "Naked Citadel," pp. 70–72. Two other women admitted to the Citadel soon after were also sexually harassed. Several male cadets admitted their involvement in the harassment and intimidation of the female cadets and were punished.

27. See Strikwerda and May, "Male Friendship and Intimacy," p. 118. The suggestion that the term "conversative" is connected to "converse" is not meant to be historically grounded. Various dictionaries indicate that there once was a use of conversative that was connected to conversation.

28. I have played racketball and squash in this way for the past twenty years. Each new partner I have had has expressed reluctance to give up keeping score and other trappings of competitive play, but each of my partners has also come to embrace the cooperative style of play and to prefer it.

29. It is common for elite athletes to say that they are competing against their own previous best times or games.

30. At VMI, the first-year students are called rats to let them know that they are the lowest members of the academy. See Juliette Kayyem, "The Search for Citizen

Soldiers: Female Cadets and the Campaign against the Virginia Military Institute," *Harvard Civil Rights–Civil Liberties Law Review*, 30 (1995): 247–49.

31. On this general topic, see May, "Legal Advocacy," chap. 8 of *The Socially Responsive Self.*

32. See the fascinating discussion of the importance of instilling a sense of positive reciprocity as a way of combating hatred and prejudice in Ervin Staub, *The Roots of Evil: The Origins of Genocide and Other Group Violence* (Cambridge: Cambridge University Press, 1989), esp. pp. 259–60 and 281–84.

33. See Strikwerda and May, "Male Friendship and Intimacy," esp. pp. 120–23.

34. See section V, Inclusion and Male Solidarity, in Chapter 6: Sexual Harassment and Solidarity.

35. See section II, The Testosterone Excuse, in Chapter 1: Anger, Desire, and Moral Responsibility.

36. For more discussion of my views about socialization, see May, *The Socially Responsive Self*, chap. 4.

37. See Chapter 3: Sexuality and Confession.

38. See Chapter 6: Sexual Harassment and Solidarity.

39. Again see Faludi, "Naked Citadel," for many examples of this sort.

40. For a defense of this form of channeling, see David Blankenhorn, *Fatherless America* (New York: Basic Books, 1994), esp. pp. 116–17.

Chapter 8. A Progressive Male Standpoint

1. Unlike some in the feminist standpoint movement, I will use the term "standpoint" in a fairly broad way to cover considerations of both knowledge and practice. Indeed, I use the term standpoint as a rough equivalent for situated knowledge, contrary to some of the main adherents of feminist standpoint epistemology.

2. Sandra Harding has developed a feminist standpoint epistemology that shares many features with the view I articulate. Among her many writings on this topic, I recommend "Rethinking Standpoint Epistemology: 'What Is Strong Objectivity?' " in *Feminist Epistemologies*, ed. by Linda Alcoff and Elizabeth Potter (New York: Routledge, 1993). Alcoff and Potter's introduction to this collection, gives a good, brief overview of the general projects that fall under the label of feminist epistemology. See esp. pp. 1–4.

3. Many women who are feminists wish to reserve the label "feminist" for women's progressive views of gender, whereas some other women are willing to use the label "feminist" in a broader way to describe progressive views of gender by both women and men. Not wanting to enter into the merits of the positions in this debate, I have chosen simply to use the label "progressive" rather than "feminist" for the view of masculinity I describe, but I believe that my view could also legitimately be called "feminist."

4. One of my personal favorites is Iris Young, *Throwing Like a Girl and Other Essays in Feminist Philosophy and Social Theory* (Bloomington: Indiana University Press, 1990), which has wonderful essays on being pregnant, having breasts, and throwing like a girl.

5. A progressive male standpoint also here has some features in common with what feminists mean by standpoint epistemology, where the standpoint of the knower, his or her experiences and biases, are crucial for the status of the knowledge alleged.

6. In some cases, personal experience can blind one to what is really going on, as when one regards one's experiences as self-certifying. A man who has been discriminated against may feel that this experience gives him an insight into all forms of discrimination. As I will explain later, there is always a need for critical reflection on this experiential base before experience can be a legitimate source of understanding.

7. One of the best and most accessible accounts of this view is put forth by Bertrand Russell in *The Problems of Philosophy* (1912; Oxford: Oxford University Press, 1970).

8. For a good discussion of moral saliency, see Barbara Herman, "The Practice of Moral Judgment," in her book *The Practice of Moral Judgment* (Cambridge: Harvard University Press, 1993).

9. W. V. Quine, an otherwise model behaviorist, allows that introspection is an important source of data. See Roger Gibson, *The Philosophy of W. V. Quine* (Tampa: University of South Florida Press, 1986), pp. 195–96.

10. At least in part this has to do with limits on our attention spans. But also it has to do with limitations on sustaining an idea which was itself based on something not very vivid.

11. Nancy Hartsock, "The Feminist Standpoint: Developing the Ground for a Specifically Feminist Historical Materialism," in *Feminism and Methodology*, ed. Sandra Harding (Bloomington: Indiana University Press, 1987).

12. In a later section I argue that a person who has been subject to oppression may have an easier time achieving a progressive standpoint than someone who has not had this experience. On first sight, this might appear to be a bias that one must have, as opposed to what I have just said about eliminating biases. But as will become clear, being a member of an oppressed group does not give one a bias so much as it eliminates various biases.

13. See Hartsock, "Feminist Standpoint."

14. I here assume that women will not be biased against male experience more than men are biased in favor of it. Men have a clear self-interested basis for favoring their own experience. Women do not have a correspondingly strong interest in disfavoring male experience.

15. I am grateful to Ed Soule for help with this point.

16. See my discussion of this point at the end of Chapter 5: Rape and Collective Responsibility.

17. For a good discussion of the motivational dimension of morality, and the debate between those who think that motivation is internal and those who think it is external to moral judgments, see David Brink, *Moral Realism and the Foundation of Ethics* (Cambridge: Cambridge University Press, 1989), chap. 3.

18. I am grateful to Tom Digby for help on this point.

19. Indeed, many studies show that men have trouble expressing their feelings and sustaining intimate relationships even though they want to do so. See Strikwerda and May, "Male Intimacy and Friendship."

20. See Greenspan, *Practical Guilt*, esp. chaps. 1 and 6.

21. There will also be other things that are necessary to end traditional patterns of male socialization. Various collective and institutional efforts will have to go hand in hand with individual men choosing to educate their sons differently. I have discussed some of these collective and institutional changes in previous chapters.

22. See especially May and Strikwerda, "Fatherhood and Nurturance."

23. See Susan Faludi, *Backlash* (New York: Crown, 1991).

24. Some of these points are discussed at greater length in the collection of essays edited by David M. Rosenthal and Fadlou Shehadi, *Applied Ethics and Ethical Theory* (Salt Lake City: University of Utah Press, 1988).

25. There are already a few good books in this domain. Stoltenberg, *Refusing to Be a Man*, is a good example. A new journal, *masculinities*, is also proving to be a good source of new scholarship by men taking a progressive male standpoint. It is interesting, though, that even in this journal, there are as many women as men writing. Indeed, all the articles in the Summer 1995 issrue were written by women.

26. Also see May et al., eds., *Rethinking Masculinity*, for a number of attempts to fill out such a sketch.

27. These are each the subject of chapter-length treatment in earlier parts of this book.

Bibliography

Adkins, Arthur W. H. *Merit and Responsibility*. Oxford: Clarendon Press, 1960.

Alexander v. Yale University, 459 F. Supp. 1 (D. Conn. 1977), 631 F.2d 178 (2d Cir. 1980).

Aristotle. *Nicomachean Ethics*. Translated by Terence Irwin. Indianapolis: Hackett, 1985.

Bar On, Bat-Ami. "Marginality and Epistemic Privilege." In *Feminist Epistemologies*, edited by Linda Alcoff and Elizabeth Potter. New York: Routledge, 1993.

Bart, Pauline B. and Margaret Jozsa. "Dirty Books, Dirty Films, and Dirty Data." In *Take Back the Night*, edited by Laura Lederer. New York: William Morrow, 1980.

Beneke, Timothy. *Men on Rape*. New York: St. Martin's Press, 1982.

Berggren, Erik. *The Psychology of Confession*. Leiden: E. J. Brill, 1975.

Betcher, R. William and William S. Pollack. *In a Time of Fallen Heroes*. New York: Atheneum, 1993.

Blankenhorn, David. *Fatherless America*. New York: Basic Books, 1994.

Bly, Robert. *Iron John*. Reading, Mass.: Addison-Wesley, 1990.

Bordo, Susan. "Reading the Male Body." *Michigan Quarterly Review* (1994): 696–737.

Boyle, Patrick. "Parvitas Materiae in Sexto." In *Contemporary Catholic Thought*. Lanham, Md.: University Press of America, 1987.

Brink, David. *Moral Realism and the Foundation of Ethics*. Cambridge: Cambridge University Press, 1989.

Brownmiller, Susan. "Making Female Bodies the Battlefield." *Newsweek*, 4 January 1993, 37.

Bunch, Charlotte. "Women's Rights as Human Rights: Toward a Revisioning of Human Rights." *Human Rights Quarterly* 12 (November 1990). Reprinted in *Applied Ethics: A Multicultural Approach*, edited by Larry May and Shari Sharrat. Englewood Cliffs, NJ: Prentice-Hall, 1994.

Caban v. Mohammed, 441 U.S. 380 (1979).

Callahan, Daniel. "Bioethics and Fatherhood." *Utah Law Review* 3 (1992): 737.

Candib, Lucy, and Richard Schmitt. "About Losing It: The Fear of Impotence." In *Rethinking Masculinity*, edited by Larry May, Robert Strikwerda, and Patrick Hopkins. 2d ed. Lanham, Md.: Rowman and Littlefield, 1996.

Card, Claudia. "Rape as a Terrorist Institution." *Violence, Terrorism, and Justice*, edited by R. G. Frey and Christopher Morris. New York: Cambridge University Press, 1991.

Catechism of the Catholic Church, Liguori, Mo.: Liguori Publications, 1994.

Clatterbaugh, Kenneth. *Contemporary Perspectives on Masculinity*. 2d ed. Boulder, Colo.: Westview Press, 1997.

Cohen, Daniel I. A. "The Hate That Dare Not Speak Its Name." *Law and Philosophy* 13 (1994): 236–37.

Condron, M. K. and D. E. Nutter, "A Preliminary Examination of the Pornographic Experience of Sex Offenders, Paraphiliacs, Sexual Dysfunctional Patients, and Controls Based on Meese Commission Recommendations." *Journal of Sex and Marital Therapy* 14 (1988): 285–98.

Corne, S., et al. "Women's Attitudes and Fantasies about Rape as a Function of Early Exposure to Pornography." *Journal of Interpersonal Violence* 7 (1992): 454–61.

Devlin, Patrick. *The Enforcement of Morals*. Oxford: Oxford University Press, 1965.

Dixon, Norman F. *Preconscious Processing*. New York: John Wiley and Sons, 1981.

Dolgin, Janet L. "Just a Gene: Judicial Assumptions about Fatherhood." *UCLA Law Review* 40 (1993): 650–52.

Donnerstein, Edward, and Daniel Linz. "Mass Media, Sexual Violence, and Male Viewers: Current Theory and Research." *American Behavioral Scientist* 29 (May–June 1986). Reprinted in *Men Confront Pornography*, edited by Michael S. Kimmel. New York: Meridian Books, 1990.

Faludi, Susan. *Backlash*. New York: Crown, 1991.

——. "The Naked Citadel." *New Yorker*, 5 September 1994, 62–81.

Fausto-Sterling, Anne. *Myths of Gender*. New York: Basic Books, 1992.

——. *Harm to Others*. Oxford: Oxford University Press, 1984.

Feinberg, Joel. ——. *Offense to Others*. Oxford: Oxford University Press, 1985.

Feshbach, Seymour, and Neal M. Malamuth. "Sex and Aggression: Proving the Link." *Psychology Today* 12 (November 1978): 110–22.

Fischer, W. A. and G. J. Greneir, "Violent Pornography, Antiwoman Thoughts, and Antiwoman Acts: In Search of Reliable Effects." *Journal of Sex Research* 31 (1994): 23–38.

Forman, Deborah L. "Unwed Fathers and Adoption: A Theoretical Analysis in Context." *Texas Law Review* 72 (April 1994): 967–1045.

Foucault, Michel. *The History of Sexuality*, vol. 1. New York: Vintage Books, 1978.

Gerzon, Mark. *A Choice of Heroes*. New York: Houghton Mifflin, 1982.

Gibbard, Allan. "Moral Judgment and the Acceptance of Norms." *Ethics* 95 (October 1985): 5–21.

——. *Wise Choices, Apt Feelings*. Cambridge: Harvard University Press, 1990.

Gibson, Roger. *The Philosophy of W. V. Quine*. Tampa: University of South Florida Press, 1986.

Gilmore, David. *Manhood in the Making: Cultural Concepts of Masculinity*. New Haven: Yale University Press, 1990.

Goldman, Alan H. *Justice and Reverse Discrimination*. Princeton: Princeton University Press, 1979.

Greenberg, Blu. "Female Sexuality and Bodily Functions in the Jewish Tradition." In *Women, Religion, and Sexuality*, ed. by Jeanne Becher. Philadelphia: Trinity Press International, 1990.

Greenspan, Patricia. *Practical Guilt*. New York: Oxford University Press, 1995.

Griffin, Susan. "Rape: The All-American Crime." *Ramparts* (September 1971): 26–35. Reprinted in *Women and Values: Readings in Feminist Philosophy*, edited by Marilyn Pearsall. Belmont, Calif.: Wadsworth, 1986.

Gutman, Amy, ed. *Multiculturalism: Examining the Politics of Recognition*. Princeton: Princeton University Press, 1994.

Haliczer, Stephen. *Sexuality in the Confessional: A Sacrament Profaned*. New York: Oxford University Press, 1996.

Harding, Sandra. "Rethinking Standpoint Epistemology: 'What Is Strong Objectivity?' " In *Feminist Epistemologies*, edited by Linda Alcoff and Elizabeth Potter. New York: Routledge, 1993.

Harris, George W. "Fathers and Fetuses." *Ethics* 96 (April 1986): 596.

Harris v. Forklift Systems, Inc. 114 S.Ct. 367 (1993).

Hart, H. L. A. *Law, Liberty, and Morality*. Stanford: Stanford University Press, 1963.

Hartsock, Nancy. "The Feminist Standpoint: Developing the Ground for a Specifically Feminist Historical Materialism." In *Feminism and Methodology*, edited by Sandra Harding. Bloomington: Indiana University Press, 1987.

Hassan, Riffat. "An Islamic Perspective." In *Women, Religion, and Sexuality*, edited by Jeanne Becher. Philadelphia: Trinity Press International, 1990.

Held, Virginia. *Feminist Morality*. Chicago: University of Chicago Press, 1993.

——. "The Obligations of Mothers and Fathers." In *Mothering: Essays in Feminist Theory*, edited by Joyce Trebilcot. Totowa, N.J.: Rowman and Allanheld, 1983.

Herman, Barbara. "The Practice of Moral Judgment." In *The Practice of Moral Judgment*. Cambridge: Harvard University Press, 1993.

Hoagland, Sarah Lucia. "Separating from Heterosexualism." In *Feminism and Community*, edited by Penny Weiss and Marilyn Friedman. Philadelphia: Temple University Press, 1995.

Hudson, Liam, and Bernardine Jacot. *The Way Men Think: Intellect, Intimacy, and the Erotic Imagination*. New Haven: Yale University Press, 1991.

Hughes, John C., and Larry May. "Sexual Harassment." *Social Theory and Practice* 6. (Fall 1980): 249–80.

In Re Raquel Marie X, 559 N. E. 2d 418 (1989).

Jordan, Pat. "Belittled Big Men." *New York Times Magazine*, 10 December 1995, 68–75.

Kayyem, Juliette. "The Search for Citizen Soldiers: Female Cadets and the Campaign against the Virginia Military Institute." *Harvard Civil Rights–Civil Liberties Law Review* 30 (1995): 247–49.

Keen, Sam. *Fire in the Belly*. New York: Bantam Books, 1991.

Kimmel, Michael. "Masculinity as Homophobia." In *Theorizing Masculinities*, edited by Harry Brod and Michael Kaufman. Thousand Oaks, Calif.: Sage, 1994.

Koop, C. E. "Report of the Surgeon General's Workshop on Pornography and Public Health." *American Psychologist* 42 (1987): 944–45.

Kutchinsky, Berl. "The Effects of Easy Availability of Pornography on the Incidence of Sex Crimes: The Danish Experience." *Journal of Social Issues* 29 (1973): 163–181.

——. "Legalized Pornography in Denmark." In *Men Confront Pornography*, edited by Michael S. Kimmel. New York: Meridian Books, 1990.

Lacqueur, Thomas W. "The Facts of Fatherhood." In *Conflicts in Feminism*, edited by Marianne Hirsch and Evelyn Fox Keller. New York: Routledge, 1990.

LaFollette, Hugh. "Licensing Parents," *Philosophy and Public Affairs* 9 (Winter 1980).

——. "Real Men." In *Rethinking Masculinity*, edited by Larry May, Robert Strikwerda, and Patrick Hopkins. 2d ed. Lanham, Md.: Rowman and Littlefield, 1996.

Langton, Rae. "Speech Acts and Unspeakable Acts." *Philosophy and Public Affairs* 22 (Fall 1993): 293–330

Lehr v. Robertson, 463 U.S. 248 (1983).

Lepowsky, Maria. "Gender in an Egalitarian Society." In *Beyond the Second Sex*, edited by Peggy Reeves Sanday and Ruth Gallagher Goodenough. Philadelphia: University of Pennsylvania Press, 1990.

Lipsyte, Robert. "An Ethics Trial: Must Boys Always Be Boys." *New York Times*, 12 March 1993, B11

Long, Vonda Olson. "Relation of Masculinity to Self-Esteem and Self-Acceptance in Male Professionals, College Students, and Clients." *Journal of Counseling Psychology* 36 (1989): 84–87.

McGraw, Carol, and Mike Eisenbath, "God's Guys." *St. Louis Post-Dispatch*, 28 June 1995, E1, 5.

MacIntyre, Alisdair. *After Virtue*. Notre Dame, Ind.: University of Notre Dame Press, 1981.

MacKinnon, Catharine. "Pornography, Civil Rights, and Speech." *Harvard Civil Rights–Civil Liberties Law Review* 20 (1985): 1–70.

——. "Turning Rape into Pornography: Postmodern Genocide." *Ms.* July–August, 1993, 30.

Matsuda, Mari J., Charles R. Lawrence, III, Richard Delgado, and Kimberle Williams Crenshaw. *Words That Wound*. Boulder, Colo.: Westview, 1993.

May, Larry. *The Morality of Groups*. Notre Dame, Ind.: University of Notre Dame Press, 1987.

——. *Sharing Responsibility*. Chicago: University of Chicago Press, 1992.

——. *The Socially Responsive Self*. Chicago: University of Chicago Press, 1996.

May, Larry, and James Bohman. "Masculinity, Sexuality, and Confession." *Hypatia* 12 (Winter 1997): 138–54.

May, Larry, and Marilyn Friedman. "Harming Women as a Group." *Social Theory and Practice* 11 (Summer 1985): 207–34.

May, Larry, and John C. Hughes. "Is Sexual Harassment Coercive?" In *Moral Rights in the Workplace*, edited by Gertrude Ezorsky. Albany: State University of New York Press, 1987.

May, Larry, and Robert Strikwerda. "Fatherhood and Nurturance." *Journal of Social Philosophy* 22 (Fall 1991): 28–39.

——. "Men in Groups: Collective Responsibility for Rape." *Hypatia* 9 (Spring 1994): 134–51.

May, Larry, Robert Strikwerda, and Patrick Hopkins, eds. *Rethinking Masculinity*, 2d ed. Lanham, Md.: Rowman and Littlefield, 1996.

Meritor Savings Bank v. Vinson, 477 U.S. 57, 106 S.Ct. 2399, 91 L.Ed.2d 49 (1986).

Metcalf, Andy, and Martin Humphries, eds. *The Sexuality of Men*. London: Pluto Press, 1985.

Miedzian, Myriam. *Boys Will Be Boys: Breaking the Link between Masculinity and Violence*. New York: Doubleday, 1991.

Mill, John Stuart. *On Liberty*. 1859. Indianapolis: Hackett, 1978.

Moore, Robert, and Douglas Gillette. *The Warrior Within: Accessing the Knight in the Male Psyche*. New York: William Morrow, 1992.

Morrow, Lance. "Men: Are They Really That Bad?" *Time*, 14 February 1994, 56–57.

Navarro, Mireya. "Appeals Court Rebuffs Lesbian in Custody Bid." *New York Times*, 31 August 1996, A7.

Oates, Joyce Carol. "Rape and the Boxing Ring." *Newsweek*, 24 February 1992, 60.

Okin, Susan Moller. *Justice, Gender, and the Family*. New York: Basic Books, 1989.

Parent, W. A. "A Second Look at Pornography and the Subordination of Women." *Journal of Philosophy* 87 (April 1990): 205–11.

Peterson, Susan Rae. "Coercion and Rape: The State as a Male Protection Racket." In *Feminism and Philosophy*, edited by Mary Vetterling Braggin, Frederick Elliston, and Jane English. Totowa, N.J.: Littlefield, Adams, 1977.

Pleck, Joseph H. *The Myth of Masculinity*. Cambridge: MIT Press, 1981.

Porter, Roy. "Does Rape Have a Historical Meaning?" In *Rape: An Historical and Social Enquiry*, edited by Sylvana Tomaselli and Roy Porter. Oxford: Basil Blackwell, 1986.

Post, Tony, et al. "A Pattern of Rape." *Newsweek*, 4 January 1993, 32–36.

Prosser, William, and W. Page Keeton. *On Torts*. 5th ed. St. Paul: West, 1984.

Radford, Jill. "Policing Male Violence, Policing Women." In *Women, Violence, and Social Control*, edited by Jalna Hanmer and Mary Maynard. Atlantic Highlands, N.J.: Humanities Press, 1987.

Rosenthal, David M., and Fadlou Shehadi. *Applied Ethics and Ethical Theory*. Salt Lake City: University of Utah Press, 1988.

Russell, Bertrand. *The Problems of Philosophy*. 1912. Oxford: Oxford University Press, 1970.

Sadker, Myra, and David Sadker. *Failing at Fairness: How America's Schools Cheat Girls*. New York: Charles Scribner's Sons, 1994.

Sanday, Peggy Reeves. "Androcentric and Matrifocal Gender Representation in Minangkabau Ideology." In *Beyond the Second Sex*, edited by Peggy Reeves Sanday and Ruth Gallagher Goodenough. Philadelphia: University of Pennsylvania Press, 1990.

——. "Rape and the Silencing of the Feminine." In *Rape: An Historical and Social Enquiry*, edited by Sylvana Tomaselli and Roy Porter. Oxford: Basil Blackwell, 1986.

Schneider, Elizabeth. "Describing and Changing: Women's Self-Defense Work and the Problem of Expert Testimony on Battering." *Women's Rights Law Reporter* 9 (1986): 213–41.

Scott, Joan W. "Experience." In *Feminists Theorize the Political*, edited by Judith Butler and Joan W. Scott. New York: Routledge, 1992.

Scully, Diana. *Understanding Sexual Violence.* Boston: Unwin Hyman, 1990.

Seidler, Victor J. *Unreasonable Men: Masculinity and Social Theory.* London: Routledge, 1994.

———. ed. *The Achilles Heel Reader.* London: Routledge, 1991.

———. ed. *Men, Sex, and Relationships.* London: Routledge, 1992.

Shafer, Carolyn M., and Marilyn Frye. "Rape and Respect." In *Feminism and Philosophy,* edited by Mary Vetterling-Braggin, Frederick Elliston, and Jane English. Totowa, N.J.: Littlefield Adams, 1977.

Shanley, Mary. "Unwed Fathers' Rights, Adoption, and Sex Equality: Gender-Neutrality and the Perpetuation of Patriarchy." *Columbia Law Review* 95 (January 1995): 60–103.

Soble, Alan. *Pornography.* New Haven: Yale University Press, 1986.

Sommers, E. K. and J. V. Check. "An Empirical Investigation of the Role of Pornography in the Verbal and Physical Abuse of Women." *Violence and Victims* 2 (1987): 189–209.

Stanley v. Illinois, 405 U.S. 645 (1972).

Staub, Ervin. *The Roots of Evil: The Origins of Genocide and Other Group Violence.* Cambridge: Cambridge University Press, 1989.

Sterba, James. *Contemporary Social and Political Philosophy.* Belmont, Calif.: Wadsworth, 1996.

Stoltenberg, John. *Refusing to Be a Man.* New York: Meridian Books, 1990.

Strawson, Peter. "Freedom and Resentment." 1962. Reprinted in *Perspectives on Moral Responsibility,* edited by John Martin Fischer and Mark Ravizza. Ithaca: Cornell University Press, 1993.

Strikwerda, Robert, and Larry May. "Male Friendship and Intimacy." *Hypatia* 7 (Summer 1992): 110–25.

Sunstein, Cass R. "Words, Conduct, Caste." *University of Chicago Law Review* 60 (Summer–Fall 1993): 795–844.

Tamburinus, Thomas, S. J. *Explicationes in Decalogum.* Vol. 2. Lyons, 1651.

Taylor, Charles. *Sources of the Self.* Cambridge: Harvard University Press, 1989.

Thalberg, Irving, and Deborah Pellow. "Imagining Alternatives." *Philosophical Forum,* 11 (Fall 1979): 1–17.

Thomas, Laurence. "On Sexual Offers and Threats." In *Moral Rights in the Workplace,* edited by Gertrude Ezorsky. Albany: State University of New York Press, 1987.

Thornhill, Randy, and Nancy Wilmsen Thornhill. "The Evolutionary Psychology of Men's Coercive Sexuality." *Behavioral and Brain Sciences* 15 (1992): 363–75.

Tiger, Lionel. *Men in Groups.* New York: Marion Boyars, 1984.

Trebilcot, Joyce. *Mothering: Essays in Feminist Theory.* Totowa, N.J.: Rowman and Allanheld, 1983.

United States v. Commonwealth of Virginia (VMI), 766 F. Supp. 1407 (W. D. Va. 1991).

Vadas, Melinda. "A First Look at the Pornography/Civil Rights Ordinance: Could Pornography Be the Subordination of Women?" *Journal of Philosophy* 84 (September 1987): 487–511.

Waits, Kathleen. "The Criminal Justice System's Response to Battering: Understanding the Problem, Forging the Solutions." *Washington Law Review* 60 (1985). Reprinted in *Feminist Jurisprudence*, edited by Patricia Smith. New York: Oxford University Press, 1993.

Warshaw, Robin. *I Never Called It Rape*. New York: Harper and Row, 1988.

Wilcox, B. L. "Pornography, Social Science, and Politics: When Research and Ideology Collide." *American Psychologist* 42 (1987): 941–43.

Wittemore, Anne Marie. "Single Gender Education and the Constitution." *Loyola Law Review* 40 (1994): 261–62.

Woodhouse, Barbara Bennett. "Hatching the Egg: A Child-Centered Perspective on Parents' Rights." *Cardozo Law Review* 14 (1993): 1747–1828.

Young, Iris. *Throwing Like a Girl and Other Essays in Feminist Philosophy and Social Theory*. Bloomington: Indiana University Press, 1990.

Zaretsky, Eli. "Female Sexuality and the Catholic Confessional." In *Women, Sex, and Sexuality*, edited by Catherine R. Stimpson and Ethel Spector Person. Chicago: University of Chicago Press, 1980.

Zillman, Dolf, and Jennings Bryant. "Pornography, Sexual Callousness, and the Trivialization of Rape." *Journal of Communication* (Autumn 1982). Reprinted in *Men Confront Pornography*, edited by Michael S. Kimmel. New York: Meridian Books, 1990.

Index

Citadel. *See* Military
Collective responsibility:
  distributional, 90, 92, 94
  nondistributional, 91
  for rape, 87–97
  See also Shared responsibility
Community:
  moral code, 74–78
  regulating pornography, 74–78
  sentiments and pornography, 59
Confession:
  and confessional writing, 53, 57
  as "progressive confessional," 55–57
  See also Catholic Church;
    Socialization
Consciousness raising, 80

Devlin, Patrick, 74–77
Dialogue:
  and conversative socialization, 127–
    130, 132
  and emotions, 17
Diversity, value of, 119–122, 150
Domestic violence, and military, 9

Epistemology:
  as defined by male voice, 136
  and empathy, 137–139
  feminist standpoint, 135, 140
  and the justification of beliefs, 146–
    148
  of traditional male viewpoint, 140
  See also Progressive male standpoint
Emotions:
  control of, 9, 12–14, 17
  reasonableness of, 16–20
  See also Anger; Responsibility; Sexual
    desire

Fatherhood. *See* Paternity
Faulkner, Shannon, 127
Feinberg, Joel, 61–63
Feminism:
  and "consciousness raising," 57, 80
  and equality, 39–40

and infantilizing men, 29
as movement, and confession, 53
and patriarchy, 91
and social learning theory of rape,
  84–85, 87
Foucault, Michel, 48

Gender discrimination, 65, 141; *See
  also* Group harm
Gibbard, Allan, 16–17
Gilmore, David, 119
Group harm:
  of pornography:
    as affecting status, 70–74
    as caste-like discrimination, 68–70
    as defamation, 66–67
    definition of, 63–65
    and law, 66, 69
    and reputation, 66–67, 69
    as set-back to interests, 64–65,
      74–78
    as subordination, 67–68, 70
  of rape, 94–95
  of sexual harassment, 105–108
    based on historical dominance,
      107–111
    as discrimination, 100–111
    as limiting options, 101–102, 104
    and sexual orientation, 108–111
Guilt, 8, 15, 22, 53
  for rape, 88
  and sexual aggression, 54, 145
  and sexuality, 47
  socializing power of, 145

Harm:
  conceptualizing of, 61–63
  as set-back to interests, individual,
    61–63
  See also Gender discrimination;
    Group harm
Harris v. Forklift, 102–105
Hart, H. L. A., 76
Hartsock, Nancy, 139–141
Held, Virginia, 38–41

Larry May is Professor of Philosophy at Washington University, St. Louis.
He has authored and edited many books, most recently *The Socially
Responsive Self*, and *Rethinking Masculinity*, 2d edition.